Ezra Pound and Senator Bronson Cutting

EZRA
POUND
AND SENATOR BRONSON
CUTTING

A POLITICAL CORRESPONDENCE
1930–1935

Edited by E. P. Walkiewicz and Hugh Witemeyer

University of New Mexico Press
Albuquerque

Library of Congress Cataloging-in-Publication Data

Pound, Ezra, 1885-1972.
Ezra Pound and Senator Bronson Cutting :
a political correspondence, 1930-1935
edited by E.P. Walkiewicz and Hugh
Witemeyer. — 1st ed.
p. cm.
Includes bibliographical references and index.
ISBN 0–8263–1584-4
1. Pound, Ezra, 1885-1972—Correspondence.
2. Cutting, Bronson M., 1888-1935—Correspondence.
3. Poets, American—20th century-Correspondence.
4. Legislators—United States—Correspondence.
5. United States—Politics and govenment—20th century.
6. World politics—20th century.
I. Cutting, Bronson M., 1888-1935.
II. Walkiewicz, E.P.
III. Witemeyer, Hugh.
IV. Title.
PS3531.O82Z4824 1995
811'.52—dc20
[B]   95-4348
CIP

Designed by Sue Niewiarowski

Contents

Editors' Preface

The correspondence of Ezra Pound and Senator Bronson M. Cutting ran from 8 November 1930 to 4 April 1935. Thirty-three items have survived, twenty-six from Pound to Cutting, and seven from Cutting to Pound. All are included in the present edition. To judge from references in the extant letters, others were written that have since been lost.

The originals of thirteen of Pound's letters to Cutting are in Box 36 of the Bronson M. Cutting Papers, Manuscript Division, Library of Congress. Carbon copies of thirteen other letters from Pound to Cutting are in the Ezra Pound Archive, Beinecke Rare Book and Manuscript Library, Yale University. The originals of Cutting's letters to Pound are also in the Pound Archive. We are grateful to the Manuscript Division of the Library of Congress and to Dr. Patricia C. Willis, Curator of the American Literature Collection of the Beinecke Library, for providing photocopies of these letters, which have served as copytexts for the present edition. All photocopies have been checked against the source documents.

Our edition also includes seventeen items that Pound contributed in 1935, under the title "Ez Sez," to Senator Cutting's newspaper, the Santa Fe *New Mexican.* Although they are not part of the correspondence between the poet and the senator, these editorials are nevertheless important to the history of the Pound-Cutting relationship and interesting in their own right as representative examples of Pound's political journalism. For copytexts of "Ez Sez," we have used the facsimile edition of *Ezra Pound's Poetry and Prose: Contributions to Periodicals,* arr. Lea Baechler, A. Walton Litz, and James Longenbach, 11 vols. (New York: Garland, 1991), and microfilm copies of the *New Mexican* housed in the New Mexico State Library. Carbon copies of Pound's typescripts for the "Ez Sez" pieces are in the Pound Archive, as are carbon copies of two letters, reproduced in Chapter Four, from Pound to E. Dana Johnson, editor of the *New Mexican.* The typescript of Pound's obituary on Cutting, here given in Chapter Four, is also housed in the Pound Archive. The senator's photograph was reproduced by the Library of Congress from a print in the Cutting Papers, and his caricature comes from the *Syracuse Journal* for 14 April 1934; a copy of it is also to be found among the Cutting Papers.

The correspondence and the editorials appear in separate chapters and are chronologically arranged. Incomplete dates on some letters have been supplemented from textual and contextual evidence, and all dates provided by the editors have been placed in square brackets. The format of dates has been standardized so that days precede months, and months (except May, June, and July) are abbreviated. A few pages found with letters 8, 27, and 30 in the Pound Archive defy placement in the sequence; we have inserted editorial notes in square brackets to indicate that these pages may not belong to the letters with which they are published here. Similarly, we have inserted bracketed notes in letters 6, 8, 9, 10, 13, 17, and 30 to indicate that the beginning or the end of a page is missing from the copytext, invariably a carbon copy by Pound of an original that is now lost.

In transcribing the texts of the letters and editorials, we have employed the following guidelines. Every item has been reproduced as completely as the extant copytext allows; no editorial abridgements have been made. Every letter is preceded by a headnote that gives its number in the present edition, its original form and length, and the location of the copytext. To designate epistolary forms, we have used the following abbreviations: TLS (typed letter signed), TL (typed letter unsigned), and ALS (autograph letter signed). Every "Ez Sez" column is preceded by a headnote that gives the date of its first publication in the *New Mexican* and its entry number in Donald Gallup's *Ezra Pound: A Bibliography* (Charlottesville: University Press of Virginia, 1983). The same number accompanies each column in the Garland facsimile edition of *Ezra Pound's Poetry and Prose*, vol. 6.

Some standardizations have been applied to the texts. In the letters, positions of dates, salutations, closings, and signatures have been regularized. Return addresses are reproduced, but other features of printed letterheads are not. Inside addresses are omitted from Cutting's letters to Pound but retained in Pound's letters as evidence that they were addressed to Cutting rather than another senator. Typographical errors and misspellings, including those of proper names, have been silently corrected unless they seem intended by the writer. Typed and autograph corrections and insertions have been silently incorporated. Missing words, alternate readings, and problematic transcriptions are indicated by square brackets with question marks.

Paragraphing has been standardized, as have the spacings between paragraphs, between sentences, and between words and punctuation marks within and at the end of sentences. Unpunctuated titles of books and periodicals have been italicized. Otherwise, the original grammar, punctuation, and capitalization of the letters have not been altered.

Each letter and editorial is followed by explanatory notes. Each note is keyed to the preceding text by the repetition in italics of a word or phrase from that text. The names of Ezra Pound and Bronson Cutting are abbreviated in the notes as EP and BC, respectively. If pertinent information is given elsewhere in the edition, a cross-reference directs the reader to the relevant passage. In adopting this format, we have followed several recent editions of Pound's correspondence: *Ezra Pound and Dorothy Shakespear: Their Letters: 1909–1914*, ed. Omar Pound and A. Walton Litz (New York: New Directions, 1984); *Ezra Pound and Margaret Cravens: A Tragic Friendship, 1910–1912*, ed. Omar Pound and Robert Spoo (Durham, N.C.: Duke University Press, 1988); and *The Selected Letters of Ezra Pound to John Quinn, 1915–1924*, ed. Timothy Materer (Durham, N.C.: Duke University Press, 1991).

The explanatory notes that follow each of the "Ez Sez" editorials in Chapter Four include a record of the textual discrepancies between the published versions of the columns and the typescript versions housed in the Pound Archive. These variants result from the fact that Pound's typescripts were edited by the Santa Fe *New Mexican* before they appeared in its pages. The published versions provide our copytexts, while some but not all of the typescript variants are given in the notes. We do not reproduce the newspaper's corrections of typographical errors in Pound's typescripts, of apparently unintended misspellings, of paragraphing, or of punctuation and capitalization that do not affect meaning or emphasis. However, we do note typographical errors introduced *into* Pound's texts by the newspaper's printers, and we record all words completely capitalized in Pound's typescripts but reduced to conventional lower-case settings in the newspaper printing. In many of these instances, conventional typography alters the expressive, if unorthodox, emphasis of Pound's original text. Most of the signatures and all of the Rapallo datelines at the ends of the editorials were added by the *New Mexican's* editors. Only the editorials of 26 March, 1 June, 16 August, 17 August, and 4 October 1935 are signed by Pound in their original typescript versions.

Besides texts and annotations, our edition provides background information about the interests and activities of Pound and Cutting and about the history of the issues they discussed. This contextual information is necessary to an understanding of their writings, which are often topical and allusive in nature. Thus our first chapter treats the careers of the poet and the senator prior to the beginning of their correspondence in 1930. The second chapter presents the first fifteen letters of the correspondence (1930–32), together with brief introductions to the principal issues that preoccupied the writers at the time. The third chapter contains the final eighteen letters in the correspondence (1934–35), again preceded by concise summaries of the issues which most concerned the men at that stage. The fourth chapter reproduces Pound's editorials from the Santa Fe *New Mexican;* the introduction explains how Pound came to write "Ez Sez," analyzes his rhetorical strategies, and sketches the backgrounds of recurrent topics in the series. The fifth chapter assesses the biographical and historical significance of the relationship between the senator and poet, as it is documented in the present edition. The Index lists proper names and major themes in the texts and the editorial apparatus.

This is the second of Pound's many correspondences with American political leaders to be edited, and the first to be published. It is also the first edition of any of Senator Cutting's correspondences. None of the letters in the present edition has previously been published in its entirety. We have quoted excerpts from the letters in two earlier articles: "Ezra Pound's Contributions to New Mexican Periodicals and His Relationship with Senator Bronson Cutting," *Paideuma* 9, 3 (Winter 1980) 441–59, and "Ezra Pound, Bronson Cutting, and American Issues, 1930–1935," in *Ezra Pound and America,* ed. Jacqueline Kaye (London: Macmillan and New York: St. Martin's, 1992) 166–80. Two other recent studies have likewise cited passages from the letters: Richard Lowitt, *Bronson M. Cutting: Progressive Politician* (Albuquerque: University of New Mexico Press, 1992), and Tim Redman, *Ezra Pound and Italian Fascism* (Cambridge: Cambridge University Press, 1991).

Facsimile reproductions of the "Ez Sez" editorials appear in the Garland edition of *Ezra Pound's Poetry and Prose* (1991), but ours is the first edition to annotate the pieces, place them into historical context, and provide textual variants. We were helped in this by William Bedford Clark's essay, " 'Ez Sez': Pound's Pithy Promulgations," *Antioch Review,* 37 (1979) 420–27.

The unpublished letters of Ezra Pound are copyright © 1995 by the Ezra Pound Literary Property Trust and are published by permission of New Directions Publishing Corporation, agents for the Trust, and of the Beinecke Rare

Book and Manuscript Library, Yale University. We are grateful to James Laughlin and Peggy L. Fox of New Directions for helping to arrange this permission.

We wish also to acknowledge the contributions of the following persons, who answered queries or otherwise facilitated our work: Terry Basford, Philip Burns, William Bedford Clark, Amy Fogelman, David M. Gordon, David V. Holtby, James E. Hutson, Edward Jones, Jacqueline Kaye, Richard Lowitt, Timothy Materer, Gerald Nash, Jill Patterson, Mary de Rachewiltz, Tim Redman, Orlando Romero, Richard Rudisill, Richard Salazar, Richard Taylor, and Jeffrey Walker. Without the help of these friends and colleagues, our work could not have been completed; but they are not responsible for its errors or omissions. For support of our research, Professor Walkiewicz wishes to thank the Oklahoma Foundation for the Humanities; Southwestern Bell; and the Department of English and the College of Arts and Sciences of Oklahoma State University. Professor Witemeyer wishes to thank the American Philosophical Society; the Ball Brothers Foundation of Indiana University; and the College of Arts and Sciences, the Research Allocations Committee, and the Inter-Library Loan Department of the University of New Mexico.

Finally, we would like to dedicate our work on this edition to our children: Katie, Alice, and Stephen Walkiewicz and Hazen Witemeyer.

1

The Poet and the Senator

I
The Political Poet

Ezra Pound's politics are even more infamous than his notoriously difficult poetry. People who know little else about him can recite Pound's public
actions during and after World War II. From 1941 to 1943 Pound made more
than one hundred broadcasts over Rome Radio. In them he criticized the
American government and its role in the war against the Axis powers, he
defended some of the policies of Mussolini and Hitler, and he made many
anti-Semitic statements.[1] Some of the broadcasts were monitored in Washington, and in 1943 Pound was indicted for treason by the United States
Department of Justice. He was apprehended in Rapallo, Italy, in May 1945
and held for six months in the U.S. Army's Disciplinary Training Center
near Pisa. He was then flown to Washington, where a federal court declared
him mentally incompetent to stand trial. From December 1945 to May 1958,
he was incarcerated in St. Elizabeths Hospital, a federal institution for the
criminally insane in Washington. Upon his release, he returned to Italy, where
he died in 1972, shortly after his eighty-seventh birthday. Except in a few
faint statements made near the end of his life, he never recanted the political and racial beliefs proclaimed in his broadcasts. These outrageous facts
about Pound's life are better known than any others, and give rise to the
common judgment that he was a traitor, a bigot, and a madman.

Many of Pound's words and acts can indeed never be mitigated or for-
given. Yet his politics in the years leading up to the war were far less eccentric than people usually assume. No one seeking a balanced assessment of
his allegiances and state of mind can afford to ignore his economic, political, and cultural writings of the 1930s. These include hundreds of contributions to periodicals and scores of personal correspondences with civic leaders
in Europe and North America. This branch of Pound's work has received
relatively little attention from editors, biographers, and critics.[2] Yet it shows
Pound in a different light, and suggests the need to avoid oversimplified
judgments of his activism.

The present book contributes to a reassessment of the poet's politics by documenting and summarizing one of Pound's epistolary relationships with an important American political leader. From 1930 to 1935 he corresponded with Senator Bronson M. Cutting of New Mexico (1888–1935), a wealthy newspaper owner and a rising star in the Progressive wing of the Republican party. The two men exchanged nearly three dozen letters, and Pound also contributed seventeen articles to one of Cutting's newspapers, the Santa Fe *New Mexican*. Reproduced and annotated in the present edition, these texts are representative examples of the suasive letters and articles Pound sent in great numbers to American opinion-makers during the 1930s.

How did the correspondence begin? The present chapter traces the careers of the poet and the senator up to the beginning of their contacts in 1930, showing how they were drawn together by a variety of mutual interests. We shall outline the process by which Pound, a professional man of letters, came to devote much of his time and energy to public advocacy. We shall see how Cutting, the scion of a wealthy and civic-minded New York family, became the Senate's leading spokesman for censorship reform and a hero in American intellectual and literary circles. The gap bridged by the correspondence of the political poet and the literate senator was less wide than we might expect or than it would be in the cultural environment of the 1990s.

To begin with, Pound's earlier promotion of an international modernism and his notorious allegiance to Italian fascism have tended to obscure his interest in and involvement with twentieth-century American politics. Only in the past decade or so have Pound scholars begun to examine in detail the political traditions within the poet's family and their influence upon his later activism.[3] We are now able to see Pound's lobbying of Cutting and other leaders in the context of the poet's American political inheritance.

Pound himself once wrote that "perhaps it may be held that the actions of one's ancestors, especially if recited to one in childhood, tend to influence one's character."[4] Pound's ancestors on both sides of the family influenced his character by bequeathing to him a rich legacy of civic responsibility and public service.[5] In seeking an alliance with Cutting, a Progressive western Republican, Pound was following a branch of the family tradition that stemmed from his grandfather, Thaddeus Coleman Pound (1832?–1915).

A self-made businessman and successful railroad entrepreneur, Thaddeus served as Republican assemblyman, speaker of the state assembly, lieutenant governor, and acting governor of Wisconsin. He was later elected to three consecutive terms in the United States House of Representatives. In Washington, he lived with a woman to whom he was not married, and was known for his oratorical skills, which his party relied upon in presidential elections.[6]

Pound romanticized this grandfather into a figure of almost legendary proportions. The idealization entailed an alignment of Thaddeus's politics with his own. Although Thaddeus was "an old-line Republican during most of his career," Pound focused upon the views and actions that made Thaddeus seem a radical reformer and a predecessor of the Progressive or Bull Moose Republicanism of a later generation.[7] As J. J. Wilhelm explains,

> Thaddeus Pound represented to the mature Ezra the American West in all of its untrammeled vigor and energy. He stood for what the country might have become, had it followed the basic precepts of Jefferson and Adams and not fallen prey to the selfish tactics of usurious bankers and greedy monopolists. . . . Pound saw his grandfather as the archetypal pioneer, fighting meddling politicians. . . . the Wall Street bankers, the Federal Reservists, and the robber barons running rampant in the last half of the nineteenth century, those men who were turning the Jeffersonian dream of the land belonging to everyone into the possession of the few. When he died, Thaddeus was called "a Republican of the radical type."[8]

Pound associated his ancestors with the Jefferson/Jackson ideal of frontier democracy to which Wilhelm alludes, and liked to think of himself as a Westerner by virtue of his birth in Hailey, Idaho, even though his family moved to the East Coast before he was two years old. In the 1930s, as Pound became more and more obsessed with economic reform, he even persuaded himself that Thaddeus had anticipated "the same essentials of monetary and statal economics that I am writing about today," such as stamp scrip and the existence of an evil, usurious collusion between government and bankers.[9] This cluster of values and attitudes belongs to what Richard Hofstadter has called "the Populist-Progressive tradition" in American politics, and Pound clearly aligned himself and his family with that heritage.[10]

Pound family politics remained Republican for at least two generations after Thaddeus. In a letter to Senator Cutting of 13 February 1934, Ezra describes himself as "having been brought up to suppose the republican party was THE party etc." The Pounds, like the Cuttings, were drawn to the liberal wing of the party led by Theodore Roosevelt, whose presidency from 1901 to 1909 coincided with Pound's political coming-of-age. Pound remained loyal to Roosevelt when Teddy ran again for the White House in 1912, this time as an independent candidate on the ticket of the Progressive party. Keith Tuma has shown that Pound's 1912 essay on America, entitled "Patria Mia," contains direct verbal echoes of the Progressive platform of that year. These echoes, Tuma argues, illustrate Pound's youthful "commitment to the social and political policies of the progressive wing of the Republican party."[11]

That commitment persisted. Pound viewed the election of Woodrow Wilson in 1912 as an unmitigated turn for the worse in American public life. The ascendancy of the old-guard Republicans under Harding, Coolidge, and Hoover from 1920 to 1932 did nothing to improve matters. Only when the Progressive movement was revived in 1931 by a coalition of dissident Republicans and Democrats did Pound's political hopes for his native land reawaken. On the American political spectrum, the Progressive bloc in the U.S. Senate—William Borah, Edward Costigan, Bronson Cutting, Hiram Johnson, Robert LaFollette, Jr., George Norris, Burton Wheeler, and others —was the group with which Pound identified most closely and corresponded most extensively.

Meanwhile, Pound's political views had become more radical as a result of his experience of the Great War of 1914–18. Living in London before the war, he felt that he was at the center of a "vortex," an exciting dynamic of cultural activity that promised a modernist renaissance in the arts no less momentous than the classical revival of the sixteenth century.

These high hopes were dashed by the war, which killed off a generation of artists (such as Pound's good friend, the young French sculptor, Henri Gaudier-Brzeska) and left London spiritually enfeebled. Seeking a comprehensible explanation of the incomprehensible carnage, Pound, like many of his contemporaries, embraced a conspiracy theory of economic causation. He came to believe that the war had been prolonged by the greed of those who profited from it: munitions-makers, financiers, high-ranking officers, and politicians.

In particular, Pound was drawn to Social Credit, an analysis put forward by Major C. H. Douglas in 1919 as a result of his experience in wartime manufacturing. Douglas argued that poverty and war are avoidable consequences of flaws in the existing capitalist system of distribution. Inequitable distribution of wealth, purchasing power, and credit within economically developed nations makes it impossible for them to purchase and consume all that they produce. Chronic underconsumption in domestic markets leads to international competition for foreign markets and thus eventually to war. The spanner in the machine, according to Douglas, is the control and exploitation of credit by private banks. Because private banks charge excessive interest (or usury) for the use of money and credit, prices in a given economy will always be higher than consumer purchasing power. The Social Credit solution to the problem calls for governmental control of credit and interest rates and governmental issuance of "national dividends" directly to consumers. These measures will augment purchasing power and put an end to unearned profits.[12] Douglas's program rhymed at many points with the Populist-Progressive tradition in which Pound was brought up. Pound's conversion was not, therefore, an entirely new departure.

Pound was converted to Douglas's views in the offices of A. R. Orage's *The New Age* in 1919. In the following year Pound castigated "usury age-old and age-thick" in the antiwar sections of *Hugh Selwyn Mauberley*, a poetic farewell to London.[13] He moved to Paris in 1921 and to Rapallo, Italy, in 1924, all the while retaining his American citizenship.

In Italy, Pound came to admire Mussolini's brand of National Socialism and to believe that the Italian fascist government was more likely than any other to implement the economic policies necessary to the world's material and cultural salvation. On the spectrum of Italian politics, he aligned himself with the dissident left wing of the fascist party. He never joined the party, but he saw no incompatibility between its principles and those of the American founding fathers. Until the later 1930s, he did not promote Hitler or the policies of German National Socialism.[14]

When the Depression struck, Pound was convinced that the same forces which had caused the First World War were building toward a second. He also believed that this movement of history could be reversed by the adoption of simple, sensible economic reforms. He therefore set up in Rapallo as a one-man clearinghouse, gathering information from a variety of publications and personal contacts, and transmitting essential news and the fundamental principles of his economic creed to a growing network of individuals and groups. "There is for the moment, the year, the decade," he said in 1931, "nothing for the serious American author to do but to learn what he can and to struggle to instruct those who know even less than he does."[15] Like many other artists and writers, Pound felt himself caught up by an imperative demand for political engagement.

Never modest in his ambitions, he sought nothing less than to change the consciousness of the populace and the leaders of his native land. He believed that meaningful innovation comes only from the top down, from the leadership of an enlightened elite. Yet he also recognized the importance of educating public opinion, so that it will empower or support true leaders and accept their innovations rather than others. To this end Pound campaigned on two primary fronts. On the one hand, he tried to cultivate the general public through any media—print or electronic—to which he could gain access. On the other hand, he attempted to influence individual members of the governmental establishment by the time-honored American method of direct personal correspondence. In his dealings with Senator Cutting, Pound employed both of these channels.

From 1930 to 1939 Pound contributed to a wide range of American periodicals. In 1935 alone, for example, he produced on the order of 150 articles and letters to editors, most on political and economic topics. These went to all parts of the country and all sorts of journals. Thus Pound's instigations appeared not only in such widely read organs as the *New York Sun,* the *New York World Telegram,* the *Boston Herald, Time, Esquire,* and the *New Republic;* but also in college publications, little magazines, and local newspapers in out-of-the-way places such as Oglethorpe, Georgia; Millbrook, New York; Bethlehem, Connecticut; Columbus, Mississippi; Gambier, Ohio; Olivet, Michigan; Rock Island, Illinois; Salem, Oregon; and Santa Fe, New Mexico.[16] In New Mexico alone, between 1929 and 1935, Pound placed twenty-two brief articles in three different periodicals.[17] One of the periodicals was Senator Cutting's daily newspaper, the Santa Fe *New Mexican,* in which Pound placed seventeen items in 1935 under the title "Ez Sez, Being Some Pithy Promulgations by Ezra Pound."

At the same time, he conducted a voluminous correspondence with American political leaders. No one knows exactly how many officials of the executive, legislative, and judicial branches of the United States federal government, not to mention state and local governments, Pound lobbied by mail from Rapallo during the 1930s; but the number may approach two or even three score. In a herculean effort to influence American policy and opinion, Pound sent hundreds, perhaps thousands of hortatory letters, cards, and telegrams from Italy at his own expense to highly placed public and private figures in his homeland. In these communications he did not espouse a standard fascist party line, and he acted independently, without support or encouragement from the Italian government.

Like his grandfather, Pound concentrated primarily upon the legislative branch of government. He corresponded with dozens of congressmen, three of whom became his principal contacts. His correspondence with Representative George Holden Tinkham of Massachusetts comprises one hundred letters written between 1933 and 1940; the two men met in Italy in 1936. Between 1932 and 1940, Pound likewise exchanged thirty letters with Senator William E. Borah of Idaho, whom he met in Washington in 1939. The Cutting correspondence includes thirty-three items written between 1930 and 1935; the two men never met in person.[18]

In addition to his journalism and correspondences, Pound published many other instructional writings during the 1930s. He turned out *ABC of Economics* (composed in ten days in 1933), *ABC of Reading* (1934), *Social Credit* (1935), *Jefferson and/or Mussolini* (1935), and *Guide to Kulchur* (composed in six weeks in 1935), as well as other pamphlets and essay collections.[19] This in a ten-year span that saw him publish the satiric *Alfred Venison Poems* and add forty new sections to his major creative project, a modern epic poem entitled *The Cantos*. The amount of energy he expended on these activities was considerable; the quantity of his output, impressive.

The new cantos, 31–71, reflect the poet's intense and focused engagement with American history and politics in this decade. Constituting the longest stretch of historiography in the entire poem, they include the "Chinese Cantos," bracketed by others that draw largely on the matter of America, in particular the deeds and words of Van Buren, Jefferson, and John Adams. As appropriated by Pound through the medium of his French sources, Chinese history illustrates what he sees as a universal pattern discernible as well in American history: the collapse of dynasties or cultures as a result of their falling away from the original "mission" and precepts laid down by their founding generations.

This monitory vision of history conforms to a familiar paradigm in the history of American thought. Wendy S. Flory identifies it as the tradition of the "American Jeremiad," first defined by Sacvan Bercovitch. "Like a true American jeremiah," Flory writes, Pound

> constantly reminds his readers how far they have fallen from the standards set by the Founding Fathers, how many obstacles stand in the way of the writer who is determined to produce work that is both excellent and specifically American, and, consequently, how much dedication and energy will be necessary if the obstacles are to be overcome.[20]

Speaking as a prophet in exile, Pound made many efforts, during the 1930s, to call the attention of the American public and its elected officials to the fallen state of the state, and to remind them of the careers, thought, and rhetoric of exemplars such as Adams and Jefferson. Thus, in his early letters to Cutting, Pound cites Jefferson's opinions on alcoholic beverages, the diplomatic recognition of revolutionary foreign governments, and excessive legal penalties imposed upon U.S. citizens by the federal government. In new forms, all of these historic issues were still on the national agenda.

These affinities with American political traditions did not, of course, make Pound a democrat. The Puritan myth of national covenant and national consensus has always privileged the clerisy and included an authoritarian tendency to negate individualism and persecute difference.[21] In Pound's case, the jeremiac stance entailed a profound distrust of "the democratic method of getting REPRESENTED."[22] Even as he courted Cutting and others in the Senate, Pound was wooing Mussolini, seeing in the Italian dictator both a man of action who could cut through procedural niceties and bureaucratic red tape to get things done, and a man of culture who might heed the superior counsel of a political poet.[23]

Pound lobbied U.S. senators because, in both ancient Rome and modern America, the Senate embodied the principle of aristocratic governance. He targeted Bronson M. Cutting in particular because Cutting had acquired a reputation for enlightened intellectual leadership as a result of his campaign against federal censorship in 1929–30. Soon thereafter Pound initiated a correspondence with the senator from New Mexico. In Cutting, Pound saw a congenial figure: a Progressive Republican of his own generation, with a fine literary education and a strong commitment to the maintenance of culture and the provision of economic justice.

II
THE LITERATE SENATOR

The career of Bronson M. Cutting (1888–1935) is less well known than that of Ezra Pound. Who was this literate senator from a remote corner of the Southwest that did not even become a state until 1912, the year of Pound's *Ripostes*?[24]

The Cuttings were a long-established, wealthy, and prominent New York family. The senator's father, William Bayard Cutting (1850–1912), traced his maternal ancestry to the Stuyvesants of New Amsterdam and to the Bayards, a French Huguenot family. His father's side of the family descended from Robert Livingston, a Scot who crossed the Atlantic in 1673 and by 1686 owned 160,000 acres on the Hudson River; and from the Reverend Leonard Cutting, a Cambridge-educated cleric who emigrated to the New World in 1748. Robert Fulton, inventor of the steamboat, was related to the family by marriage. The senator's mother, Olivia Peyton Murray (1855–1949), came from English families that had settled in the colonies before the Revolution.

By the last quarter of the nineteenth century, both the Cuttings and Murrays were very well to do. William Bayard Cutting took a law degree from Columbia University, of which he later became a trustee, but he never practiced law. Instead, he became president and/or director of a number of corporations, including the Southern Pacific Railroad, the Norfolk and Southern Railroad, the Santa Fe Railroad, and sundry insurance companies, banks, trust companies, and real estate conglomerates. Cutting also served as vice president of the New York Chamber of Commerce and engaged in extensive church and charity work. He was a founder of the New York Botanical Gardens, the Zoological Society, the Metropolitan Museum, and the New York Public Library.[25]

There was a strong tradition of Progressive Republican public service in the Cutting family. The senator's uncle, Robert Fulton Cutting, served as president of the Cooper Union and of the Citizens' Union, a nonpartisan organization that challenged the power of Tammany Hall. From 1895 to 1897, William Bayard Cutting was a Civil Service commissioner in the reform or "fusion" administration of Mayor William L. Strong. At this time, Cutting came to know and admire Theodore Roosevelt, who was a member of the same administration. Cutting later supported Roosevelt's campaign for the governorship of New York State. Bronson Cutting thus inherited an active political allegiance to the independent, reformist wing of the Republican party led by Roosevelt and later known as the Progressive or Bull Moose faction.

Bronson Murray Cutting was born 23 June 1888 on the family estate of Westbrook in Oakdale, Long Island. With his older brother and his two sisters, he enjoyed a cosmopolitan upbringing; by the time he was nineteen, Cutting had been to Europe five times. He began to learn French and German on these trips, and in the summer of 1906 he attended the hearing at which the Dreyfus conviction was overturned.

From 1901 to 1906 Cutting was enrolled at Groton, where he compiled an outstanding academic record in history, the classics, and modern languages and literature; he also served as editor of *The Grotonian*. In the fall of 1906, he entered Harvard University. He completed his freshman year, but took leave of absence in 1907–8 because of a bronchial illness. Returning to his studies in 1908–9, he added a passion for archaeology to his interest in classical antiquity; and he passed examinations in Greek, Latin, German, French, and English. He was later to learn Italian, Spanish, and Arabic as well.

But in November of 1909, Cutting began to hemorrhage from both lungs. He withdrew from Harvard, never to return. In February of 1910, he was sent with his sister, Justine Cutting Ward, to recuperate in Redlands, California. On 10 March his older brother, Bayard, died in Aswan, Egypt, of the same bronchial weakness. Fearing for the life of the younger son, the family took action when Bronson did not recover as rapidly as expected. He and Justine were dispatched to the deserts of the Southwest to find a more salutary climate. They reached New Mexico in May of 1910. On the railway platform, Cutting told an inquisitive fellow passenger, "I came to New Mexico to die."[26]

Instead, he flourished in the new environment. Justine later recalled their first impressions of Santa Fe.

> The place was like a little Spanish town—built around a plaza where Spanish women wore shawls and mantillas, where the men left their horses in rows around the sides of the square, where an occasional Indian in bright colors sold his wares of pottery and silver jewelry, where columns of tiny burros loaded with wood came down from the mountains and trotted through

the square. . . . Bronson never said much and never volunteered an opinion—but this time I saw clearly that he liked the place. Before we came back
to the car for supper, it was practically decided that this was the place for
the "cure."[27]

Clearly, Cutting and his sister appreciated the multicultural character of
northern New Mexico. A few months after their arrival, they were caught in
a flash flood after an especially effective corn dance at the Santo Domingo
Indian Pueblo.

In the fall of 1910, Cutting commissioned an architect to build him a
large home in the Mission Revival style on the outskirts of Santa Fe. He
moved into the house in August of 1911, dubbed it Los Siete Burros, and
threw himself into local politics as a Progressive Republican. When New
Mexico became a state in 1912, the Progressives successfully influenced
the election of the first governor. They also supported Teddy Roosevelt's
Bull Moose presidential campaign.

In the same year, Cutting bought three journals to secure his local political base. The Santa Fe *New Mexican* had the third-largest daily newspaper
circulation in the state; the *New Mexico Review* was a weekly; and *El Nuevo
Mexicano,* also published weekly, was one of the few Spanish-language periodicals in the former territory. Cutting threw the editorial influence of his
papers against the Republican old guard of Holm Bursum and Thomas Catron,
often siding with the Democrats in state and local elections. In 1916 the old
guard struck back with a libel suit against the *New Mexican,* but Cutting
fought them to a standstill in a complicated, three-year legal battle. In later
years, he and his newspapers favored direct primary elections, women's suf-
frage, a workmen's compensation law, the regulation of child labor, the creation of a state labor commission, and the establishment of a veterans' bureau.

When the United States entered World War I, Cutting was commissioned
a captain in the army and assigned to the U.S. Embassy in London as a
military attaché. His work consisted mainly of intelligence gathering, liaison with British officials, and counterespionage. At the end of the war,
Theodore Roosevelt asked Cutting to help organize American Legion posts
among New Mexico veterans.

Cutting accepted the assignment and traveled throughout the state, forming a network of personal contacts that later became the foundation of his
electoral constituency.[28] He mastered Spanish and cultivated Hispanic voters, who had traditionally been exploited or neglected by both of the estab-

lished parties. Inevitably, Cutting fell into the role of don or *patrón*, making hundreds of small loans from his personal fortune in return for the electoral support of individuals and families. Many of his closest political allies were Hispanics, such as Miguel Antonio Otero, Sr., Jesus M. Baca, and Herman Baca; and his most loyal voters resided in the predominantly Hispanic counties of northern New Mexico.

Cutting also played an active role in the social and cultural life of Santa Fe. As a vestryman of the Episcopal church, he was much involved in its affairs. He generously supported the Laboratory of Anthropology, though he refused to do the same for the Museum of New Mexico and the School of American Research, whose director, Edgar Hewett, he disliked. At first he resisted Mary Austin, but later he collaborated with her on a number of projects designed to preserve and develop the indigenous arts and crafts of New Mexico. He served on the advisory board of the Santa Fe Art School and on the regional committee administering the federal Public Works of Art program in New Mexico and Arizona. He also worked with Mabel Dodge Luhan, and he was friendly with Witter Bynner, W. W. ("Spud") Johnson, and other writers associated with *Laughing Horse* magazine.

In his prime, Cutting stood about six feet tall, weighed around two hundred pounds, had brown hair and eyes, and reminded some people of Jack Dempsey. His bronchial problems had cleared up, and his main complaint was hay fever. His assertiveness in politics notwithstanding, he was rather shy; and this reticence, combined with his Hispanic connections and with rumors about his sexual orientation, prevented him from ever being fully accepted in some Santa Fe circles. His closest New Mexico friends were his political cronies, his newspaper employees, and several members of the Bynner circle. He never married and steered clear of involvements with women. In Washington, he lived with his widowed mother. It was and still is widely assumed in Santa Fe that Cutting was discreetly homosexual. There is no conclusive evidence of this, however, and his principal biographer "lean[s] toward the view that Cutting was not gay."[29]

Among the arts, Cutting's greatest passion was classical music. He was an accomplished pianist who sometimes played all night on his Steinway, especially when he was upset. His phonograph collection at Los Siete Burros contained thousands of records, and his library was likewise extensive and varied. His taste in modern literature inclined toward realistic and adventuresome fiction; his favorite authors included Balzac, Gissing, Conrad, and Remarque.

He was not a great collector of the experimental modernists; a posthumous inventory of his library lists only the *ABC of Economics* by Pound, *Ash Wednesday* by T. S. Eliot, and *James Joyce's Ulysses* by Stuart Gilbert.[30]

Late in 1927, United States Senator Andrieus A. Jones of New Mexico died before the completion of his term in office. On 29 December, the Republican governor, Richard C. Dillon, appointed Cutting to serve in Jones's stead until the next congressional elections. (Dillon's own election was largely due to Cutting's support.) In November of 1928, Cutting was elected to a full, six-year term in his own right. He was forty years old and the second youngest man in the Senate; he had no prior experience of public office.

In Washington, Cutting found his natural allies among the Progressive Republicans from the western and midwestern states: Robert LaFollette, Jr., of Wisconsin, William Borah of Idaho, Hiram Johnson of California, George Norris of Nebraska, and others. As the Depression deepened, this group of maverick Republicans dissented from the policies of the Hoover administration and crossed party lines to vote with the Democrats on many occasions. In the spring of 1931, Cutting acted as one of the principal organizers of the nonpartisan Conference of Progressives in Washington; and in the following year he joined with other Progressive leaders to support the presidential candidacy of Franklin D. Roosevelt.

In the Senate, Cutting devoted himself to a number of Progressive causes. In his maiden speech, he urged campaign and electoral reform. He subsequently advocated the liberalization of federal laws governing censorship and copyright, and urged the diplomatic recognition of the Soviet Union. As the Depression worsened, Cutting championed a variety of federal public-assistance measures, including unemployment compensation, old-age and disability pensions, public-works projects, veterans' assistance, and federal aid to education. By 1934, he was sponsoring legislation to nationalize the banking industry. As we shall see, many of these measures form the substance of his correspondence with Ezra Pound. Perhaps the single most important piece of legislation to carry the senator's name was the Hawes-Cutting Bill for Philippine independence, which the Congress passed over President Hoover's veto in January 1933.

But it was not Philippine independence that made Cutting famous in American intellectual and literary circles. Rather, it was the debate over customs censorship in 1929–30 that earned him the reputation of being the most literate and cultured man in the Senate. Early in 1929 Spud Johnson informed the senator that customs authorities had seized three copies of D. H. Lawrence's *Lady Chatterley's Lover,* which Johnson had ordered from Florence, where the novel was published in 1928. Upon receiving an unsatisfactory explanation of the affair from the Department of the Treasury, Cutting began to look into its legal aspects. He consulted Mercer G. Johnston of the People's Legislative Service, and he later took advice from Morris Ernst, a rising young anticensorship lawyer.[31]

From these sources, Cutting learned that the earliest federal law prohibiting the importation of obscene material into the United States was the Tariff Act of 1842. The censorship power was renewed and extended in subsequent tariff bills and in the so-called Comstock Act of 1873, popularly named for its most outspoken advocate, Anthony Comstock, the crusading secretary of the New York Society for the Suppression of Vice. In 1929 the U.S. tariff law was once again up for revision. The Smoot-Hawley Bill renewed the censorship clause (Section 305) and extended its application to new categories of potentially subversive writings.

Section 305 authorized inspectors at U.S. ports of entry to impound any imports which, in their judgment, were obscene or seditious. The clause covered not only books and pamphlets but also photographs, prints, materials having to do with contraception and abortion, and lottery tickets. Among the books which at one time or another had been declared obscene were Aristophanes's *Lysistrata;* Defoe's *Moll Flanders;* Voltaire's *Candide;* Rousseau's *Confessions;* the works of Ovid, Apuleius, Rabelais, Boccaccio, Casanova, Balzac, George Moore, and Radclyffe Hall; Remarque's *All Quiet on the Western Front;* and Joyce's *Ulysses.* In August of 1928, lawyers from the Customs Bureau and the Post Office compiled a blacklist of 739 titles for use by agents in the field. Owners of confiscated material could appeal the decisions of customs officers, but such appeals were rare and seldom successful.

On 28 July 1929, Cutting fired the opening salvo of his battle against customs censorship. He issued a press release that criticized the exclusion of *All Quiet on the Western Front.* Then, on 10 October 1929, Cutting moved to eliminate Section 305 entirely from the tariff bill. For tactical reasons, he soon moderated this sweeping proposal and asked simply that books be excluded from the clause. On 11 October, with the Senate sitting as a Committee of the Whole, Cutting's motion passed by the narrow margin of 38 to 36. More than twenty senators abstained, however, so the issue was by no means settled. When the tariff bill came before the Senate for final action in March 1930, its cosponsor, Senator Reed Smoot of Utah, moved to restore books to the censorship provisions of Section 305.

Both in October and in March, the Senate debate was lengthy and impassioned.[32] It amounted to a restatement, in twentieth-century American terms, of the timeless arguments for and against censorship. Defending customs confiscations, Senator Smoot argued that they do more good than harm.

> I know it is said that much of the so-called obscene matter is literature, classical literature, and that foreign classics die along with the matter immoral in purpose, use, and tendency. Well, Mr. President, let the dead bury the dead. It were better, to my mind, that a few classics suffer the application of the expurgating shears than that this country be flooded with the books, pamphlets, pictures, and other articles that are wholly indecent both in purpose and tendency, and that we know all too well would follow the repeal of this provision. (4458)

The Mormon senator from Utah was sincere in his concern to protect the moral integrity of America against corrupting influences.[33] But his assumption that the classics are "dead" letters antagonized many Americans for whom they are alive and permanently relevant.

Advocating the abolition of customs censorship, Senator Cutting advanced the classic libertarian arguments against all forms of censorship, quoting from John Milton's *Areopagitica* and John Stuart Mill's *On Liberty*. Cutting alluded to a wide variety of classical, Renaissance, and modern authors whose lives or works have been affected by censorship, from Socrates to D. H. Lawrence. And he read into the *Congressional Record* testimonials in favor of his initiative signed by hundreds of writers, editors, and educators from all parts of the country.

Cutting argued that censorship is arbitrary, counterproductive, and undemocratic. It is arbitrary because its criteria are not fixed and objective. "There is no authoritative test of obscenity," he told his Senate colleagues. "There is no definition of it which all of us sitting here in this Chamber would agree to. It is one of the vaguest words in the English language" (4438). Furthermore, the criteria of obscenity are relative, and change with time. "The standards of decency and morality vary from generation to generation," Cutting asserted; "public opinion changes with startling rapidity, and . . . the heresies of to-day may easily become the commonplaces and platitudes of to-morrow" (4445, 4451). The sexual explicitness of some modern literature, for example, would not have offended an eighteenth-century reader, however shocking it may seem to a Victorian sensibility conditioned by "a century of comparative prudery" (4435).

Censorship is counterproductive, Cutting maintained, because "the attempt to suppress individual books simply promotes their circulation and reputation" (5489). Cutting's chief example of a book made notorious by efforts to suppress it was *Lady Chatterley's Lover*. Senator Smoot had frequently referred to Lawrence's novel as an example of precisely the type of smut that customs censorship aimed to keep out of America. "There can not be viler language, there can not be words put together so vile and rotten" as in *Lady Chatterley's Lover*, Smoot told the Senate. The novel

> is written by a man with a diseased mind and a soul so black that he would even obscure the darkness of hell. Nobody would write a book like that unless his heart was just as rotten and as black as it possibly could be. (5494)

Cutting retorted that Smoot's "interviews in the press have brought *[Lady Chatterley's Lover]* to the attention literally of millions of American citizens who would otherwise never have heard of the book." Smoot's references to the novel, according to Cutting, "induced the publication of an American edition, which is circulated widely all over the country. . . . That is what he has done; he has made this book a classic" (5490).

Finally, Cutting argued that censorship is undemocratic: "censorship has been in all ages and will always continue to be a tool of tyranny" (5499). "The doctrine of censorship is a doctrine characteristic of the Fascist government of Italy, and equally characteristic of the Bolshevist government of Russia. It has nothing to do with a democracy. A democracy, if it means anything, must be founded on the fundamental proposition that its citizens have a right to hear both sides" (4452). Without that right, Cutting asserted, "thought has ceased to be free, and its expression has equally ceased to be free" (5498).

Such arguments did not impress the most passionate southern advocates of customs censorship: Senators Coleman Blease of South Carolina, J. T. Heflin of Alabama, and Park Trammell of Florida. Senator Blease was especially eloquent: "I had rather see both the democratic form of government and the republican form of government forever destroyed if that should be necessary in order to protect the virtue of the womanhood of America" (5431).

Obscene literature, Blease contended, leads only to the penitentiary, the chain gang, or the bawdy house.

> I hope we will vote to make the importation of such literature a crime. The virtue of one little 16-year-old girl is worth more to America than every book that has ever come into it from any other country. (5432)

Blease threatened to have fired from the University of South Carolina any professor who went on record as supporting the abolition of Section 305.[34]

Cutting rejected such extreme scenarios. "I can not think that the evil effect of works of literature is by any means as far-reaching as the proponents of this sort of legislation seem to believe" (4445). In fact, as Cutting wryly noted, censors inconsistently consider themselves immune from the corrupting influence of the literature they screen. "I believe there is one clerk in the Bureau of Customs who reads all of these works. I do not know whether his morals have been injured or not. Certainly if there is anything in the theory on which this law is based he ought to be the most wicked man on the face of the earth" (4435–36).

Despite his witty and eloquent arguments, Senator Cutting could not persuade his colleagues to abolish the customs censorship of books. But he did succeed in bringing about a significant alteration in Section 305. Under a compromise resolution introduced by Senator Hugo Black of Alabama and eventually passed by the entire Senate, customs officials could initiate action for the seizure of allegedly obscene or seditious printed imports. But the adjudication of cases was vested in the U.S. district courts, and appeals were transferred to the federal appeals courts. Without this change in the tariff law, the case against Joyce's *Ulysses* would never have been tried in New York's Southern District in 1933, and Judge Woolsey would never have issued his famous ruling that *Ulysses* "is not pornographic... [and] may, therefore, be admitted into the United States."[35]

When Yvor Winters praised Senator Cutting in *Poetry* for April 1930, Ezra Pound sent a response that appeared in the June number. In it, he expresses his gratitude for Cutting's efforts and urges that a similar battle against postal censorship be joined immediately.

> In the account of Senator Cutting's speech [of 18 March 1930] that has reached me I see no mention of our postoffice. Sen. Cutting advocated exempting the classics from interference on the Hoboken docks. He said nothing about article 211 of the penal code, which confuses the classics and patent medicines and delivers both to ignorant postal clerks in Senator Smoot's home town or

anywhere else in the country. This appears to me to be a serious omission in Senator Cutting's program. He has a chance to gain still more gratitude, and if he could bring the question to a sane contemporary and enlightened conclusion he would certainly leave a permanent mark in our history. . . . At any rate Cutting has put New Mexico on the map.[36]

In fact, Cutting had already stated his intention to attack postal censorship.[37] He reiterated his determination to do so when he and Pound began to correspond in November and December of 1930.

Pound initiated the contact because he saw in Cutting a potential ally in the never-ending battle against American provincialism. Cutting responded because, although he was not well acquainted with Pound's work, he knew and respected Pound's reputation as a major American poet. The political poet and the literate senator corresponded for the next four and a half years.

2

THE EARLIER LETTERS

1930–1932

Senator Bronson M. Cutting. Courtesy of the Library of Congress.

EZRA POUND AND SENATOR CUTTING

I
INTRODUCTION

The correspondence of Pound and Cutting had two phases. The first group of fifteen letters was exchanged between November 1930 and November 1932; they belong, in other words, to the final years of the Hoover presidency. Having been prompted by the debate over customs censorship, the correspondence continued, in its initial stages, to emphasize questions of culture and cultural politics. From customs censorship, the poet and the senator turned to the issues of postal censorship, international copyright, passport regulations, Prohibition, and the diplomatic recognition of the Soviet Union. Pound had laid out this part of his program as early as 1927, when he took a stand

> against the following abuses: (1) Bureaucratic encroachment on the individual, as the asinine Eighteenth Amendment, passport and visa stupidities, arbitrary injustice from customs officials; (2) Article 211 of the Penal Code, and all such muddle-headedness in any laws whatsoever; (3) the thieving copyright law.[1]

Pound took up all of these matters with Cutting. Economic questions such as child labor and the length of the working day also arose in the earlier letters, but they remained secondary, and we have postponed their consideration to the next chapter.

Underlying Pound's prescriptions on both cultural and economic issues is a vision of healthy, unobstructed circulation within and among national communities—circulation of ideas, publications, works of art, consumer goods, money, and people. To promote that free and life-enhancing circulation, Pound lobbied for the removal of artificial legal restrictions and the creation of unimpeded channels of transmission. The goal, as he phrased it in a letter to Cutting of 9 December [1931?], was "to force an elimination of some of the more barbarous minor infamies." In their discussion of prospective reforms, Pound assumed that he and Cutting were collaborators for cultural enlightenment, working together in a never-ending Progressive crusade against entrenched and benighted forces of ignorance, fear, greed, provinciality, puritanism, and bureaucracy.

The poet's confidence was not misplaced. For his part, Senator Cutting was receptive to a number of the points in his correspondent's program. For instance, he saw eye to eye with Pound on the issues of postal censorship and international copyright and introduced progressive legislation on both subjects, as we shall see. The senator did not, however, share the poet's objection to passport regulations. When it came to Prohibition, both men were "wets," but Cutting tended to be reticent on this politically sensitive issue. On the diplomatic recognition of Soviet Russia, the senator's position was, if anything, in advance of the poet's. Despite some differences of opinion, the two men had no trouble finding enough common ground for their dialogue to expand from the issue of censorship to many of the other urgent public questions confronting the American people in the early years of the Depression.

The correspondence is issue-oriented, topical, and practical; its predominant tone is brisk and businesslike. There is little of a personal, reflective, or philosophical nature. Contexts are taken for granted, and references are often elliptical ("the XVIIIth pestilence," "the baboon law"). The writers are usually too busy to explain their positions fully to one another or to fill in the backgrounds of the issues they are discussing.

Because the correspondence is so specific in its focus, we have compiled brief general introductions to the main questions addressed in its first phase. The following historical summaries offer wider views of the day-to-day and month-to-month developments preoccupying the writers of the bulletins that passed between Rapallo and Washington in 1930–32.

A.
Postal Censorship

Pound first wrote to Cutting to urge him to follow up his partially successful campaign against customs censorship with an attack upon postal censorship. The immediate target was Article 211 of Chapter 321 of the United States Criminal Code of 1909. This law gave postal employees the right to impound obscene printed material and objects circulating through the U.S. mail and to initiate criminal prosecutions of senders and recipients. In 1928, 262 people were arrested for, and 220 convicted of, violating Article 211.[2]

Censorship of the federal post had begun in the era of the Civil War. The first law to prohibit the transmission of obscene material through the U.S.

mail was passed by Congress on 3 March 1865, primarily to stop the traffic in erotic items to soldiers in the Union army. The provision was amended and enlarged in bills of 8 June 1872 and 4 March 1873. The latter was the "Comstock Act," which, as we saw in Chapter One, also underpinned the customs-censorship provision of the tariff law. Further revisions of the postal-censorship law took place in 1876, 1888, and 1890. On 4 March 1909, the language quoted below, most of which dates from the bill of 12 July 1876, became Section 211 of Chapter 321 of the United States Criminal Code.

> Every obscene, lewd, or lascivious, and every filthy, book, pamphlet, picture, paper, letter, writing, print, or other publication of an indecent character, and every article or thing designed, adapted, or intended for preventing conception or producing abortion, or for any indecent or immoral use; and every article, instrument, substance, drug, medicine, or thing which is advertised or described in a manner calculated to lead another to use or apply it for preventing conception or producing abortion, or for any indecent or immoral purpose; and every written or printed card, letter, circular, book, pamphlet, advertisement, or notice of any kind giving information directly or indirectly, where, or how, or from whom, or by what means any of the hereinbefore-mentioned matters, articles, or things may be obtained or made, or where or by whom any act or operation of any kind for the procuring or producing of abortion will be done or performed, or how or by what means conception may be prevented or abortion produced, whether sealed or unsealed; and every letter, packet, or package, or other mail matter containing any filthy, vile, or indecent thing, device, or substance; and every paper, writing, advertisement, or representation that any article, instrument, substance, drug, medicine, or thing may, or can, be used or applied for preventing conception or producing abortion, or for any indecent or immoral purpose; and every description calculated to induce or incite a person to so use or apply any such article, instrument, substance, drug, medicine, or thing, is hereby declared to be nonmailable matter and shall not be conveyed in the mails or delivered from any post office or by any letter carrier. Whoever shall knowingly deposit, or cause to be deposited for mailing or delivery, anything declared by this section to be nonmailable, or shall knowingly take, or cause the same to be taken, from the mails for the purpose of circulating or disposing thereof, or of aiding in the circulation or disposition thereof, shall be fined not more than five thousand dollars, or imprisoned not more than five years, or both.[3]

Aimed primarily at pornography and birth-control materials, Article 211 was sometimes invoked to suppress questionable literature. That is why Pound accused the law, in his opening letter to Senator Cutting, of "confusing smutty postcards, condoms & Catullus." Pound had first run afoul of the provision when it was used to block distribution of the October 1917 issue of *The Little Review,* which contained Wyndham Lewis's controversial story, "Cantleman's Spring Mate."[4] Then, in 1919–20, the Post Office seized and burned three issues of *The Little Review,* each of which carried an installment of James Joyce's *Ulysses.*[5]

Pound immediately declared war upon Article 211. Between March 1918 and December 1930, he reprinted the full text of the law at least six times in various periodicals. Simply to read the language of the provision, Pound felt, was to see its absurdity: "its very wording proclaims a contempt for the concision and economy of the classics and a disdain of Latinity."[6] In addition to these public attacks, he lobbied against Article 211 in many private letters to U.S. officials, from the chief justice of the Supreme Court on down.

Cutting agreed fully with Pound on the issue of postal censorship. "I am just as much opposed to Article 211 of the Penal Code as I was to the corresponding section of the tariff law," he assured his correspondent in the earliest letter he sent to Rapallo (8 December 1930). And Cutting acted upon his conviction. In 1931 and 1932, he tried to help amend what he and Pound both called "the baboon law." But the revision of Article 211 proved to be altogether more difficult than the revision of Section 305 of the tariff law.

In the year following the senator's partial victory over customs censorship, a vigorous initiative was mounted against postal censorship. The campaign was spearheaded not by literary intellectuals so much as by birth-control advocates. Margaret Sanger, who had been indicted for violating Article 211 in 1914, pushed for a specifically focused amendment to the law which would exempt doctors from its anti-contraceptive provisions. Early in 1931, an amendment to this effect (S. 4582) was sponsored by Senator Frederick H. Gillett (1851–1935), a lame-duck Republican from Massachusetts.

Hearings on Gillett's bill were held before a subcommittee of the Senate Committee on the Judiciary on 13–14 February 1931. The New York *World* for 15 February 1931 (p. 2) reported that

> enemies of the Gillett Bill to open the mails to the circulation of birth control information jammed a Senate committee room today [14 February] to offer vigorous opposition to the arguments presented yesterday by Mrs. Margaret

Sanger of New York. . . . Chief among their reasons was the objection raised by Ralph Barton, counsel for the Sentinels of the Republic, who told the committee that enactment of the measure permitting a reprinting and circulation of birth control information originally printed in any foreign or domestic government publication would permit the Soviet Russian Government to flood the United States with free love literature.

The opposition groups included the American Medical Association, the American Federation of Labor, the Lord's Day Alliance, the Methodist Episcopal Board of Public Morals, the New York Society for the Suppression of Vice, the National Reform Society, the World's Purity Federation, the Southern Baptist Association, the National Council of Catholic Women, the Patriotic Society, the Purity League, the Clean Books League, the Knights of Columbus, and the International Order of Foresters. As Senator Cutting told Pound, "it is hard running up against the organizations of canned virtue" (23 January 1932).

The Gillett Bill died in 1931. In 1932, Senator Cutting himself, with the backing of the American Civil Liberties Union and the National Council on Freedom from Censorship, sponsored a wider-ranging bill (S. 3907) "to amend section 211 of the Criminal Code, as amended (relating to nonmailable matter)."[7] As *The Publishers' Weekly* reported on 2 April 1932, this bill sought to provide "the same procedure of trial by jury as is now used for printed matter coming from abroad" (p. 1561). "I am working on an amendment to the Baboon law," the senator told Pound on 23 January,

which I hope to have ready in a few days. I think the best we can hope for is to bring the procedure in line with that which I got into the Tariff Act two years ago. Of course the thing ought to be out of the criminal code altogether, but we would not have the slightest chance of eliminating it.

This amendment, too, died in the Judiciary Committee, and other bills failed in 1934 and 1935. In all, five hearings on Article 211 were held in as many years. The ban on contraceptive materials was not eliminated until 1971. The rest of Article 211 remains in force today as Title 18, Chapter 71, Section 1461 of the U.S. Code.

Having failed to move the Congress, Mrs. Sanger tried her luck in the courts, where she met with better success. In 1936, a federal court exempted doctors from the prohibition against the importation and mailing of contraceptive devices.[8]

B.
INTERNATIONAL COPYRIGHT

Between 1922 and 1940, many efforts were made in Congress to amend the copyright law of 1909 in order to allow the United States to join the International Copyright Union. Adherence to the Berne Convention for the Protection of Literary and Artistic Works, which established the Union in 1886, would have protected the creations of American authors, artists, composers, and filmmakers in most European countries and many other parts of the world.[9] By the same token, foreign works of art would have been protected from exploitation by American pirates such as Samuel Roth, who published a version of James Joyce's *Ulysses* in 1926–27 without requesting the author's permission or paying him any royalties.

One of the most important pieces of legislation designed to achieve these ends was the Vestal Bill, named after its sponsor, Albert Henry Vestal (1875–1932), Republican congressman from Indiana and chairman of the House Committee on Patents. Originally introduced in 1926, the Vestal Bill had been nearly six years in the making and had grown to a length of fifty-four pages by the time it came before the Seventy-first Congress in 1931 as H.R. 12549. The main provisions of the bill made copyright automatic and divisible and permitted the United States to join the International Copyright Union.

The Vestal Bill passed the House of Representatives on 5 January 1931 and was then taken up by the Senate. Bronson Cutting spoke in favor of the bill on 29 January in hearings of the Committee on Patents and on 28 February on the Senate floor. But the bill never came to a vote in that session of Congress because of a filibuster on an unrelated issue by Senator Elmer Thomas of Oklahoma. Pound, who had supported the Vestal Bill since at least the spring of 1927, criticized Thomas's obstructive tactics in the pages of the *Saturday Review of Literature*.[10]

When a new Congress convened in December 1931, Pound reminded Cutting that the issue was still unresolved: "copyright, probably bogging along . . . but still no harm in mentioning it" (9 December [1931?]). Representative Vestal reintroduced his bill but died of a sudden heart attack on 1 April 1932. His successor as chairman of the House Committee on Patents was Representative William Sirovich of New York. In the spring of 1932, Sirovich introduced and held hearings on a new bill of his own devising "to amend and consolidate the acts respecting copyright and to codify and amend common-law rights of authors in their works" (H.R. 10740, later revised four times and reintroduced as H.R. 10976, 11948, 12094, and 12425). This bill, too, would have allowed the United States to join the International Copyright Union. Opposed by radio broadcasters, motion picture and theater producers, and phonograph and record manufacturers, it did not pass.

In June of 1933, Senator Cutting himself introduced a simplified measure focused exclusively upon the issue of international copyright. The aim of Senate bill 1928 was "to enable the United States to enter the International Copyright Union."[11] Lengthy hearings on the bill took place before a subcommittee of the Senate Committee on Foreign Relations, which reported the measure favorably to the full Senate on 18 April 1935. Nevertheless, Cutting's initiative was not adopted. The United States remained outside the Berne Convention until 1 May 1989. Instead of entering the International Copyright Union, the U.S. government worked through UNESCO for the establishment of an alternative organization called the Universal Copyright Convention, which the U.S. joined on 16 September 1955.

C.
PASSPORT REGULATIONS

Until the Great War of 1914–18, most international travelers needed no passports. American sightseers moved freely in Europe, and European visitors toured the United States without hindrance. "Except . . . for a brief period during the Civil War, passports were not required by the United States for travel abroad by its citizens and few obstacles existed to travel by way of the passport requirements of foreign states."[12] Both Pound and Cutting grew up under this liberal dispensation and carried neither passports nor visas in their pockets when they took their earliest trips abroad.

During the Great War, the governments of the United States and most European countries, desiring to control the movements of hostile aliens, suspicious neutrals, potential spies, and displaced populations, began to impose passport and visa requirements. On 22 May 1918, during the second administration of President Woodrow Wilson, Congress adopted the Passport Control Act, intended "to prevent in time of war departure from or entry into the United States, contrary to the public safety."

This legislation made it "unlawful for any citizen of the United States to depart from or enter the United States unless he bears a valid passport."

Penalties ranged up to ten thousand dollars in fines and twenty years' imprisonment. By the same token, the act made it illegal "for any alien to depart from or enter or attempt to depart from or enter the United States except under such reasonable rules, regulations, and orders, and subject to such limitations and exceptions as the President shall prescribe."[13] The executive orders that soon took effect required any alien entering the United States to possess not only a valid foreign passport but a proper visa issued by an American consul or other accredited representative abroad. In 1919 the Passport Control Act was extended into peacetime. Terms of validity on U.S. passports and visas were set at two years or less, necessitating frequent renewals.

Pound and Cutting, who were both in London when the Passport Control Act was passed, reacted very differently to the new requirements. To comply with British wartime regulations governing alien residents, Pound had obtained his first passport in March 1916 and renewed it six months later. But he did not really become aware of the new U.S. regulations until he traveled from England to France in 1919 and found himself obliged to obtain papers from American authorities in both London and Paris.[14] He thereupon became a passionate opponent of passports and visas, denouncing them in letter after letter to the Paris editions of the *New York Herald* and the *Chicago Tribune* during the 1920s and early 1930s. In one such protest, he described the passport requirement as "a needless nuisance fostered by a blithering lot of bureaucrats."[15] Writing to Senator Cutting in 1931, Pound blamed the red tape on President Wilson. "The god damned spirit of obstruction came in with Woodie Wilsi's rough necks," he grumbled (17 February [1931]).

On this issue, however, Pound found the senator unresponsive. Throughout their correspondence, Cutting maintained a discreet silence on the subject of passports and visas. In fact, he had been very much in favor of them during the war, as a result of his experience as a U.S. military intelligence officer.

Cutting's principal duties as Assistant Military Attaché to the U.S. Embassy in London from August 1917 to February 1919 included counterespionage and liaison with British military intelligence agencies. In the confidential report he wrote to the acting director of U.S. military intelligence upon leaving London in 1919, Cutting recalls that, when he arrived some eighteen months earlier, "the lack of proper control over persons traveling to the United States was probably the most serious feature of the intelligence situation in England. . . . Before March 1918 there was no control whatever." He welcomed the imposition of passport and visa requirements as a way of restricting "the number of doubtful characters who were getting across the Atlantic." He was personally involved in screening visa applications in London, and although he was critical of the inefficient way the system worked in practice, he definitely approved of it in principle.[16]

It is no wonder, then, that when Pound derided passports in their correspondence twelve years later, his complaints struck no responsive chord in the once-uniformed and decorated bosom of the senator. Cutting firmly believed that passports were necessary to safeguard the security of the nation.

D.
Prohibition

The Eighteenth Amendment to the Constitution of the United States prohibited the manufacture and sale of any drink containing more than 0.5 percent alcohol. Prohibition took effect on 16 January 1920 and remained the law of the land until 5 December 1933, when the Eighteenth Amendment was repealed by the Twenty-first. In January and February of 1931, measures both to strengthen and to weaken Prohibition were pending before Congress.

The Eighteenth Amendment struck Pound, who had lived in France and Italy since shortly after its passage, as simply barbarous, inconceivable in a truly civilized nation. He himself was a light drinker, especially in comparison with many members of the "lost generation" of Americans who frequented Paris during the early twenties. Nevertheless, Pound was an outspoken "wet." He stated his views in a letter to the editor of the New York *World* for 14 February 1931: "As a camouflage for corruption prohibition has been useful to the worst elements in American politics and to no other element at any time whatsoever" (p. 8). After eleven years of protest, Pound's impatience with Prohibition was exceeded only by his boredom.

In his correspondence with Senator Cutting, Pound is so weary of the issue that he can summon little more than grumbling abuse of "the XVIIIth pestilence" (3 February 1931), "the 18th infamy" (17 February [1931]), "the dirty XVIIIth amendment" (20 March 1931), and "the 18th catastrophe" (13 November [1932]). In one letter, however, he rouses himself enough to send Cutting a quotation from the letters of Thomas Jefferson, in which the founding father encourages the consumption in America of lightly taxed "cheap wines" as "a great gain to the treasury, and the sobriety of the country" (17 February [1931]). Still, it took nearly three more years for Pound's compatriots to achieve a Jeffersonian awareness of the virtues of *vin plonk.*

Cutting's position on Prohibition was more equivocal than that of his correspondent. Like Pound, Cutting was temperate in his personal drinking habits. But he enjoyed a glass of good wine, and was something of a connoisseur of French and German vintages. The wine cellar at Los Siete Burros was said to be "perhaps the finest . . . in the Southwest."[17] According to Brian Boru Dunne, a Santa Fe friend, Cutting was of the opinion that "a little good wine and a little good beer could do no harm to the average human being."[18]

Because Prohibition was such a sensitive and divisive political issue, however, Cutting did not become a militant "wet." Within the Progressive wing of the national Republican party, there was little consensus on the question. Although some of Cutting's allies opposed the Eighteenth Amendment, Senator William Borah of Idaho, the most prominent and vocal member of the faction, was fiercely "dry." Borah managed to get a strong endorsement of Prohibition inserted into the Republican national platform of 1928. Herbert Hoover, the party's presidential candidate in that year, accepted the plank, spoke of Prohibition as a noble experiment, and was elected by a wide margin over his Democratic opponent, Governor Al Smith of New York, a known "wet." Bronson Cutting, running in his first statewide election in 1928, sensed the tenor of the times. He, too, accepted his party's national platform, endorsed its presidential candidate, ran as a "dry," and won a full term in the Senate. New Mexico had voted overwhelmingly in favor of Prohibition in 1917, and the editorial policy of Cutting's newspaper, the Santa Fe *New Mexican,* remained ardently "dry" throughout the 1920s.[19]

Not until the mood of the nation began to swing against Prohibition in the early 1930s did Cutting change course on the issue. In 1932, he endorsed Franklin D. Roosevelt, who ran for the presidency on a repeal platform. In an International News Service poll released on 25 November 1932, just two weeks after Roosevelt's election, Cutting went on record as favoring the legalization of 2.75 percent beer.[20] The editorial policy of the *New Mexican* shifted from "dry" to "wet," and in September 1933 state voters went on record in favor of repeal.[21] By the time Cutting stood for reelection in 1934, Prohibition was history and he did not have to take a campaign position on it, one way or the other. If Pound had hoped that the senator would take up cudgels against the Eighteenth Amendment, he was disappointed. Cutting, who always chose his fights carefully, was too shrewd a politician to risk his career on such a treacherous issue.

E.
DIPLOMATIC RECOGNITION OF THE SOVIET UNION

After the Russian Revolution of October 1917, the United States refused to recognize the communist government of the Soviet Union for more than sixteen years. But the crisis of Western capitalism in the early 1930s awakened new interest in the Russian experiment. Much of this interest centered upon the comparative success or failure of the five-year economic plan that had commenced in 1928. Both Pound and Cutting were caught up in the great national debate over the significance for America of the Soviet political and economic system. Although neither man believed that socialism would suit the United States, both favored the diplomatic recognition of the Soviet government.

Senator Cutting had some firsthand knowledge of Russia, having spent several weeks there during the summer of 1930. He went on a fact-finding junket with Senators Burton Wheeler of Montana and Alben W. Barkley of Kentucky. The solons arrived in Russia on 11 August. They spent one week in Moscow and one in Leningrad, where they conducted discussions with the State Planning Commission, the Council of Trade Unions, and education authorities. The visitors also went to a great many rural villages. Cutting was impressed by the enthusiasm of the people he met, if not by their efficiency. He disliked the apparatus of state surveillance and control.[22]

Nevertheless, the trip convinced Cutting that the Soviet system was there to stay and that the United States had little to fear and much to gain from a dialogue with it. On 31 January 1931, he put this case to the National Republican Club in New York City. His speech, in which Pound had a hand, was printed a week later in the *Congressional Record* under the title "Recognition of Russia."

Cutting began by citing the analogy of Thomas Jefferson's diplomatic recognition of Republican France in 1793. He went on to argue that "the Russian experiment, like it or not, is one of the fundamental events in world history. We can not ignore it and we can not cope with it through lack of recognition or through suppression or through misrepresentation."[23] Pound's contribution to the speech was a quotation from Jefferson, whose works he was then culling in preparation for the writing of Cantos 31–33. The quotation does not appear in printed versions of Cutting's speech, but the senator acknowledged its receipt and use in a letter to Pound of 6 February 1931. "Thanks for record of yr/ speech," Pound replied in turn. "I (so far as I see) agree. I mean we both think there is no Russian peril once they and 'we' have a clear idea of the other's position" (17 February [1931]).

From such an episode, we can see why Pound believed that he might influence national policy through his personal correspondence with the men at the head of the government. He might act as informal adviser and research assistant, turning up historical precedents that could be quoted to make contemporary reforms seem less radical. With Cutting's encouragement, he continued to provide data for debating purposes, although there is no evidence that the senator actually used any of the additional ammunition he received from Rapallo.

Pound participated in the discussion of Soviet communism in other ways as well. He skirmished with Marxist intellectuals in the pages of left-wing little magazines, two of which were editorially associated with Cutting's home state of New Mexico. In *Morada,* Pound took on Mike Gold and the *New Masses;* while in *Front,* he crossed swords with communist playwright Sergei Mikhailovich Tretyakow.[24] In February 1931 Pound sent Cutting a copy of the second number of *Front,* as if to show him the lively doings of some of his own constituents. Four years later, as we shall see, the senator opened the pages of his own newspaper, the Santa Fe *New Mexican,* to a series of editorials from Rapallo on a variety of economic, political, and cultural topics.

On the issue of diplomatic recognition, as on the question of Prohibition, the poet and the senator were about three years ahead of their times. Cutting was unable to sway mainstream Republican opinion, and the United States did not recognize the Soviet government until 17 November 1933, after President Roosevelt had assumed office.

In the first phase of their correspondence, then, Pound and Cutting found common ground on a number of cultural issues. Pound argued for the removal of legal restrictions upon, and the creation of unimpeded channels for, the circulation of ideas, publications, works of art, people, and goods. Thus he opposed customs and postal censorship, passport regulations, and

Prohibition, whereas he favored international copyright and the diplomatic recognition of Russia. Cutting agreed with Pound on at least three of these causes, and actively promoted them while in office. During the period of their correspondence, the reformers saw victories on the issues of customs censorship, Prohibition, and the recognition of Russia. But they lost the battles over postal censorship and international copyright. Their struggles continued beyond the Hoover years into the first phase of the New Deal.

II
THE LETTERS

1. TL, carbon copy, 1p., Beinecke Library

8 Nov. 1930

My dear Senator Cutting

Article 211 of the Penal code was, as I have had occasion to remark "obviously made by gorillas for the further stultification of imbeciles". The late Chief Justice Taft was somewhat shocked at this expression but I see no reason to soften it.

As the recent election has purged the senate of some of the worst fauna which you had against you in the debate of March 18th. wd. it not now be possible to rise on some quiet day and move the repeal of that idiot "article" (the one confusing smutty post cards; condoms and Catullus.)?

I know there are formalities of "procedure" etc. but they are not subject for conversation between serious men.

/ /

I shd. be very glad if your secretary cd; find time to send me sections of the *Congressional Record* when any bills affecting literature or any attempts to civilize the country are under discussion. And perhaps a list of the literate members of the senate (this last I shd. treat as a confidential communication, meaning that I wd. NOT mention the source of my information).

very truly yours

Notes on Letter 1

(8 Nov. 1930)

Article 211. See the Introduction to Chapter Two, pp. 24–27, above. EP here echoes his own description of the article as "a law obviously framed by baboons for the further stultification of imbeciles"; see "And the Remainder," *Hound & Horn* 3, 3 (April–June 1930), 417–20; rpt., *Ezra Pound's Poetry and Prose*, 5: 214. For a poetic version entitled "Damnation to Bureaucrats," see also EP's letter of 8 May 1930 to Judge Beals of the Washington State Supreme Court, first published in *Hyperion* 3, 3 (Fall 1973) [4–6], and rpt., *Ezra Pound's Poetry and Prose*, 10: 88–89. EP often referred to Article 211 as "the baboon law," an allusion to the Tennessee law against the teaching of evolution in the public schools; see "The Irish Censorship," *Chicago Tribune* (Paris), 15 December 1928, p. 4; rpt., *Ezra Pound's Poetry and Prose*, 5: 88. The phrase also referred to those who condoned or supported Article 211, whom EP considered to be "little better than apes"; see "From Ezra Pound," *Chicago Tribune* (Paris), 26 May 1928, p. 4; rpt., *Ezra Pound's Poetry and Prose*, 5: 30.

Taft. William Howard Taft (1857– 1930) was president of the United States from 1909 to 1913 and chief justice of the United States Supreme Court from 1921 to 1930. EP wrote to him on 30 December 1927, attacking the passport system, and again on 11 December 1928, attacking Article 211: "It is inconceivable it shd. have been passed by anything save an assembly of baboons and imbeciles" (Pound Archive). Taft replied in two perfunctory letters to EP dated 24 January and 24 December 1928 (Taft Papers, Manuscript Division, Library of Congress).

recent election. In the congressional elections of 1930, both Senator Blease of South Carolina and Senator Heflin of Alabama (see Letters 7 and 15 below) lost their seats. They had opposed BC in the Senate debate of 17–18 March 1930 on customs censorship; see Chapter One, pp. 18–19 above.

2. ALS, 2pp., Beinecke Library

9 Dec. 1930

United States Senate
Washington, D.C.

Dear Mr. Pound,

As to condoms & Catullus:

On returning here I saw your letter. I am just as much opposed
to Article 211 of the Penal Code as I was to the corresponding
section of the tariff law. Owing to an anomaly of our constitution
the fauna whom you mention, though retired by the voters, are still
with us; and the House contains hundreds of their stripe. There is
no use trying anything of this kind till the new Congress (72nd)
which starts next December, and which promises to be
considerably more liberal.

As for "literacy", I don't suppose you are interested in people
like Moses & Bingham & Dave Reed, who sin against the light.
That leaves Borah & Norris & LaFollette & Hiram Johnson &
Tydings & Wheeler & Walsh of Montana & I suppose Dwight
Morrow, & not much else. But don't say that I said so.

Sincerely,

Bronson Cutting

Notes on Letter 2

(9 Dec. 1930)

an anomaly. Though elected on 4 November 1930, the Seventy-second Congress did not legally take office until March 1931 and did not actually convene until December 1931. By then, eleven of the elected congressmen, including Dwight W. Morrow (see note below), had died. The Twentieth Amendment to the U.S. Constitution, sponsored by Senator George W. Norris of Nebraska (see below) and ratified in February 1933, eliminated the anomalous delay of which BC speaks. The amendment stipulates that the members of an incoming Congress shall take office on 3 January following its election. The amendment had the effect of ending "lame-duck" sessions of outgoing congresses, which had traditionally been held in the first three months of the new year following November elections.

"literacy". EP mentions this list of senators in Cantos 86, 98, and 102; in the *Saturday Review of Literature* 8, 8 (29 August 1931), 92; in *Contempo* 1, 9 (15 September 1931), 1–2; in "The European in America," *Poetry* 41, 5 (February 1933), 273–75; in "L'economia ortologica—Il problema centrale," *Rassegna Monetaria* 34, 7–8 (July–August 1937), 711; and in *Guide to Kulchur* (1938; new ed., Norfolk, Conn.: New Directions, 1952), 260. The magazine pieces are reprinted in *Ezra Pound's Poetry and Prose*, 5: 319; 6: 11–12; and 7: 221.

Moses. George Higgins Moses (1869–1944) was Republican senator from New Hampshire from 1918 to 1933. EP corresponded with him in February and March of 1934 (Pound Archive).

Bingham. Hiram Bingham (1875–1956) served as Republican senator from Connecticut in 1925–33. He was well known as a historian of South America and the explorer of Machu Picchu.

Dave Reed. David A. Reed (1880–1953) served as Republican senator from Pennsylvania in 1923–35.

Borah. Independent Republican William Edgar Borah (1865–1940) represented Idaho from 1907 to 1940. He was one of the Senate's most influential members. EP frequently corresponded with Borah during the 1930s (Pound Archive).

Norris. Progressive Republican George William Norris (1861–1944) represented Nebraska in the Senate in 1913–43.

La Follette. Progressive Republican Robert Marion LaFollette, Jr. (1895–1953) of Wisconsin served in the Senate from 1925 to 1947.

Johnson. Progressive Republican Hiram Warren Johnson (1866–1945) was California's senator from 1917 until his death. EP corresponded with him in 1934 (Pound Archive).

Tydings. Democrat Millard E. Tydings (1890–1961) represented Maryland in the Senate from 1927 to 1951.

Wheeler. Burton Kendall Wheeler (1882–1975) was Democratic senator from Montana in 1923–47. He was the vice presidential candidate of the Progressive party in 1924. EP corresponded with him from April 1936 to April 1940 (Pound Archive).

Walsh. Democrat Thomas J. Walsh (1859–1933) represented Montana from 1913 to 1933. He led the Senate investigation into the Teapot Dome scandal and was President Roosevelt's first choice for the post of attorney general. Walsh died two days before the Roosevelt administration took office.

Dwight Morrow. Republican banker Dwight Whitney Morrow (1873–1931) was elected to the Senate from New Jersey in 1930 but served only ten months before he died unexpectedly in October 1931. He worked for J. P. Morgan and Company from 1914 to 1927, when he became United States Ambassador to Mexico. He was also the father-in-law of Charles Lindbergh. BC knew Morrow personally and called upon him at the embassy in Mexico City. In *The Cantos*, EP misnames him "Dwight L. Morrow," probably conflating the senator's name with that of Dwight L. Moody (1837–1899), a famous American evangelist.

3. TLS, 1p., Beinecke Library

8 Jan. 1931

United States Senate
Committee on Military Affairs

My dear Mr. Pound:

Many thanks for your good letter of December 22d.

The Jefferson quotation is very apt, and I shall be glad to get
anything worth while from John Adams, not merely with regard
to article 211, but on any other subject which is still alive.

As to article 211, there has been quite a move to bring it at least
into accordance with the present state of the similar clause in the
Tariff Act. There is no chance of accomplishing anything in the
present Congress, and my feeling has been that we should leave it
until the new Congress. But some of our friends think we should
make a start even now, in order to get some publicity. At any rate,
something will be started fairly soon.

Please do not hesitate to write whenever you have anything on
your mind. You will understand if at times you get only brief
and perfunctory replies.

Very sincerely yours,

Bronson Cutting

NOTES ON LETTER 3

(8 Jan. 1931)

your good letter of December 22nd. We have not found this letter in the Pound Archive or the Cutting Papers.

4. TL, carbon copy, 2pp., Beinecke Library

3 Feb. 1931

EZRA POUND
RAPALLO
VIA MARSALA, 12 INT. 5

Dear Senator Cutting

My last outbreak left here a few hours before I recd. your letter of
whatever the date was. In accordance with that I shall put down
citations from Jefferson's correspondence (disparate and
heteroclite) which strike me as having a chance of being useful.
You can file 'em acc/ whatever system (if any) you use.

"ALL <u>EXCESS</u> OF PUNISHMENT IS A CRIME"

This is as official as anything can be, it is Jefferson as secretary of
state, to Carmichael and Short instructing them re/ an extradition
treaty with Spain.

Vol. VIII (bound up with vol. VII) of *Writings of T.J.* edited by
Lipscomb, pub; by Jefferson Memorial assn. Page 333

The underlining is Jeffersons. I have put the sentence in caps.
merely to make it apparent in this note.

On p. 255; of the same vol. in a letter to Washington Jeff. speaks
of "acts render'd criminal by tyrannical laws only".

Both these citations seem to me too good to waste on trivial
occasions, but wd. certainly apply to damnable idiocies of
punishing booksellers under asininity 211. and to any conceivable
punishment given anyone under the XVIIIth. pestilence.

So much for criminals. Secondly and probably irrelevantly//

As "no American" has any principles, in the sense that almost no one ever thinks anything down to its root; wd. it be feasible occasionally to kill off or at least throw one or two of the most objectionable solons by more sweeping or general questions (obviously must be sudden act): "Just what does the gent from (child labour district or wherever it might be) suppose that the state is for?"

No use against the downy old scoundrels who are sure it was created for their personal use, but some of these southern lyricists who still perfume the debates with selections from poesy about twilight etc....

Thirdly

Jefferson vol. IX. p. 424/ and beginning of same letter

"immense consequence that the states retain as complete authority over their own citizens."

citation not specific; but idea that jurisdiction from courts outside state causes confusion.

Please dont take time out to answer this. I shall undoubtedly send irrelevant items, but if one citation in ten is of any use, I shall be satisfied.

I see that Vestal has got his copyright bill half way through, and that *N. Y. World* is raising filibusterous obstruction re/ detail. Surely the sensible thing wd. be to get it through now and make additions later (even in 1950) rather than lose it all.

Notes on Letter 4

(3 Feb. 1931)

My last outbreak. Apparently a letter of 21 January 1931, which has not survived. BC refers to it in Letter 5 below.

Jefferson's correspondence. EP quotes from *The Writings of Thomas Jefferson*, Monticello Edition, ed. Andrew A. Lipscomb et al., 20 vols. (Washington D. C.: Thomas Jefferson Memorial Association, 1903–4), 8: 333 (letter of 24 April 1792 to Messrs. Carmichael and Short) and 255 (letter of 7 November 1791 to President Washington); and 9: 424 (letter of 7 September 1797 to Colonel James Monroe reading, "It is of immense consequence that the States retain as complete authority as possible over their own citizens"). EP was culling the works of Jefferson in preparation for a series of lectures at the University of Bocconi in Milan and for the writing of Cantos 31–33.

XVIIIth pestilence. The Eighteenth Amendment to the U.S. Constitution, which mandated Prohibition; see the Introduction to Chapter Two, pp. 31–33 above.

child labour district. See Letter 7 below.

southern lyricists. See Letter 15 below.

Vestal. On Representative Albert H. Vestal and his copyright bill, see the Introduction to Chapter Two, pp. 28–29 above.

N. Y. World. The New York *World* published two editorials on the Vestal Bill on 10 January 1931 (p. 10) and 14 January 1931 (p. 14). The former argued that "it is to be regretted that a measure with so many good features should also be cluttered with indefensible restrictions on the importation of certain classes of foreign books." The latter proposed an amendment to the bill.

5. TLS, 1p., Beinecke Library

6 Feb. 1931

United States Senate
Committee on Military Affairs

My dear Mr. Pound:

This will acknowledge your letter of January 21st. I shall see that
you get the *Record* once in a while.

I have not yet had time to read Grinko's book, but was in Russia
last summer, and had a chance to see the five year plan in action.

I used your Jefferson quotation in speaking at the National
Republican Club the other day. The enclosed version, as printed in
the *Record,* does not contain the quotation, as it is merely the
advance version which was given out for release.

Believe me always

Sincerely yours,

Bronson Cutting

Notes on Letter 5

(6 Feb. 1931)

Grinko's book. Grigory Fedorovich Grinko, *The Five-Year Plan of the Soviet Union: A Political Interpretation* (New York: International Publishers, 1930).

Russia. On BC's trip to Russia in August 1930 and his speech of 31 January 1931 advocating the diplomatic recognition of the Soviet Union, see the Introduction to Chapter Two, pp. 33–34 above.

6. TL, carbon copy, 2pp., Beinecke Library

17 Feb. [1931]

My dear Senator:

Thanks for record of yr/ speech. I (so far as I see) agree. I mean we
both think there is no Russian peril once they and "we" have
a clear idea of the other's position. If you don't receive copies of
FRONT within a week or so, please let me know. I am trying to
start an argument with Tretyakow. I.e. the editor *says* T. is going
to answer my reply to T.

/ / / /

I suppose it wd. be as much as a "seat" is worth to enquire of the
supporters of the baboon law (211) just what THEY imagine to be
the advantage [of?] ten children and misery plus a bit of paper
from the registry office over "free love" on an income?

(This apropos the newspaper reports re/ debate on the birth control
side of case). Syndically speaking I am more concerned with the
question of Catullus. . . .

/ / / /

Re/ the 18th infamy. I find this / Jefferson to Gallatin (T.J. vol. 11
(eleven) p. 216. June 3, 1807

"I am persuaded that were the duty on cheap wines put on the
same ratio with the dear, it wd. wonderfully enlarge the field of
those who use wine, to the

[rest of page cut off]

The introduction of a very cheap wine (St George) into my neighborhood, within two years past, has quadrupled in that time the number of those who keep wine, and will ere long increase them ten fold. This wd. be a great gain to the treasury, and to the sobriety of our country.

red ink mine.

re the enquiry in my second paragraph, it cd. be quoted. Even a senator might have received a letter containing the enquiry. (not from me. It would NOT do for a senator to be suspected of receiving my correspondence, not YET . . .

/ / / / / / / /

I enclose a hysterical document from (though you might not on internal evidence suspect it,) a A.P. correspondent. I think I have done all that can be expected of me re/ the passport imbecility. The god damned spirit of obstruction came in with Woodie Wilsi's rough necks. Consular behaviour improved under Coolidge but the dept. is not yet wholly purged, nor are we yet as well off as the English.

Mussolini simply gave a comprehensive order re/ frontiers, to the effect that travelers were not to be subjected to needless annoyance. An Englishman through

[rest of page cut off]

Notes on Letter 6

(17 Feb. [1931])

FRONT. A Marxist literary-political journal edited by Sonja Prins and others and published in The Hague. EP contributed a "Credo" and an "Open Letter to Tretyakov, kolchoznik" to the first number (December 1930, pp. 11, 124–26). The latter was a response to a "Report" in the same issue (pp. 45–52) by Russian poet, playwright, and theorist Sergei Mikhailovich Tretyakov (1892–1939?), who had spent a year on a collective farm and urged other writers to do likewise. See E. P. Walkiewicz and Hugh Witemeyer, "Ezra Pound's Contributions to New Mexican Periodicals and His Relationship with Senator Bronson Cutting," *Paideuma* 9, 3 (Winter 1980) 447–48.

the birthcontrol side of the case. On the opposition of birth-control advocates to Article 211, see the Introduction to Chapter Two, pp. 26–27 above.

18th infamy. The Eighteenth Amendment to the U.S. Constitution, which mandated Prohibition; for the positions of EP and BC on this issue, see the Introduction to Chapter Two, pp. 31–33 above.

T.J. vol. 11. For *The Writings of Thomas Jefferson,* see Letter 4 above. A great believer in the salubrious qualities of wine, Jefferson kept a large cellar at Monticello and made a point of taking some every day.

passport imbecility. On the modern history of U.S. passport regulations and the attitudes of EP and BC toward those regulations, see the Introduction to Chapter Two, pp. 29–31 above.

Woodie Wilsi. President Woodrow Wilson (1856–1924), during whose second term in office the Passport Control Act of 1918 was adopted.

Coolidge. Calvin Coolidge (1872– 1933) was president of the United States from 1923 to 1929.

Mussolini. Benito Mussolini (1883– 1945) was premier of Italy from 1922 to 1943 and leader of the Italian Fascist party.

7. TL, carbon copy, 1p., Beinecke Library

19 Feb/ [1931?]

Senator Cutting

Re/ baboon law

Page 237 of Shepards "Van Buren" there is an ambiguous
reference which might mean that artcl/ 211 started with the
attempt to prevent circulation of abolitionist literature in the
slave states. 1835.

at any rate it has all the spirit of the worst slave holders.

For purposes of imparting atmosphere of ignominy. Child=labour
states (Blease, Heflin species etc/)

At any rate bill to give power to excessive power to postmasters
dates to Dec. 1835.

glorious centenary?

Notes on Letter 7

(19 Feb/ [1931?])

Shepard's "Van Buren". In *Martin Van Buren* (Boston: Houghton, Mifflin, 1888) Edward M. Shepard reports that in December 1835 "a bill was introduced making it unlawful for any postmaster knowingly to deliver any printed or pictorial paper touching the subject of slavery in states by whose laws their circulation was prohibited" (236). Although the proposal came directly from President Andrew Jackson himself and was sponsored in the Senate by John C. Calhoun of South Carolina, it was opposed by Daniel Webster and Henry Clay as a violation of the First Amendment to the Constitution. Calhoun's bill was defeated on 8 June 1836; see Lindsay Rogers, *The Postal Power of Congress: A Study in Constitutional Expansion* (Baltimore: The Johns Hopkins Press, 1916), 104–15. Shepard compares the measure to "the present prohibition of the use of the post-office for obscene literature" (237), but he does not suggest a direct historical connection between the two pieces of legislation.

Child-labour states. Until the Fair Labor Standards Act of 1938, child labor was regulated by the individual states. Many of the southern states, where children were widely employed in agriculture and the textile industry, imposed no regulations and resisted all federal legislation on the subject. See the Introduction to Chapter Three, pp. 88–89 below.

Blease. Democratic Senator Coleman Livingston Blease (1868–1942) represented South Carolina from 1925 to 1931. He opposed child labor laws, factory inspections, and compulsory school attendance for children. For more information on Blease, see Chapter One, pp. 18–19, and Letter 1 above, and Letter 15 below.

Heflin. Democratic Senator James Thomas Heflin (1869–1951) represented Alabama from 1920 to 1931. Nicknamed "Tom–Tom" for his rousing style of oratory, he was an outspoken advocate of customs censorship and a leading congressional critic of Mussolini.

8. TL, carbon copy, 5pp.?, Beinecke Library

20 Mar. 1931

To Sen Cutting

Thanks for *Cong. Record* of 28 ult.

Brookhart's speech against Meyer seems to me very important. Have long thought Wilson wrecked the govt. but lacked detailed information. There is no reason why the Federal Reserve Board shd. be a private instrument of the executive.

Woodrow made . The president appoints the board and the board appoints the president (nominating, I take it; the candidates of both parties). That effectively bitches the Jeffersonian system. Destroys balance between execut. judic. and legislature.

If the papers report you correctly, you have said the constitution etc// Introduction of the fourth power: money, banks agan.[?] labor obviously upsets the original balance of the three other powers. Fed. Res. Board certainly more powerful than, let us say; the cabinet.

There is NO reason why the board shd. not be

A. elective

B. distributed either to geographic sections of the country
or
C. among the various major interests, say corn, cotton, cattle, manufactures as well so that they cd. put the screws on industries that treated the men too rough, and onto the child labour states.

D. There is no reason why the board shd. not sit as a committee of the senate.

E. or that tribunes of people shd. not be present at the board meetings to report AT ONCE all attempts at malfeasance to congress.

F. No reason why the board (in part or as a whole) shd. not be removable at the pleasure of congress. NOT for crime, and by impeachment but simply because their policy was unsatisfactory in a given case. (This wd. supply your (? as reported in *N.Y. World*) idea of something like responsibility of European cabinets, and quick effect of general disapproval.

I dont mean that all these changes can be made, but a selection from them cd. be applied.

Brookhart shd. be made to see that his idea of nationalizing railroad or *any* single industry is naif by comparison. (all the supernumerary bureaucracy; red tape etc.) ineffective UNTIL you have democratized the credit control, and unnecessary when you have. (mere audit wd. [squeeze and create & chg. efficiency ?]

[rest of page cut off]

the controllers of an industry's credit.

I dont want to disperse these suggestions in a mere magazine article. The dirty XVIIIth amendment, was obviously put thru about the same time to disthracht the attention of the roughnecks. (which is one on Mr Borah and his desiccated friends). Also divided the parties inside, brought general govt. into contempt, self=contradictory; etc . . . giving free hand to Wall St.

Ut sup/ I dont want to disperse this in mere talk. Am keeping a carbon but I shall not print anything till I have your opinion; and I think that it wd. be well to have an opinion from Senators Brookhart and Norris. Idea too useful for campaign issue; to be wasted in gas, and also those forming the nucleus of whatever movement is to be made during the next twelve years shd. agree among themselves before laying selves open to filibustering discussion of details. Say they openly advocate tribunes sitting on board; and threaten to move for making the board elective if they aren't given tribunes, or removability at congress' pleasure. Etc.

I dont trust Borah, too much rhetorical ballyhoo. Not a word of rhetoric in all Brookhart's speech, unless the frequent "Mr President" is such (? trick of delivery; or trying to keep Curtis awake, or to see if ANY of it was entering the paleozoic skull?).

[The following page may not belong to letter 8.]

God preserve us from any confederation with the french at the top of it. They are the worst governors in Europe. Nous avons le genie pour la mauvais organisation; this long= suffering murmur from a french woman struggling past the three [sets of bureaucrats ?] necessary to struggle past to get into a french theatre. is good for their whole mess thru centuries.

From the death of Henri. IV; or of Francois II. as you choose no decent french king, the utter imbecility of the french ct. life thru centuries; as cf/ cinvilazation of small italian courts.

Napoleon thorough scoundrel, sympathy sob=stuffing biographers most you can say of his govt. was picturesque or dramatic;

Worst bureaucracy. decadence architecture and sculpt. (public arts . . . . .

decent french; brave homme. in railway 3. in walking the country roads; OUT of govt.

the occ. fonctionnaire who tacitly apologizes for his job. as brit. [curate ?] visiting a poet by stealth.

[The following page may not belong to letter 8.]

P.S. private

P.S. One might formulate three accusations.

I. The benefit from machinery is not distributed to the public but is allowed to stagnate in a few hands.

II. Stagnate is the word. Not only does the benefit of machines *in being* stagnate, but the potential development is blocked. Every engineer knows that factories etc. do not improve "the plant" etc. because they wouldn't know what the hell to do with the product.

III. Circulation of credit, or better; the acceleration of credit circulation does not keep pace with the development of machinery. Remedy here wd. in great measure settle the other difficulties, or at least tend to improve 'em.

Notes on Letter 8

(20 Mar. 1931)

Brookhart's speech. Republican Senator Smith Wildman Brookhart (1869–1944) represented Iowa in 1922–26 and again in 1927–33. He favored abolition of the gold standard, nationalization of railroads and toll bridges, and representation of agricultural and labor interests on the Federal Reserve Board. He opposed President Hoover's nomination of millionaire investment banker Eugene Isaac Meyer (1875–1959) to the Federal Reserve Board on the grounds that Meyer, as managing director of the War Finance Corporation during World War I, had used public funds to speculate in government bonds and was, in general, "a disciple of the philosophy of the Mellon family." See Brookhart's speeches in the *Congressional Record* 74, 6 (24–25 February 1931), 5839–50, 5922–31. Passages from the second speech (pp. 5922–23) appear at the end of EP's Canto 33, first published in *Pagany* 2, 3 (July–September 1931), 49–53; rpt., *Ezra Pound's Poetry and Prose*, 5: 305–8. A letter from EP to Brookhart of 18 March 1931 is published in EP's *Impact: Essays on Ignorance and the Decline of American Civilization*, ed. Noel Stock (Chicago: Henry Regnery, 1960), 269–70. EP writes: "Your speech against Meyer . . . seems to me very important. Parts of it at any rate seem to me the most important historical document of the period I have come upon." Meyer's appointment was nevertheless confirmed by the Senate; he served from 1931 to 1933.

Federal Reserve Board. Created in December 1913 during the first administration of President Woodrow Wilson, the Federal Reserve Board, which controls the supply of credit in the United States, was reshaped by Congress in 1933–35, but not along the democratic lines suggested by Senator Brookhart and EP.

the papers. We have not been able to locate the newspaper reports to which EP refers.

Borah. Senator Borah was an ardent supporter of Prohibition; see the Introduction to Chapter Two, p. 32, and Letter 2 above.

Curtis. Republican Charles Curtis (1860-1936) of Kansas was vice president of the United States from 1929 to 1933 and ex-officio president of the Senate. He had represented Kansas in the Senate from 1907 to 1913 and again from 1915 to 1929.

Nous avons. This anecdote is repeated in EP's *Guide to Kulchur* (1938; new ed., Norfolk, Conn.: New Directions, 1952): "*Nous avons le génie pour la mauvais organisation*, said a French woman, as we had to pass three desks, exchange two sets of coupons, pay tax in small change in order to use a free ticket to a premiere performance at I suppose the what's-its-name theatre, with a square front near the Arc de Triomphe" (186–87).

Henri IV. Henri IV ruled France from 1589 to 1610. EP credited him with lifting the city duties or *octroi* on the importation of books into Paris; see *The Selected Letters of Ezra Pound to John Quinn 1915–1924*, 22, 25. The reign of François II lasted only from 1559 to 1560.

9 Oct. 1931

Bronson Cutting Esq.

My Dear Senator

I don't know what publications we have in the U.S. in the nature of the *Revista di Dirit. Agricola* and *Diritto Commerciale.* Have been seeing Sraffa, supposedly their best light and edtr. of the latter. He has refrained from calling me an imbecile and even suggested that I have a crack at reviewing for him, tho' I spose he wd. keep me on historic stuff rather than theory.

I made out a little plan for pore ole England which I dont suppose anyone in Eng. will print. It can't be so idiotic or so irrelevant to the U.S. as its wildest proposition, namely against short selling seems now to have the sanction of the U.S. Chamber of commerce.

The other essential was the shortening of the working day. I wonder really whether anyone in America has taken the trouble to detach Marx tenth chapter from the rest of his sometimes indefinite writing.

I shd. like to see you go to the White House on so simple and lucid an issue. It is time someone took it up. I don't know ANY honest argument against it. Hoover's last blah is not an answer; but an hypodermic. Credit must have SOME connection with labour; work done.

I thought my notes were theoretic as far as America was concerned, but now Lamont and Al S. are *reported* to be yapping about dole, which is the god damndest idiocy that ever emerged from even a British brain.

It is the only thing I have against Lamont; and

[rest of page cut off]

England will continue to sag: but her way out wd. be to abolish the dole: cut the working day even to four hours (though any length that can permit two shifts comfortably wd. help, and wd. allow the "plants" to make superprofits when there are any to be made).

The wage cd. (and shd.) remain the same (i;e; same figures on the paper paid the workers), and instead of dole they cd. give subsidy to firms which cd *prove* by audit that they cdnt. afford it. This subsidy shd. be made in jetons (like the small coin the french have used ever since the war with no scandal and no howls from the conservative side). Money (fiat money) having value only inside the country.

NOTE that no piece of this money cd. *get into circulation* save as a certificate of work done.

If you do not see the implications I will write out details but I dont think I need do so.

Money (paper) resting partly on gold and partly on work DONE is cert/ better than money resting on part gold and a large hunk of vacuum.

The short day is so obviously the remedy for unemployment that I know of no honest man who can deny it, and in

[rest of page cut off]

a lucid or apparently honest or in fact ANY answer against it.

I want two words on a postcard in answer, if you've the time. And shd. also like to know how Dexter Kimball is regarded outside academic circles. (head of a dept. at (I think Cornell) and has written on Industrial Economics).)

Cd/ yr/ secretary send me some sort of Dept. Interior (Land Office) publication showing how much land is still open for settlement in the U.S. . . . want it for correlation with J. *Q.* Adams)

Literates now down to 8.

Notes on Letter 9

(9 Oct. 1931)

Sraffa. Angelo Sraffa, a citizen of Rapallo, was a jurist, a professor at the University of Milan, and a founder of the Università Commerciale Luigi Bocconi in Milan, where EP lectured in 1933 on economics and American history. EP corresponded with Sraffa from May 1932 to November 1936 (Pound Archive).

Marx tenth chapter. In the tenth chapter of *Das Kapital* (1867), German political economist Karl Marx (1818–1883) sets forth his concept of "relative surplus value." He argues that, under capitalism, advances in the productivity of labor lead not to higher wages or a shortening of the working day but only to an increase in commodities, a lowering of prices, and an increase in employers' profits. In "Economia ortologica — Le basi etiche," *Rassegna Monetaria* 34, 9–10 (September–October 1937), 1104, EP maintains that "in Chapter X of *Das Kapital* . . . Marx is a pure historian when he protests against the excessive length of the working day"; see *Ezra Pound's Poetry and Prose*, 7: 252. This translation of EP's Italian is taken from Tim Redman, *Ezra Pound and Italian Fascism*, 149.

Hoover. Herbert Clark Hoover (1874–1964) was president of the United States from 1929 to 1933.

Lamont. Thomas W. Lamont (1870–1948) was a partner in the New York banking house of J. P. Morgan. He appears in EP's Canto 19 as "Tommy Baymont." Lamont was the most active patron of Mussolini's regime in the American business community. In 1926, he secured a loan of 100,000,000 dollars to the Italian government.

Al S. Progressive Democrat Alfred E. Smith (1873–1944) was governor of New York in 1919–21 and 1923–29. In 1928 he was the Democratic candidate for president of the United States.

cut the working day: On EP's plan to shorten the working day, see the Introduction to Chapter Three, pp. 89–90 below.

Kimball. Dexter Kimball (1865–1952) was an engineer who specialized in machine design and an educator who helped to make engineering part of the scientific curriculum of American universities. From 1920 to 1936 Kimball was dean of the College of Engineering at Cornell University. He was also the author of *Industrial Economics* (1929), which EP cites in "Machines," *New Review* 1, 4 (Winter 1931–32), 291–92; in "The Depression Has Just Begun," *Contempo* 1, 16 (15 January 1932), 1, 4; in "'Abject and Utter Farce,'" *Harkness Hoot* 4, 2 (November 1933), 6–14; in "The Bear Garden," *New Democracy* 1, 7 (25 November 1933), 6; and in Canto 38, first published in the *New English Weekly* on 28 September 1933. See *Ezra Pound's Poetry and Prose*, 5: 327, 336–37; and 6: 75, 87–95, 106. To Milton Abernethy and A. J. Buttitta, the editors of *Contempo*, EP wrote: "The problem of production is solved. Dexter Kimball knows it is solved. . . . Kimball ("Industrial Economics") more than admits that the real problem is distribution" (Pound Archive). EP corresponded with Kimball in 1935 (Pound Archive).

10. TL, carbon copy, 5pp., Beinecke Library

9 Dec. [1931?]

My Dear Senator

With the power in both houses so nearly even wd. it not be an opportune time to force an elimination of some of the more barbarous minor infamies?

I don't know whether you want [to] help kick out the "administration gang" or are struggling to save us from worse, or whether the "subjects" shd. be riz in the auguster house or in the private conclaves.

1. Baboon law or art 211 of the penal code.

2. (copyright, probably bogging along . . . but still . . . no harm in mentioning it)

You cd. probably get at least momentary attention by opening with "And the judge said: "Mr; . . . . , I am sorry that this have been brought as a civil and not as a criminal action.". But that was in another country, and besides, the chink is dead. (At least I suppose so, the plaintiff was well on in years, at the time.)

[lines missing?]

who regard both dem/ and rep/ gangs as sons of almost indistinguishable bitches.

Can't make out if credit for a little marginal civilization wd. save or damage either party. But the narrow majority ought to [be ?] made use of.

Dem/ party, cd. be reminded of Wilson's push for bureaucracy and the passport infamies (but the rep/ under the crook and the lemon did almost nothing to alleviate and Herbert hasn't even yet eliminated).

If he is such a damn fool as to stay dry he deserves all he gets. That issue no longer one for the intelligentsia.

What about attracting a little cooperation from elements of govt. that do NOT want publicity? I can't see that elimination of 211 wd. be noticed at all if done quietly. Obviously bigots cd. stink if it were made an issue; but if agreed in quiet/ some formula// The wording of 211 representing obsolete phase of human understanding; the following will be substituted/

"cheap smut, publications designed to pervert and corrupt (no underlining of designed) but it does the business statements contrary to medical knowledge or unsustained by serious medical opinion.

How or why the people controlling the situation and sitting on it in smug self=satisfaction expect to escape the infamy that has been the lot of their likes.

Take it that neither Pound, Williams, or Eliot get 50 dollars a month out of America in respect to their literary work not only has it been impossible at various times for them to do so, but they probably have not averaged that over the past 20 years, and despite their present position or recognition the conditions have not changed.

The people responsible are not only the publishers but the various tribes of parasites infesting the weekly reviews, the Canbys, Van Dorens, Benets etc. (Old Villard merely a dunderhead with a few fixed ideas late 80s. liberal and no knowledge of or interest in literature. Minor figures of the feeding critics; general cohesion of and blather of minor inferiority complexes.

first question not whether they can "help it" but whether they are full of satisfaction with the conditions. 2 whether they have even considered trying to improve things.

If P/E/and W/ not victims like Poe it is because they have been more disgusted than depressed by the obstructionism.

manifestoes are a bit out of the mrkn line, etc. Taupin is a prof/ and foreigner, I dont know how much weight he cd. carry in a lit/ manifest/ or whether he wants to write in the weaklies??

R. Johns is I think convinced that I ought to be upheld. Foster who runs "Fifth Story Window", is disposed to righteousness.

It is not a very heavy phalanx wherewith to try a coup d'etat.

O DAMMMMM I was about to outline a few things that OUGHT to be said// mebbe I'll have to write 'em myself. I dont see (from here) why I shd/ expect a thin line of younger 'eros to commit hari=kari.

Johns might use something as an editorial. He has, I hear; a inkum of his own. and dont have to hunt jobs from the muckers.

I suppose what is blocking me is the aversion from mentioning by name a list of people who ought to be beneath my attention; and who individually are of no god damned importance whatever. Yet taken en masse they produce an general infamy. (with bland and selfsatisfied unconsciousness). And if killed tomorrow wd. we suppose be replaced by something no better. idiots are always replaceable; the supply is without bourne ETC/

ON THE OTHER HAND one of the funniest things in the reports from Sovietica is the naif horror (hoRRRRRor) of some of the grabbers at finding a superintendent, a engineering boss or clothing store manager working for the same pay as mere under-lings, whereas in our own beatified and perfect state most of the best artists and writers have spent most or all of their lives working for considerably less pay than the plumber or milk=man.

AND YET AGAIN, there is no use carrying one's mind sewed up in a bag. Given a reasonable term of overproduction (of houses, living room, material comforts) would not the "worst features" of Russia 1931 disappear?

Are the horrors reported by Hank Wales etc. due to some Russian hogging all the best and locking it up, or simply to there not being any more for anyone?

Notes on Letter 10

(9 Dec. [1931?])

the power in both houses. When the Seventy-second Congress convened on 7 December 1931, the Democrats controlled the House of Representatives by only five votes and the Republicans controlled the Senate by only one. Under these circumstances, the bloc of insurgent Republicans to which BC belonged constituted an important swing vote. The "administration gang" was still that of President Hoover.

And the judge. The missing name here is that of Herbert Hoover. EP's source is John Hamill, *The Strange Case of Mr. Hoover under Two Flags* (New York: William Caro, 1931) 190. Hamill reports, not altogether accurately, a 1905 lawsuit in London in which an English mining company, for which Hoover worked as an engineer, was adjudged to have obtained property in China through fraudulent misrepresentations. EP's paraphrase of the judge's remarks is invented and inaccurate, but he repeats it in Canto 97, in letters to James Laughlin (3 February 1934), Viola Baxter Jordan (7 February 1934), and Olivia Agresti (3 September 1954), and in one of the unpublished "Ez Sez" manuscripts (Pound Archive). See Ben D. Kimpel and T.C. Duncan Eaves, "Herbert Hoover and the London Judge," *Paideuma* 9, 3 (1980) 505-07, and *Ezra Pound and James Laughlin: Selected Letters*, ed. David M. Gordon (New York: New Directions, 1994) 23-24.

But that was in another country. EP echoes the words of Barabas in Christopher Marlowe's *The Jew of Malta*, Act IV, scene i (1633). Confessing to fornication, Barabas extenuates the deed by saying, "but that was in another country;/ And besides, the wench is dead." T. S. Eliot quotes the same lines in the epigraph to his poem "Portrait of a Lady" (1915).

Wilson's push. See Letter 6 and the Introduction to Chapter Two, pp. 29-30 above.

the crook and the lemon. Republican President Warren G. Harding (1865-1923), whose administration from 1921 to 1923 was plagued by corruption, and his successor, the dour Calvin Coolidge (see Letter 6 above).

Williams or Eliot. American poets William Carlos Williams (1883-1963) and T. S. Eliot (1888-1965), both friends of EP.

Canbys. Henry Seidel Canby (1878-1961) edited the *Saturday Review of Literature* from 1924 to 1936 and chaired the board of judges of the Book of the Month Club from 1926 to 1961.

Van Dorens. Carl Van Doren (1885-1950) was literary editor of *The Nation* from 1919 to 1922 and of *Century* from 1922 to 1925. His brother, poet and novelist Mark Van Doren (1894-1972), was literary editor of *The Nation* from 1924 to 1928. Both were professors of English at Columbia University. Irita (Mrs. Carl) Van Doren (1891-1966) edited the *New York Herald Tribune Book Review* from 1926 to 1963.

Benets. William Rose Benet (1886-1950) was a founder and associate editor of the *Saturday Review of Literature* from 1924 to 1950. His brother Stephen Vincent Benet (1898-1943) was a poet and novelist.

Villard. Oswald Garrison Villard (1872-1949) was owner and editor of *The Nation* (New York) from 1918 to 1932. He was a pacifist, a cofounder of the National Association for Advancement of Colored People, and a prominent critic of Italian fascism. In "American Notes," *New English Weekly* 7, 12 (4 July 1935), EP speaks of "the old Garrison Villard, hoakum, tea-and-toast American liberals" (226). And in the same column one week later, EP says, "Garrison Villard impedes truth by lack of curiosity. Some of mankind's worst enemies are these petrified ossified reformers of yester year" (245). See *Ezra Pound's Poetry and Prose*, 6: 301, 302.

victims like Poe. The American writer and journalist Edgar Allan Poe (1809-1849) was poorly paid for his books and for his contributions and editorial services to various periodicals, including the *Southern Literary Messenger* of Richmond, Virginia; *Burton's Gentleman's Magazine* and *Graham's Magazine* of Philadelphia; and the *Evening Mirror, Broadway Journal,* and *Godey's Lady's Book* of New York. To the end of his brief and troubled life, Poe dreamed of owning and editing a literary journal that would embody the highest critical standards.

Taupin. René Taupin (1904–1981) taught at Hunter College in New York from 1934 to 1966. He was the author of *L'Influence du symbolisme francais sur la poésie américaine (de 1910 à 1920)* (Paris: H. Champion, 1929); *Essais indifférents pour une esthétique de l'inspiration* (Presses universitaires de France, 1932); *Le Style Apollinaire* (Les Presses modernes, 1934); and *La France au XVIIIe siècle* (Les Editions des presses modernes, 1940).

Johns. From 1930 to 1933 Richard Johns (1904–1970) edited *Pagany,* a Boston and New York literary magazine to which EP contributed an essay and three Cantos.

Foster. Harvey N. Foster, a young broker in Hartford, Connecticut, was an editor of *Fifth Floor Window,* a literary magazine that appeared irregularly in 1931–32.

ON THE OTHER HAND. This paragraph and the next two are quoted directly from EP's "Fungus, Twilight or Dry Rot," *New Review* 1, 3 (August-September-October 1931), 112–16; rpt., *Ezra Pound's Poetry and Prose,* 5: 316.

Hank Wales. Journalist Henry Wales (1888–1960) worked on the Paris staff of the *Chicago Tribune.* For several months in 1931, he lived and traveled in Russia, assessing the achievements of the Five-Year Plan, which began in 1928. His reports appeared frequently in the Paris edition of the *Tribune* between 10 March and 15 July. Wales described acute shortages of food, fuel, clothing and other consumer goods, school facilities, and transportation.

11. TL, carbon copy, 2pp., Beinecke Library

23 Dec. [1931?]

EZRA POUND
RAPALLO
VIA MARSALA, 12 INT. 5

My Dear Senator

In the somewhat irrelevant levity of my morning (strictly private)
correspondence I have been brought (also with eye on yesterdays
paper/ re/ you and Ham; Lewis) been brought I was about to say;
to advocate the starting of a nice little club for the 12 literates in
the senate. . . . . with me and Benito as honorary members. (Its all
right, I mean I shall qualify by my Cavalcanti in a few weeks,
and we are startin my Prolegomena unt/ to be folio about size
of Albertus Magnus' his woiks.

I was [a ?] little puzzled as to "who else"? There is the new
Harvard Prof. of Poesy (most suitable, and in glittern' not to say
blighting and annihilatin' contrast with Yale). Hauptmann wd. give
no trouble and looks well as postcard or (wd. on postage stamp).
Yeats, has as you may know, been a senator; though he is (vide
"Packet") rather against my taking it up. Cocteau wd. be an highly
ornamental addition and have the advtg/ of being wholly
incomprehendable to the electorate).

und so weiter/

 Xmas greetin's.

(As for the practical irony; extreme delicacy of which is due to
B.C. or H.L. of introducing Mssrs. Mooney and Fall . . .

Did it rise from Lewis' alleged fondness for latin authors?

Oh yes (parenthesis). Honourary founder of that club/ Matt. Quay;
on grounds of the legend that he used to read Euripides in his
bawth where Penrose cdn't see him.

Notes on Letter 11

(23 Dec [1931?])

Ham; Lewis. The *New York Herald* (Paris) reported on 22 December 1931 (p. 1) that BC and Democratic Senator James Hamilton Lewis (1863–1939) of Illinois had asked President Hoover to pardon Albert B. Fall (see note on Fall below). Lewis had a reputation in the Senate for elegant speches ornamented with literary references. He served in the Senate from 1913 to 1919 and again from 1930 to 1939. In 1932, he was a candidate for the Democratic presidential nomination.

Benito. For Benito Mussolini see Letter 6 above. EP's high opinion of Mussolini's literary perspicacity was confirmed when they met on 20 January 1933 and Il Duce pronounced *A Draft of XXX Cantos* to be "divertente"; see Canto 41.

my Cavalcanti. EP's edition of *Guido Cavalcanti Rime* (Genova: Edizione Marsano) appeared in late January 1932. He first published translations of Cavalcanti (c. 1255–1300), one of his favorite medieval Italian poets, in 1910–12.

my Prolegomena. EP's *Prolegomena I: How to Read Followed by The Spirit of Romance Part I* (Le Beausset, France: F. Cabasson) was published in June 1932.

Albertus Magnus. In the Abbé Auguste Borgnet's edition of 1890–92, the works of St. Albertus Magnus (c. 1200–1280) occupy thirty-eight quarto volumes.

Prof. of Poesy. T. S. Eliot (see Letter 10 above) was Charles Eliot Norton Professor of Poetry at Harvard University in 1932–33. His appointment was announced on 15 December 1931.

Hauptmann. German dramatist Gerhard Hauptmann (1862–1946) stayed at the Albergo Rapallo in 1928 and 1929. EP mentioned him to George Yeats in a letter of 20 January 1928 and introduced him to W. B. Yeats in March 1929. See Ann Saddlemyer, "George, Ezra, Dorothy and Friends: Twenty-Six Letters, 1918–1959," *Yeats Annual No. 7*, ed. Warwick Gould (London: Macmillan, 1990), 11-12.

Yeats. Irish poet and playwright William Butler Yeats (1865–1939) served as a senator of the Irish Free State from 1922 to 1928. His *A Packet for Ezra Pound* (Dublin: Cuala Press, 1929) contains an open letter "To Ezra Pound," which begins: "My dear Ezra/ Do not be elected to the Senate of your country. I think myself, after six years, well out of that of mine. Neither you nor I, nor any other of our excitable profession, can match those old lawyers, old bankers, old business men, who, because all habit and memory, have begun to govern the world" (33).

Cocteau. Jean Cocteau (1889–1963), French avant-garde poet, novelist, dramatist, filmmaker, and critic.

Mooney. Probably Thomas J. Mooney (1882–1942), radical socialist and labor-union organizer. In January 1917, Mooney was convicted, on what later proved to be perjured eyewitness testimony, of participation in the bombing of the San Francisco Preparedness Day parade of 22 July 1916, in which ten persons died. Although Mooney's sentence was commuted in November 1918 from death to life imprisonment, he was held in prison until 7 January 1939, when he received a pardon from the governor of California. In the early 1930s, Mooney's case was often in the news, as he appealed for a new trial and petitioned for executive clemency. In "Publishers, Pamphlets, and Other Things," *Contempo* 1, 9 (15 September 1931), 1–2 (rpt., *Ezra Pound's Poetry and Prose*, 5: 319), EP cites Mooney's continuing imprisonment as a symptom of America's decay.

Fall. Albert Bacon Fall (1861–1944) was Republican senator from New Mexico in 1912–21 and secretary of the interior under President Harding in 1921–23. In the latter office, Fall leased the Great Teapot Dome federal oil reserves in Wyoming to Harry F. Sinclair of the Continental Trading Company and the Elk Hill reserves in California to Edward L. Doheny of Pan American Petroleum. Fall was convicted in 1929 of accepting a 100,000-dollar bribe from

Notes on Letter 11 continued

Doheny. From 21 July 1931 to 9 May 1932, Fall was incarcerated in the New Mexico State Penitentiary, where he served nine months and twenty-one days of a one-year sentence. His case is mentioned in Canto 38 (1933): "And the secretary of the something/ Made some money from oil wells." Although BC did not as a rule have much to do with old-guard New Mexico Republicans, he was fond of Fall and his family; see Richard Lowitt, *Bronson M. Cutting*, 191–92, 203, 205–6, 377.

Matt. Quay. Republican Matthew Stanley Quay (1833–1904) represented EP's home state of Pennsylvania in the Senate during the poet's formative years (1887–99, 1901–4). Quay owned a fine library and read the Greek and Latin classics in their original languages.

Penrose. A protégé of Quay, Boies Penrose (1860–1921) served as Republican senator from Pennsylvania from 1897 until his death.

12. TLS, 1p., Beinecke Library

23 Jan. 1932

United States Senate
Committee on Military Affairs

My Dear Mr. Pound:

Please excuse the delay in answering your two letters written in December. We are so busy with a mass of legislation, mostly futile, that it is hard to keep up with my correspondence.

The Copyright Bill failed at the end of the last session, in spite of all my efforts to the contrary. It was defective in many particulars, and I hope it will be amended in such a way, and at an early enough date, to avoid the usual filibuster. Unless one has actually worked on this type of measure, it is inconceivable how many complications come up.

I am working on an amendment to the Baboon law, which I hope to have ready in a few days. I think the best we can hope for is to bring the procedure in line with that which I got into the Tariff Act two years ago. Of course the thing ought to be out of the criminal code altogether, but we would not have the slightest chance of eliminating it. Also there is a tactical advantage in leaving the criminal feature, because in that shape it would go to the semi-liberal Judiciary Committee instead of to the hopeless Post Office Committee.

I am afraid we can hardly get by with the word "designed", but if I see a chance I shall try to work it in.

Don't be too hopeful. It is hard running up against the organizations of canned virtue.

Write me when you get a chance.

Sincerely yours,
Bronson Cutting

NOTES ON LETTER 12
(23 Jan. 1932)

Copyright Bill. See Letter 4 and the Introduction to Chapter Two, pp. 28–29 above.

an amendment to the Baboon law. Senate Bill 3907 was designed "to amend section 211 of the Criminal Code, as amended (relating to certain nonmailable matter)." See the Introduction to Chapter Two, p. 27 above.

Tariff Act. On BC's struggle to amend the Smoot-Hawley Tariff Act of 1930, see Chapter One, pp. 16–19 above.

13. TL, carbon copy, 3pp., Beinecke Library

11 Feb. 1932

Hon.
Bronson Cutting

My Dear Senator

Yours 23d. ult. recd. and contents registered in memory. *Yes.* I had observed from rept/ of Copyrt/ Com/ that the extent of the proposed act was already somewhat in excess of the four words applied to the matter in the King James version.

Is there anything yr/ somewhat hysterical correspondent or ANY individual can do re/ "the dole". I thought that imbecility was beyond American compass, and hope the Paris edtn. of the *Chicago Tribune* is exaggerating.

Even supposing their report is 40% true, LaFollette must be off his chum.

Payment to non=producers for non=productivity can not be the answer. The four hour day is no more sensational now than the eight hour day was in 1850. Edison, Stalin, Ford, Mussolini and any number of thoughtful men have seen it as at any rate the strongest of possible palliatives, and the one necessitating the least damn bureaucracy and fiddling.

Probably the most efficient length of working day wd. be one permitting two shifts of men. 6 or 7 a.m. to 12, and 12 to 5 or 6 p.m. getting the long day from the machines.

The figures printed on the day's wage

[rest of page cut off]

at least *some* purchasing power regularly for some work done.

Without perpetual and increasing unemployment, (to keep DOWN wages), to feed hypocrites and bums and destroy the will to be useful.

(In fact with England in front of one, and NO lessons learned since the panic of 1837 (eighteen thirty seven). Dole spelling slavery and MORE g.d. bureaucracy with augmenting depreciation of currency, followed in Eng. by wage cuts ANYhow.

And I suppose, once the subject is in the air, sob=stuff, human=goo [?] and tremendous courage needed to stand against the current, and every demagogue yelling to the national treasury fer soup fer his own gang!! End democracy, "failure of democracy" etc. BEFORE any adequate preparation for ANY other system whatsoever has been made.

Corriere della Sera says day in Moscow is 5 hours and half. Fascio here *arranging* that people be kept employed, all waiters take a day off, to let other waiters work. Was in print shop other day when central phoned in: "how many men?" "How many *can* you etc."

May be paternalism but very intelligent use of it.

Also "benefica", land improvement. Did I recommend you to get "U.R.S.S. In Construction" now got agency "Amkniga" 19 W. 27th St. New York.

I don't think anybody can afford to miss it. Printed in *either* Eng/ Fr/German or russ.

[rest of page cut off]

The Macmillan Report (old stuff.) I only read it a few weeks ago because I supposed it wd. be BUNK, and it was. Interest mainly in old Bradbury's final note of dissent, which (stripped of parliamentary anglican trimmings) amounted to saying just that: "This is a lot of hooey, an' damnd if I sign it.)

/ / /

WHAT I WD. BE GRATEFUL FOR: if you can spare three
minutes, tell me whether there is ANY periodical in America,
or ANY group, however small, to which it is worth sending,
or with which one can discuss serious ideas on economics.
(No; not the *Noo Rebooblik*).

As far as I can see, some labour rag might print part of what I
might write, but the American labourites and pseudo/bolcheviki
seem to have NO idea whatever of American institutions or in what
way modern economic ideas wd. really affect them. They don't
know enough to know a difference of opinion with Federal Reserve
Board is DIFFERENT from a dif/ of op/ with an icon=kissing
imbecile like Nic. II.

etc.

If any points in these notes of mine strike you as TOO blitheringly
idiotic, I wd. also be glad of castigation or reference to printed
exposition (however tedious) of what you consider sane view.

Even some of "New Economists" are trying to worm around the
dole, calling it a "dividend" ("base form of dividend", BALLZ)
Apple off the tree that aint there.

in contrition for
length of this note

Notes on Letter 13

(11 Feb. 1932)

four words. EP refers to the Mosaic commandment in the King James translation of the Old Testament: "Thou shalt not steal."

"the dole". The report that alarmed EP appeared in the *Chicago Tribune* (Paris) on 9 February 1932, under the title "Demand for Dole to Aid Jobless Grows in U. S." The article said, in part, "Demands for direct aid from the Federal Government for the unemployed are becoming increasingly insistent as the need develops. Fears are being expressed that . . . Congress will be swayed by a strong humanitarian appeal. . . . It is possible that Congress may be swayed from its conviction that a dole would be harmful by an emotional appeal and a great mass of expert testimony demonstrating the grave character of the unemployment crisis" (3). Senators Edward P. Costigan of Colorado (1874–1939) and Robert M. LaFollette, Jr., of Wisconsin (see Letter 2 above) had cosponsored a bill to provide 375 million dollars in federal grants to the states for unemployment relief. Although BC supported the bill, it was defeated in the Senate on 16 February 1932. For the differences of opinion between EP and BC on this issue, see the Introduction to Chapter Three, pp. 90–91 below.

the four hour day. See Letter 9 above and the Introduction to Chapter Three, pp. 89–90 below.

Edison, Stalin, Ford. Thomas Alva Edison (1847–1931), American inventor of the phonograph and the incandescent light; Joseph Stalin (1879–1953), head of the Russian communist party and ruler of the Soviet Union; and Henry Ford (1863–1947), American automobile manufacturer and pioneer of assembly-line mass production.

panic of 1837. The bank panic of 1837 occurred during a depression that began in England at the end of 1836, spread to the United States, and lasted until 1843. American state banks, which had overextended credit for speculative investments, abruptly began to call in their loans. In May 1837, most banks suspended specie payment. This led to a general moratorium on public works, widespread unemployment, and a demand for more stringent banking laws.

Corriere della Sera. Between 17 January and 7 February 1932, this influential Milan newspaper carried a ten-part report on Soviet Russia by Cesco Tomaselli.

U.R.S.S. U. S. S. R. in Construction, ed. G. L. Platakov (Moscow: State Publishing House of the RSFSR) was a serial publication in four languages. Volume I, number 1 appeared in 1930. EP cites it in "The Depression Has Just Begun," *Contempo* 1, 16 (15 January 1932), 1, 4; rpt., *Ezra Pound's Poetry and Prose,* 5: 335.

Macmillan Report. Hugh Pattison, Baron Macmillan (1873–1952) was chairman of a fourteen-member Treasury committee established in November 1929 to investigate the causes of the Depression and to ascertain, in particular, whether the banking and financial systems were helping or handicapping industry and trade. EP said Lord Macmillan's mandate was "to look into the sins of the British Financial system" (*"Ezra Pound Speaking": Radio Speeches of World War II,* ed. Leonard W. Doob [Westport, Conn.: Greenwood Press, 1978], 34). The *Committee on Finance & Industry: Report,* 2 vols. (London: His Majesty's Stationery Office, 1931), recommended the strengthening of Bank of England control over the national monetary system, increase of liquid assets and credit, and separation of the issuance of bank-notes from reserve holdings of gold. EP glances at these conclusions in Canto 46 (1936), and in "American Notes," *New English Weekly* 8, 1 (17 October 1935), he describes the report as "a belated, but official recognition of the minimum sanity required of governments, a low elevation, beneath which humanity can henceforth be prohibited from sinking"

(5; rpt., *Ezra Pound's Poetry and Prose*, 6: 322). Former Chancellor of the Exchequer John Swanwick, Baron Bradbury (1872–1950) dissented (1: 263–81) from the committee's report, which he thought radical and dangerously inflationary, even though he himself, as National Insurance Commissioner in 1914, had issued several hundred million pounds' worth of paper scrip money popularly known as "Bradburys" because not enough official currency was in circulation to meet the nation's economic needs at the beginning of the Great War. EP recalls "Bradbury's" in his *ABC of Economics* (London: Faber and Faber, 1933), 82.

Nic. II. Nicholas Romanov (1868–1918), last Tsar of Russia, was deposed in 1917 and murdered by the Bolsheviks in the following year.

"New Economists". The main Social Credit organization in New York City called itself the New Economics Group.

14. TL, carbon copy, 1p., Beinecke Library

12 Feb. 1932

Hon. Bronson Cutting
U.S. Senate

My dear Senator

I am sending you Hattersley's "This age of Plenty". Chapters 1
to 12 inclusive are worth reading. Chap. 13, off in the blue.

Gives Douglas more or less in relation to other contemporaries
THE GIST OF THE MATTER, pages 83 to 85

This is really the nucleus of Douglas thought. It is what was NOT
understood 14 years ago. Call it Douglas' great discovery. Being in
simple algebraic equation and NEEDING THOUGHT even those
who read C.H.D. and "understood him" often failed to get the
emphasis.

ONCE that concept is understood "everything else follows".
Or any man who can THINK can do his own thinking from there
on. Hattersley goes wobbly, and most of the writers of articles get
weak because, given the root, twists of one branch or another *can*
occur, but are NOT essential.

Douglas not a highbrow theorician. Was head of Westinghouse in
India, until he noticed too much.

Notes on Letter 14

(12 Feb. 1932)

"This age. In *This Age of Plenty—Its Problems and Their Solution* (London: Sir Isaac Pitman and Sons, 1929), Charles Marshall Hattersley expounds the economic views of Major C. H. Douglas and Professor Frederick Soddy (see Letter 27 below). A Cambridge-trained mathematician and lawyer, Hattersley belonged to the West Riding Douglas Social Credit Association in Yorkshire. In a letter of 24 April 1934 to the San Francisco Social Creditor, David Warren Ryder, BC says: "I have read Hattersley's book and several of Major Douglas's . . ." (Cutting Papers, Box 20).

Douglas. Clifford Hugh Douglas (1879–1952) was an English engineer and a manager of the British Westinghouse Company in India. After the Great War, during which he attained the rank of major in the Royal Flying Corps, Douglas turned his attention to economics, formulating his theory of Social Credit in books entitled *Economic Democracy* and *Credit Power and Democracy* (both 1920). EP was first converted to Douglas's economic ideas in 1919 in the offices of A. R. Orage, whose journal, *The New Age,* published a number of articles by Douglas.

algebraic equation. Douglas's "A + B theorem" purported to demonstrate mathematically that, under the existing credit system, the prices of goods would always exceed the purchasing power of consumers.

15. TL, carbon copy, Gaudier letterhead, 2pp., Beinecke Library and Library of Congress

13 Nov. [1932]

E. POUND
RAPALLO
VIA MARSALA 12–5

The Hon. Bronson Cutting

My Dear Senator:

Does the right of petition still exist? and if so what is the colour of the red tape.

In view of the slightly cheering results of election (limit of human or american patience, despite Renan's gloomier view/ no party cd. survive the sequence Harding, Calvin and Herbie.)

Ebbene I submit the enc/ as petition. It is at least as considerable as the poesy of S.C. that appears in the *Cong. Record.*

A few things ought to go OUT along with the 18th. catastrophe.

yrs. devotedly

Sfar as I'm concerned you can add a 4th clause/ for erection of tablets of infamy to Blease, Smoot k.t.l. I saw quote of a comic speech by Sausageface Fatboy saying that you and a few other very wicked men BELIEVED that Mr Roosevelt was the man to carry through etc. etc.

Can such things be. Also Herbie as book lover!! how llate, but how llovely. More'n a poem by Ella Wheeler and a belated reprieve of seven black boys for not committing rape wuz needed.

RESOLVED that no cockeyed sonvabitch be allowed to call himself a economist (even though a member of the Haavud or other beanery faculty) until he have pubkly answered the follerink kweschunz:

1. What is an auxiliary currency?

2. When money is rented, who ought to pay the rent, the fellow who has it on the day the rent falls due, or some bloke who aint got it?

3. What is the effect of every factory, every industry creating prices faster than it emits the power to buy?

E.P.

Notes on Letter 15

(13 Nov. [1932])

election. On 8 November 1932 Democrat Franklin Delano Roosevelt (1882–1945) was elected president of the United States, thus ending twelve consecutive years of Republican government under Presidents Harding, Coolidge, and Hoover.

Renan's gloomier view. Joseph Ernest Renan (1832–92) was a French historian and critic. In his *ABC of Reading* (New Haven, Conn.: Yale University Press, 1934), 180, EP quotes Renan as saying, "Il n'y a que la bêtise humaine qui donne une idée de l'infini" (nothing but human stupidity conveys a sense of the infinite). We have not identified the source of the quotation.

petition. The three questions in this "petition" were later published in "E. P.'s Suspicions," *Chicago Tribune* (Paris), 31 March 1934, p. 4, and incorporated into his 1934 Volitionist questionnaire; see letter 30 below.

the poesy of S. C.. During the Senate debate on customs censorship in March 1930 (see Chapter One, pp. 17–19 above), poetry was quoted not by Senator Blease of South Carolina but by his allies, Senators J. T. Heflin of Alabama (see Letter 7 above) and Park Trammell of Florida.

Blease, Smoot. For Senator Blease, see Chapter One, pp. 18–19, and Letters 1 and 7 above. Republican Reed Owen Smoot (1862–1941) represented Utah in the Senate from 1903 to 1933. He was chairman of the Senate Finance Committee, cosponsor of the Smoot-Hawley Tariff Bill of 1930, and a staunch defender of customs censorship; see Chapter One, pp. 17–18 above.

a comic speech. Speaking in New York's Madison Square Garden on 31 October 1932, President Hoover named Senators Norris, LaFollette, Cutting, Long, and Wheeler, along with William Randolph Hearst, as revolutionary "exponents of a social philosophy different from the traditional philosophies of the American people" (*New York Times*, 1 November 1932, p. 12). All of the individuals mentioned by Hoover supported his opponent, Franklin D. Roosevelt, in the 1932 presidential election.

Sausageface Fatboy. EP calls Hoover "the fat man" in "By All Means Be Patriotic," *New English Weekly* 1, 25 (6 October 1932), 589; rpt., *Ezra Pound's Poetry and Prose*, 5: 378.

Herbie as book lover. In "What the President Reads: Notes on a Visit to the White House," *Saturday Review of Literature* 9, 10 (24 September 1932), 117–20, Christopher Morley profiles "Herbert Hoover as the scholar, the man of culture, the lover of books . . . possibly more interested in humane letters than any President we've ever had." In their interview, Hoover tells Morley that "perhaps what this country needs is a great poem. Something to lift people out of fear and selfishness. . . . 'John Brown's Body' was a step in the right direction." Hoover also praises Rudyard Kipling's "Recessional" and Edwin Markham's "The Man with a Hoe," but he does not mention the popular American poet Ella Wheeler Wilcox (1855–1919).

black boys. Nine young black men were convicted of raping two white women in Scottsboro, Alabama, in 1931. On appeal, the United States Supreme Court overturned their conviction and ordered a re-trial. This decision was announced on 7 November 1932, the day before the national presidential election. No reprieve by President Hoover was involved. In a letter to the editor of the *Chicago Tribune* (Paris) published on 8 May 1932, EP refers to "the Scotsborough [*sic*] frame up" (4; rpt., *Ezra Pound's Poetry and Prose*, 5: 350).

3

THE LATER LETTERS

1934–1935

I
INTRODUCTION

Between November of 1932, when Roosevelt was elected president, and February of 1934, the end of his first year in office, the poet and the senator exchanged no letters that have survived. Then the correspondence resumed and continued until April of 1935, a few weeks before Cutting's death. This later cluster of communiqués, comprising seventeen letters and a cablegram, thus coincides almost exactly with the second year of the New Deal.

In this phase, the focus of the correspondence shifts from cultural to economic matters. Censorship takes a back seat to schemes for reviving and reforming the depressed economy. Instead of cultural literates, Pound now asks Cutting for a list of "senators or living reps/ capable of understanding simple economic arithmetic" (15 May 1934). The two men continue to chat about politicians, businessmen, and academics, past and present; but these individuals are of interest almost exclusively for the positions they take on economic issues. Personalities as such matter far less than ideological alignments.

Like millions of other people, the poet and the senator are concerned primarily with the distribution of economic welfare and purchasing power. Among welfare issues, they canvass the questions of child labor, the length of the working day, unemployment compensation, and public works. Among remedies for the deflated economy, they consider entitlement programs such as federal old-age pensions, veterans' bonuses, guaranteed annual incomes, and national dividends; monetary reforms such as the devaluation of the dollar and the issuance of stamp scrip; and the restructuring of credit banking. Many legislative proposals on these topics were pending before Congress, and a number of the specific reforms sought by Pound and Cutting already had influential sponsors in Washington.

Pound continues to promote his vision of the free and healthy circulation of life's material and cultural goods. He inherits this vision from the dissident tradition of romantic, vitalist economics that runs from John Ruskin to guild socialism to Social Credit and fascist corporatism; it is best summarized in Ruskin's famous pronouncement, "There is no wealth but life."[1] From this perspective, any person, practice, or institution which impedes the circulation of vital wealth is an "obstructor of distribution," in the language of Pound's Hell Cantos, an enemy of life to be adjured and reformed or damned and removed.[2] The role of government, in the mixed economy that Pound projects, is to foster circulation by minimizing bureaucracy, by restraining the practices of private interests when they harm the public welfare, and by performing certain functions essential to the survival and growth of the community, such as the provision of health care and the regulation of money and credit.

Once again, Cutting is receptive to some, though not all, of Pound's program. Their disagreements have to do more with means than with ends. For Cutting was also a distributionist in economics, and he agreed with much of the Social Credit critique of capitalism, especially with its analysis of private banking. Although he was not a full-fledged Douglasite, the senator had cordial relations with a number of British and American Social Creditors, some of whom saw him as an undeclared champion of their cause and a prospective presidential candidate.

In the second phase of their correspondence, Pound assumes a somewhat greater familiarity. He relaxes into the inimitable Ezratic epistolary style that distinguishes most of his later letters. Yet he continues to speak as a concerned American citizen, seeking to reform the system from within rather than transform it from without. Although he occasionally mentions Mussolini and fascist policies, he seldom tries to debate them with or sell them to Cutting as models for America. Anti-Semitism crops up in only one letter near the end of the correspondence, having to do with the Rothschild family (2 January 1935). Pound is clearly trying to operate within an American political and rhetorical consensus to which Cutting also already subscribes.

The overall tone of the letters thus remains collegial. Yet they contain signs of mounting impatience and frustration on Pound's part. By 1934, an appointed coterie of intellectuals and academics had come to play a significant advisory role in the government of the United States. Because Pound had long dreamed of belonging to such a coterie, an undertone of rivalry and envy is audible in many of his references to New Deal personnel: "why the hell aint I putt where I cd/ edderkate some of the bloody bastuds," he asks on 12 June 1934. No longer content with the role of research assistant, the political poet writes as a would-be Brain-Truster. His stance, in the words of Philip J. Burns, is that of "a political advisor, strategist, and would-be aide, who offers his services out of a developing friendship, a common philosophy, and a desire to put this philosophy into action at the highest levels of national government."[3]

Since the second phase of the correspondence is no less specific in its focus than the first, we have again compiled brief general introductions to the main issues addressed in the letters. Our summaries provide historical contexts for some of the particular questions that preoccupied the poet and senator in 1934 and 1935. The summaries are preceded by an account of the hiatus in the correspondence between 1932 and 1934.

A.
THE END OF
THE HONEYMOON

From February 1932 to February 1934, only one surviving letter passed between Pound and Cutting. It is dated 13 November 1932, five days after the election of Franklin Delano Roosevelt to the presidency of the United States. Despite their Republican allegiances, both Pound and Cutting backed Roosevelt for the office. Their mutual hope that a new leader could solve America's problems helps to account for the gap in a correspondence driven by those problems. There seemed little point in talking further until Hoover was deposed and his successor tried.

By 1934, the honeymoon was over. The New Deal was a year old, and the nation was still in the grip of the Depression. For different reasons, both Pound and Cutting had grown disillusioned with the new president's programs. Acting in loyal opposition once again, the dissenters resumed their correspondence.

Pound's hopes for the new president ran high and were slow to die. Writing to Cutting in the wake of the election, Pound describes the results as "slightly cheering," and concedes that "no party cd. survive the sequence Harding, Calvin and Herbie" (13 November 1932). Sixteen months later, he reiterates his sense of Roosevelt's superiority to the leaders of the Republican ascendancy of 1921–33.

> I suppose as between gentlemen, an' descending four centimetres from the speech of the CURIA, we may assume that the three preceding INCUMBENTS of the White House were simple goddam shits, and that F. D. is NOT of that category. (23 March 1934)

In Pound's book of political judgments, "F. D." retained his exemption for a surprisingly long time.

Even after Pound turned against Roosevelt's policies, he continued to believe in the man. The flaws of the New Deal Pound tended to blame upon the president's appointees: "In fact F. D. as near the light as most of 'em. IF he cd. shed Farley!!! and Hull (OH Hull!!!)" (15 May 1934). Not until the later 1930s did Pound's dislike of Roosevelt's administration extend to the president himself. It then turned nasty.[4]

Cutting, meanwhile, had a more complex and ambivalent relationship with the new president. The two had known and liked each other since childhood—since, as Roosevelt once said, the senator "wore short pants."[5] They had attended the same schools, Groton and Harvard, and their class backgrounds were similar.

Given these bonds, Cutting had personal as well as political reasons for crossing over to support Roosevelt after he had obtained the Democratic presidential nomination in 1932. Other Progressive Republican senators from the western and midwestern states did the same thing. They had lost faith in Hoover, whom Cutting had endorsed in 1928; they wished to drive the Republican old guard from office; and they wanted to back a sure winner.

Cutting appeared with Roosevelt in front of three thousand people when the candidate's campaign train stopped for an hour in Lamy, New Mexico, on the morning of 27 September 1932. On 26 October, Cutting made a major radio broadcast from Denver, in which he criticized Hoover's performance in office and endorsed Roosevelt. Along with Senators Norris, LaFollette, Wheeler, and Long, Cutting was attacked in turn by Hoover in a speech at Madison Square Garden on 31 October. "I saw quote of a comic speech by Sausageface Fatboy saying that you and a few other very wicked BELIEVED that Mr. Roosevelt was the man to carry through etc. etc.," Pound exclaimed with mock incredulity (13 November 1932).

Roosevelt carried New Mexico and soon thereafter offered Cutting a position in his cabinet: the secretaryship of the interior. Cutting would have been the first New Mexican to hold the post since Senator Albert B. Fall, who fell from grace in the Teapot Dome scandal. After a well-publicized hesitation, Cutting declined the job. The truth is that he had no desire for an executive or administrative position in government; he loved the Senate and the independence he enjoyed there. The secretaryship went instead to Harold L. Ickes.

Cutting's honeymoon with the new president lasted only a few months. Roosevelt's first budget, the so-called Economy Act of 1933, was conservative in principle. It addressed the economic crisis by reducing rather than increasing federal expenditures. Among the cuts it proposed was a severe reduction in pensions for veterans suffering from service-related disabilities and for widows and dependents of veterans.

This Cutting could not accept. Many of his constituents were disabled veterans, lung patients who, like himself, had come to New Mexico because of their disability. Furthermore, Cutting's political career was built upon the contacts he had made as an American Legion organizer.[6] Among the many issues that engaged the senator's energies during his time in office, none was closer to his heart than veterans' benefits.

Cutting therefore spearheaded the successful Senate fight of June 1933 to restore the eliminated funds to the appropriations bill. In doing so, he felt torn between two loyalties. On 2 June he spoke on the Senate floor as follows.

> I certainly do not wish that any word I have said should be interpreted as a personal criticism of the President of the United States. I suppose I have known Franklin D. Roosevelt longer than any man on this floor. I have known him nearly 40 years. I regard him with the highest affection and admiration. I deserted my own party affiliations in order to support him for the Presidency. I admire the courage he has displayed in handling the affairs of the country in a time of need, even though I may disagree with some of the details of his program.

Nevertheless, Cutting persisted in his opposition. In March 1934 he again made a key speech when Congress overrode the president's veto and passed the Independent Offices Appropriations Bill, which contained sharp increases in allowances for disabled veterans. This was the first time a Roosevelt veto had been overturned.[7]

In addition to suffering legislative defeat, Roosevelt was personally offended by some of his old friend's tactics, such as displaying pathetically disabled veterans and implying that the administration lacked compassion for their sufferings. Roosevelt saw these theatrics as an attempt to humiliate him, for which no amount of verbal stroking could compensate. Relations between the president and the senator were never the same after this episode, which became known in Cutting's circle as "the unforgivable offence."[8]

In the week before the Senate vote of 28 March, Cutting dined at the White House. He was then informed that he would have the president's support in his 1934 campaign for reelection to the Senate only if he changed parties and ran as a Democrat.[9] When Cutting declined this offer, James A. Farley went to New Mexico in July to help the Democrats organize for the autumn campaign.

The party chose an able candidate, U.S. Representative Dennis Chavez, who ran with the president's blessing and came within twelve hundred to thirteen hundred votes of unseating the incumbent. Chavez charged Cutting with electoral illegalities, and asked the Democratically controlled Senate not to seat him. While flying back to Washington to answer these charges and to vote on another measure affecting veterans, Cutting died in a plane crash on 6 May 1935. In the irrationality of their grief, some of his admirers blamed the president for his death.

It is unlikely that Pound knew much about the rift between Cutting and Roosevelt, for Cutting did not talk about it in his letters to Rapallo. Although their disillusionment with FDR and the New Deal had different grounds, there was one important similarity between the two critics. Cutting grew disenchanted not because the New Deal went too far but because it did not go far enough. The same is true of Pound.[10] We turn now to some of the welfare and fiscal issues on which the administration was moving too slowly to please the poet and the senator in 1934–35.

B.
CHILD LABOR

The most pressing welfare issues of the early 1930s had to do with labor, above all with the achievement of full employment under decent working conditions. One facet of the question was the continuing exploitation of child labor in the United States. During this period, the regulation of child labor was still left to the individual states. In many rural states, especially in the South and Southwest, children were widely used in agriculture and the textile industry, and there were few restrictions upon the conditions of their employment.

Pound viewed this situation as a national disgrace and suggested to Cutting that he embarrass his southern colleagues in Senate debate by alluding to the history of slavery in their region, thus "imparting atmosphere of ignominy" to their reactionary arguments (19 February 1931). This tactical advice went unheeded, Cutting doubtless judging it likely to be counterproductive.

A child labor amendment to the Constitution passed the Congress but was not ratified by enough states to become law. The amendment was rejected by a single vote in the New Mexico House of Representatives on 4 February 1935 and by a larger margin in the Senate on 7 February.[11] These actions prompted the opening sentence of Pound's first editorial in the Santa

Fe *New Mexican:* "The failure to stop child labor in New Mexico makes rotten reading for the foreign observer" ("Ez Sez," 26 March 1935; see Chapter Four, pp. 185, 187 below). Not until the Fair Labor Standards Act of 1938 did child labor come effectively under federal regulation.

C.
THE LENGTH
OF THE WORKING DAY

For the problem of mass unemployment, Pound's short-term solution was to spread what work there was by abbreviating the working day. If shifts were cut from, say, eight hours to four, twice as many workers could be employed in the available jobs. Full wages could be paid to each of the two shifts, with government subsidies for employers who could not otherwise afford to meet doubled payrolls. Pound maintained that such a system had succeeded in parts of Italy, and that it was preferable to an inequitable and demoralizing dole on the British model.

Pound advanced these ideas in letters to Cutting of 9 October 1931 and 11 February 1932, as well as in a newspaper interview of 15 October 1931.[12] In the *ABC of Economics* (1933), he writes:

> the shortening of the working day (day of paid labour) is the first clean cut to be made. I admit it is not the whole answer, but it would go a long way to keep credit distributed among a great part of the population (of any country whatsoever) and thereby to keep goods, necessities, luxuries, comforts distributed and in circulation.[13]

The final clause of this passage is a succinct statement of the vision that informs most of Pound's economic writings.

On this issue, Pound's thinking was by no means out of key with his time. His proposal resembles one put forward early in 1933 by Senator Hugo Black of Alabama (S. 5267). Black advocated a six-hour working day and a five-day working week; his aim was to spread the existing jobs among 25 percent more workers. Black's plan had the support of many unions and of William Green, president of the American Federation of Labor. It passed in the Senate, but was superseded by President Roosevelt's National Industrial Recovery Act.[14]

Pound knew of Black's plan and gave it favorable mention on at least two occasions; one was in the "American Notes" column of the *New English Weekly* for 9 May 1935.

Senator Black, of Alabama, deserves more publicity than he gets. Thirty-hour week won't distribute MORE purchasing power, but it would spread out what it does distribute. It is one of the coming sanities.

Cutting also favored the thirty-hour week.[15]

D.
UNEMPLOYMENT COMPENSATION
AND PUBLIC WORKS

Pound favored unemployment relief, such as government subsidies for a shorter working day or for public-works projects; but he opposed unemployment compensation, such as a government dole paid directly to the jobless. The dole system, which had been instituted in Britain and would soon be adopted in the United States, seemed to Pound demoralizing, inequitable, and inefficient.

His view of "the degradation of the DOLE" is forcefully stated in Pound's pamphlet *What Is Money For?* (1939). There he speaks of "the infamy of the British system wherein men who are out of jobs are paid money taken from men who do work, and where the out-of-works are rendered progressively UNFIT to work or to enjoy the sensations of living."[16] The work ethic is central to Pound's critique of unemployment compensation. "Payment to non-producers for non-productivity can not be the answer," he mutters in a letter to Cutting; "to feed hypocrites and bums and destroy the will to be useful . . . Dole spelling slavery and MORE g.d. bureaucracy" (11 February 1932).

For his part, Cutting did not draw such a sharp distinction between unemployment compensation and other forms of unemployment relief. He was one of the Senate's earliest and most outspoken advocates of massive, federally funded relief programs—mixed programs such as were later implemented during the New Deal. "What we do need is an immediate expansion of employment on a colossal scale by the Federal Government," he was quoted as saying in November 1932.[17] In the final year of the Hoover administration, Cutting introduced a bill (S. 4737) to appropriate five billion dollars for unemployment relief of various sorts. He also supported the Costigan-LaFollette Bill, which sought a more modest 375 million dollars for emergency assistance and public works. Both of these proposals failed, but they helped to prepare the way for the creation of Roosevelt's Civil Works Administration in 1933 and the famous Works Progress Administration in 1935. It was the responsibility of government, Cutting believed, to augment the purchasing power of the disadvantaged; deficit spending worried him less than human suffering.

EZRA POUND AND SENATOR CUTTING

Pound did not object in principle to the creation of new wealth by government spending on public works. After all, Mussolini's reclamation of Pontine marshland for new agriculture and housing was a result of just such spending. What Pound disliked was the system of deficit financing by which the government borrowed money for public projects from private banks. "RE public works," he told Cutting. "The line I am taking HERE is that it is 'monstrous that every time the state creates real wealth (as the new city Sabaudia etc. or new fields that will grow grain) it gets into debt to particular individuals'" (19 April 1934). The state, in Pound's view, should have an exclusive right to create and to channel credit for the nation's benefit. By the beginning of 1934, as we shall see, Cutting had come to share this view.

The question of deficit finance brings us to the many proposals for reinflating the economy and restructuring the nation's monetary and credit systems that were being canvassed by Americans in 1934 and 1935. There was a growing consensus that the causes of the Depression had more to do with poor distribution and underconsumption than with underproduction; if that were true, then the problem of poverty amidst plenty could best be alleviated by an increase in consumption and a decrease in savings. In a speech of 5 March 1934, Roosevelt himself called for "an increase in the purchasing power of the people."[18] By what mechanism could this new purchasing power be channeled to consumers for spending rather than hoarding?

The second year of the New Deal saw an extraordinary variety of proposals designed to achieve this end. Some envisioned the creation of permanent or temporary federal entitlement programs such as old-age pensions, guaranteed annual incomes, national dividends, or veterans' bonuses. Others offered monetary solutions such as the abandonment of the gold standard, the remonetization of silver, the devaluation of the dollar, or the issuance of scrip currency. Still others proposed a radical restructuring of the nation's financial institutions, from the Federal Reserve System to the local bank on the corner. Many people favored some combination of these measures.

Organizations lobbying on behalf of their pet proposals ranged from Francis Townsend's Old Age Revolving Pensions clubs to Huey Long's Share Our Wealth crusade to Father Charles Coughlin's National Union for Social Justice to Upton Sinclair's campaign to End Poverty in California (EPIC) to C. H. Douglas's Social Credit movement to Hugo Fack's Free Economy drive.

When Pound and Cutting resumed their correspondence in February 1934, they canvassed a mind-boggling array of plans and planners. "I don't know what chance we have of getting on a sound basis in the near future," Cutting tells Pound. "I fear we are going to continue 'experimenting' for another year at least" (8 March 1934). His prophecy was accurate.

E.
OLD-AGE PENSIONS
AND VETERANS' BONUSES

Like public works, a number of proposed entitlement schemes attacked the problems of welfare and reinflation simultaneously. One of these was a plan for a system of federal old-age pensions. Early in 1934, Dr. Francis Townsend of Long Beach, California, founded an organization called Old Age Revolving Pensions, Ltd. Within a year, Townsend clubs had sprung up all over the United States. By January 1935, Representative John S. McGroarty had introduced a bill in Congress (H.R. 3977) embodying Townsend's national pension program.

According to the plan, retired persons over the age of sixty and without criminal records were to receive a monthly pension of two hundred dollars, to be funded by a national tax of 2 percent on all business transactions. Recipients must not be employed and must spend their two hundred dollars in the United States within one month, thus increasing consumer demand within the depressed national economy. The Townsend plan did not get through Congress, but alternative legislation creating the Social Security pension system was adopted in August 1935, partly in response to the public pressure Townsend's plan had generated.

Neither Pound nor Cutting favored the Townsend plan. Pound describes it as "the last and LARGEST red herring," a superficial remedy that does not go to the heart of the problem.

> The cholera inherent in the pension idea is that it encourages men to PUT OFF the use of plenty; to submit patiently to infamy under the exploitation system. Sixty years of injustice for the sake of a bribe at the end is NOT good enough.[19]

Cutting saw the human need for old-age pensions but opposed the idea of using them on a massive scale to stimulate economic recovery. In June 1934 he introduced a bill of his own (S. 3803) to appropriate a relatively modest

220 million dollars for an "old-age compensation fund." This money would be paid out to bring the incomes of senior citizens earning less than 480 dollars a year up to that level if they were disabled by illness or accident.[20]

On the other hand, Cutting was by no means opposed to a massive, one-time bonus payment to veterans of World War I. Congress had originally promised to pay this bonus in 1945, but by 1934 many members were pushing for earlier payment as an emergency solution to the problem of insufficient purchasing power. In January, Senator Arthur R. Robinson of Indiana sought to amend the so-called Gold Bill so that a fund of two billion dollars, which was to have been used by the secretary of the treasury to stabilize the dollar on the international market, would be awarded instead to veterans. Cutting, of course, supported Robinson's amendment.

Although Pound had urged full and immediate payment of the bonus in 1922, he now opposed it, and sent a strongly worded letter to the senator from Indiana on 22 April 1934.[21] "Art. R. Robinson seems a gentle soul (prob. shocked as hell by my langwidge)," Pound tells Cutting somewhat apologetically three weeks later (15 May 1934). Like Cutting, however, Pound stuck to his guns on this issue, even if it meant disagreeing with a friend. Early payment of the veterans' bonus seemed to the poet no less tangential to the fundamental causes of the Depression than was the Townsend plan.

F.
HUEY LONG AND THE "SHARE OUR WEALTH" PLAN

Another entitlement proposal that attracted considerable public attention in the second year of the New Deal was Huey P. Long's "Share Our Wealth" plan. Long, a populist demagogue who had been elected to the Senate from Louisiana in 1932, mounted a national campaign for a radical family-assistance scheme that envisioned a massive redistribution of American income from rich to poor. "Share Our Wealth" proposed to take by taxation all incomes over one million dollars and inheritances over five million dollars, and to redistribute that money in homestead allowances of five thousand dollars and guaranteed annual incomes of two thousand dollars for every family in the country. The plan entailed a wild overestimate of the amount to be gained from taxing the rich, which is why Pound describes it to

Cutting as "dividing what he [Long] peels off where it AINT" (4 April [1935]).

Despite his conviction that "Share Our Wealth" was a "silly idea," Pound had a high opinion of the charismatic Long as a leader of the opposition to Roosevelt's programs. The historian W. E. Woodward told Pound in a letter of 7 March 1935 that Long "has a splendid education—brilliant mind—quick thinker—with the manners and speech of a ward politician or a street corner orator."[22] Pound repeated this assessment in the *New English Weekly* and the London *Morning Post*.[23] So enthusiastic was he that, on 13 April, he sent an extraordinary letter out of the blue to Long, in which he offered to serve as secretary of the treasury in Long's cabinet when the Kingfish entered the White House. The correspondence of the two men continued on a more even keel until 18 August.[24]

After Cutting's death in May, Long became Pound's principal candidate for a Social Credit president. But Long himself died on the tenth of September, after being shot on the eighth. Pound published further items about him in the *New English Weekly* for 12 and 26 September; in the latter, he wrote: "With Cutting gone, and The Kingfish murdered, the American people will have to do its own saving of itself."[25]

Pound thus linked the senators, as Hoover had done in his 1932 Madison Square Garden speech. There were grounds for such an association; Cutting and Long often supported one another in Senate debates, and Cutting's newspaper, the Santa Fe *New Mexican*, gave much favorable coverage to Long's activities throughout the spring of 1935.[26] The fact is, however, that Cutting, although he sometimes agreed with Long, did not like the flamboyant and ambitious southerner; their backgrounds and styles were scarcely less opposed than those of aristocrat and tribune in ancient Rome. When Pound joshes Cutting about "yer frien' Huey the Kingfish" (4 April [1935]), he inadvertently touches a nerve; for, according to Hugh Russell Fraser's memoir of Cutting, "his greatest fear was that Huey, who admired him, would be his friend."[27]

6.
DEVALUATION
OF THE DOLLAR

Will the Kingfish ever "see MONEY?" Pound asked Cutting (4 April [1935]). Many reformers saw the monetary system as one of the main causes of the Depression. In addition to welfare and entitlement programs, they

EZRA POUND AND SENATOR CUTTING

advocated bold experiments with money itself to jump-start the stalled economy. Ardent silverites such as Senator Elmer Thomas of Oklahoma worked successfully to get the United States off the international gold standard and on to a bimetallic system. Advocates of the "commodity dollar" such as Professor George Warren also recommended abandonment of the gold standard, together with devaluation of the dollar against foreign currencies. Partisans of scrip money wished to see a supplementary paper currency put into circulation to stimulate consumption. The silver question did not interest Pound, who believed that the value of money should have no relationship to metals at all; but the other two schemes attracted his attention. He opposed devaluation of the dollar and favored the use of scrip currency.

It seemed to many observers that the role of the dollar on the international market directly affected the performance of the domestic economy. In 1933 George Frederick Warren, professor of agricultural economics at Cornell University, and Frank A. Pearson published a book entitled *Prices.* In it, they advocated abandonment by the U.S. of the gold standard, adoption of the principle of a "commodity dollar," and devaluation of the dollar against foreign currencies by massive purchases of gold in the international market. These measures would, they believed, bring about a rise in depressed U.S. agricultural prices.

The Warren-Pearson thesis strongly influenced the thinking of President Roosevelt and his cabinet when they first came into office. Acting upon the economists' recommendation, Roosevelt and Secretary of the Treasury Henry Morgenthau devalued the dollar by 40 percent in late 1933 and early 1934; they did so by the systematic buying of gold from other countries at a high, fixed price.

The Warren-Pearson policies were consistent in many ways with Social Credit principles.[28] Pound complimented Warren for having "debunked one fake"—that is, the gold standard (see Letter 17 below). Nevertheless, Pound opposed devaluation of the dollar. He did so largely because it affected his family's finances directly and adversely. His father, Homer, who had retired from his job with the United States Mint in Philadelphia, moved to Rapallo in 1930. Homer's pension, paid in U.S. dollars, lost 40 percent of its exchange value when those dollars declined against foreign currencies. From Pound's point of view, the devaluation amounted to unjust confiscation.[29] "Devaluation of dollar as now practiced/ is fairly near to simple dishonesty," Pound complained to Cutting on 23 March 1934. "This present idiotic administration is already robbing my pore and 74 year aged father of 40% of his pension (god damn 'em) for no reason save that Warren is hick/ mind and that Frankie is wandering about picking gooseberries." Characteristically, the critic blames the president's advisors rather than the president himself.

Cutting did not respond to Pound's protest, and we do not know his views on the devaluation issue.

H.
STAMP SCRIP

If monetary remedies were to be pursued, Pound favored the issuance of stamped scrip currency of the sort advocated by German businessman Silvio Gesell. Stamp scrip was paper money valid only for domestic use and not linked to the international value of gold. The currency itself was to be taxed periodically by means of a stamp purchased and affixed to each bill by whoever was holding it at the time. The stamp requirement, Gesell argued, would encourage spending and discourage hoarding. By promoting the rapid circulation of money through many hands, stamp scrip would increase consumption through the multiplier effect. Gesell's plan was tried for a time in the Austrian community of Wörgl near Innsbrück. It was also approved for implementation in the principality of Monaco.[30]

Gesell's concept was taken up by an American economist, Professor Irving Fisher of Yale. His book, *Stamp Scrip* (1933), attracted the attention of several congressmen, the most important of whom was Senator John Hollis Bankhead II of Alabama.[31] On 20 February 1933, Bankhead and Representative Samuel B. Pettengill of Indiana cosponsored "a bill (S. 5674) to provide for the issuance of stamped money certificates" by the United States Treasury.[32] Bankhead proposed, as Pound later explained it in "A Visiting Card" (1942), "an emission of dollar bills up to a limit of a milliard [*i.e.*, one billion] dollars."[33] To remain valid, each bill was to be stamped weekly with a two-cent stamp purchased from the Post Office. The experiment "started in Austria and Germany," Bankhead told the Senate, "but Professor Fisher has taken it up and I am adopting it from him."

Bankhead's bill died in the Senate Committee on Banking and Currency in March, and two subsequent attempts to obtain Senate consideration of stamp scrip also failed.[34] Pound thought the original bill might have fared better if the amount of scrip to be issued and the frequency of its stamping had been less.[35] He nonetheless praised the senator's initiative repeatedly, affirming that Bankhead "rose to very considerable greatness in the debate on his bill."[36] Once again, a reform close to Pound's heart nearly attracted the serious attention of the Congress.

Pound was accordingly disappointed when Bankhead ceased to press the stamp-scrip issue after 1933. The poet attributed the senator's silence to the pressure of vested interests. "Who told Bankhead not to mention stamp scrip *again*?" Pound asks Cutting on 23 March 1934. Who has scared him "into the timber" (23 February 1934)? Cutting neither answered the question nor, so far as we know, commented upon stamp scrip. His silence on the issue may mean that the senator was not an enthusiast.

I.
NATIONAL DIVIDENDS
AND PRICE CONTROLS

Despite his disapproval of the dole, Pound advocated another form of direct public-assistance payments to increase consumer purchasing power. Instead of old-age pensions, veterans' bonuses, or guaranteed annual incomes, Pound favored national dividends, a concept derived from the Social Credit economics of Major C. H. Douglas. National dividends would be issued directly to consumers by the government on the strength of its own authority to create and manage the nation's credit. The money would not, in other words, be borrowed at interest from private sources. Two birds could be killed with one stone, Pound thought, if the dividends were issued as stamp scrip: "I am at moment preaching a blend of Mussolini's horse sense, plus Doug/ via Gesell, and with the divs pd/ in stamp scrip," Pound tells Cutting in August 1934, in a succinct summary of his current economic program.

Direct payments would eliminate profiteering by middlemen. "Why shouldn't the nation's credit be distributed per capita to the citizens instead of being 'allocated' by special favour either to banks or to groups of 'employers'?" Pound asks Cutting (8 March 1934). The dividend would have a pump-priming effect, as Pound explained to readers of *Esquire* magazine in 1935; it "would circulate and bring life into adjacent industries. It would obviously be an increase in purchasing power."[37]

To prevent the dividend from being swallowed by inflation, Pound would institute price controls, which had their theoretical rationale in the Social Credit concept of the "Just Price" and which had already been put into practice in Italy. "Here we have the price of meat, bread etc. posted up on the walls of the market etc," Pound tells Senators Borah and Cutting, "and people do NOT have to pay more" (7 June 1934).

Like stamp scrip, the national dividend had backers in Washington and came before the Congress as a specific legislative proposal. In March 1934, the *New English Weekly* published "the text of a Bill for the establishment of Social Credit in the United States now under consideration by members of the Senate, Congress, and the Administration."[38] The bill had been drafted by the New Economics Group, the principal Douglasite organization in New York City. On 22 August 1935, Representative T. Alan Goldsborough of Maryland introduced a modified version of the bill to the House (H.R. 9216). The bill eventually died in the House Banking Committee, but not before it had received extensive hearings in 1936 and 1937.[39]

Pound read the draft bill in the *New English Weekly* and objected to a minor feature of it that would have affected his own interests. The bill's provision for a "national consumers' dividend amounting to $12.50 monthly" stipulated that it be paid "to every qualified voter resident in the United States, its territories and possessions." This wording would have disqualified Pound and other American citizens living abroad from receiving a monthly stipend. Pound wrote immediately to Senator Cutting, asking him to plug the loophole.

> Some dirty dog has gone and discriminated against citizens who broaden the mind by travel and foreign contact (vide proposed Soc/ Credit Bill. N.E.W. 22. March p. 532. col. 2. From which I request you strike OUT the words "voter resident in" and replace 'em with common decency by "citizen of." (23 March 1934)

In other respects, however, Pound apparently approved of the bill.

To judge once again from his silence on the matter, Cutting may not have been a partisan of national dividends. As we have seen, he was a more ardent advocate of other forms of public assistance. Even if he rejected this plank of the Social Credit platform, however, Cutting was highly receptive to the Social Credit critique of the banking industry.

J.
The Nationalization of Credit Banking

According to Major Douglas, the control of credit and the charging of interest on credit by private bankers are the main causes of economic scarcity in modern society. "The present trade depression," Douglas declared during the slump of 1920, "is directly and consciously caused by the concerted action of the banks in restricting credit facilities."[40] All other expenditures paid out by a given producer, such as wages, salaries, and dividends, reenter the economy as purchasing power. The interest paid on credit loans, Douglas argued, does not; it is hoarded as usurious profit by the bankers and thus removed from the total amount of money available to consumers.

In order to repay his loans, the producer must reckon both principal and interest into the price of his products, but the interest payments never return to prospective consumers of those products. By a process of deduction which Douglas termed his "A + B theorem," he calculated that, so long as private bankers profit from the creation of credit, prices will inevitably outstrip purchasing power in the economy as a whole. Most people will never have enough money to buy what they help to produce. As Pound phrases it in a letter to Senator Borah, "what is the result of every factory, every industry, under present (dog dratted idiotic system) producing prices faster than it emits the power to buy..???" (undated copy sent to Cutting; see Letter 17 below). Underconsumption leading to massive economic depression—that is clearly the answer Pound has in mind. The principal rationale for the national dividend was that it would help to bridge this gap between prices and purchasing power.

In his response to Pound's query, Cutting seems to accept the critique underlying it; he calls it "a question to which the answer is . . . obvious" (8 March 1934). The payment to bankers of interest on the national debt was of particular concern to Cutting. "What does the government do," he asked,

> when it goes to the rescue of its needy and starving citizens? It floats loans through the banks. It pays interest to private organizations for the use of its own credit. The thing becomes still more preposterous when we realize that an enormous proportion of the relief expended by the government has gone to the aid of great banking institutions. So that actually the govern-

ment is getting itself into debt to the banks for the privilege of helping
them to regain their stranglehold on the economic life of the country.

This analysis led Cutting to conclude that "commercial banking and issuing
of credit should be exclusively a governmental function. Private financiers
are not entitled to any profit on credit."[41] Pound had been saying the same
thing for years.

Although he could sound like one, Cutting was not a Social Creditor—
not even in secret. He did not espouse Douglas's national dividend or just
price. Moreover, as a matter of practical politics, Cutting believed that he
would significantly narrow his national constituency if he were to announce
an allegiance to Social Credit or "to introduce a bill as an orthodox Douglas
proposal."[42] He was well aware that Social Credit had ardent opponents as
well as exponents. To a lady who asked, "Will you be the plumed knight of
Social Credit?" he answered gallantly but evasively, "I have been in close
touch with representatives of the New Economics Group, and like many
others, I have been deeply interested in the theories which they support."[43]
The careful wording reminds us that, on national issues anyway, Cutting was
by temperament a nonjoiner.

He nevertheless found the Social Credit explanation of the causes of the
Depression intellectually compelling. "While I am not necessarily committed to the mechanics of the Douglas plan," Cutting told San Francisco Social Creditor David Warren Ryder in April 1934, "I think that the analysis of
the present situation is entirely sound." That Cutting understood that analysis is suggested by his remark, in the same letter, that he has read "several"
of the Major's works as well as C. M. Hattersley's exposition of Douglas's
ideas in *This Age of Plenty* (1929).[44] Pound had mailed Hattersley's book to
the senator along with his letter of 12 February 1932. Whether at Pound's
instigation or independently, by the beginning of 1934 Cutting had clearly
done his Social Credit homework.

Avowed Social Creditors were thus intellectually congenial to Cutting.
They were also politically valuable as an interest group whose support he
wished to retain. Pound was by no means the only Douglasite lobbyist with
whom Cutting cultivated cordial relationships. He had no dealings with John
Hargrave and the Green Shirt Movement, but the senator corresponded with
A. R. Orage and entertained him and his followers in Santa Fe.[45] Cutting
contributed both money and copy to Orage's *New English Weekly* and to *New
Democracy*, respectively the leading British and American Social Credit jour-

nals of the day.[46] He corresponded with West Coast Social Credit groups in Pasadena and San Francisco.[47] And he hosted a buffet-supper reception for C. H. Douglas when the Major visited Washington during his 1934 world tour. To this reception on 26 April, Cutting invited around three dozen potentially receptive congressional colleagues, but the uncharismatic Douglas did not dazzle. "I am afraid there were few conversions," Cutting reported dryly to Pound. "As an expositor, the Major is a little less aggressive than is customary in his partibus infidelium" (24 May 1934).

Cutting himself, however, waxed aggressive on behalf of governmental control of credit banking. In January 1934, he publicly advocated the creation of a central bank that would absorb the existing Federal Reserve System and "monopolize the credit system of the country for the benefit of the public not for the benefit of the bankers."[48] In March, using language that smacked of Social Credit, he inveighed against "the wild gyrations of private banking control" over credit, recommended the abolition of this "uncontrolled and capricious power," and vowed that "unless the administration presents a bill depriving bankers of this power, I myself shall introduce such a measure. Private control of credit must be abolished."[49] In May, he said on NBC radio, "The creation of a national bank which will eventually have a monopoly of the issuance of credit is, to my mind, the most vital issue of the country today."[50] And in June, Cutting and Representative Wright Patman of Texas laid before the Congress a bill to effect these purposes.

The intentions of Senate bill 3744 were "to regulate the value of money in pursuance of article 1, section 8, paragraph 5 of the Constitution of the United States; to create a Federal Monetary Authority; to provide an adequate and stable monetary system; to prevent bank failures; to prevent uncontrolled inflation; to prevent depressions; to provide a system to control the price of commodities and the purchasing power of money; to restore normal prosperity and assure its continuance."[51] Drafted in consultation with a group of economists working under Dr. Robert M. Hutchins at the University of Chicago, the bill provided for the nationalization of the sixty-five hundred member institutions of the twelve Federal Reserve banks; this was to be accomplished through the purchase of the federal reserve stocks held by the member banks. Ten thousand non-Federal Reserve banks would eventually be brought into the system as well. His goal, Cutting told G. L. Moody of Las Cruces, New Mexico, was "to put the Government in control of the banking business of the United States."[52] The Cutting-Patman proposal ultimately lost out to the less radical Roosevelt-Eccles Federal Reserve Reform Bill of 1935. In 1939, some features of Cutting-Patman were resurrected in a Patman-Voorhis banking bill (H.R. 4931); but it, too, died in committee.

Pound had a few cavils about Cutting's bill, as did other Social Creditors; it was not, as Cutting admitted, entirely "orthodox from a Social Credit point of view."[53] Yet Pound supported the measure; once again, a key part of his economic program seemed tantalizingly close to serious congressional consideration. Resuming the familiar role of research assistant, Pound sends Cutting information on historical precedents for the communal control of credit, luminous details derived from the researches into the history of Italian banking which inform Cantos 40–44 (12 June 1934).

Pound began to tell friends that "Cutting is now openly Douglasite," and he later claimed that the senator "was finally for Social Credit."[54] These were overstatements; Cutting would not have proclaimed himself a Social Creditor even if he had lived longer. But in 1934–35, he gave Douglasites good reason to believe that their cause had indeed found its plumed knight. "Wanted:" Pound advertised in the *New English Weekly* after Cutting's death, "his successor as Social Credit leader in the Senate."[55]

In the second phase of their correspondence, then, Pound and Cutting tried to unravel some of the worst economic tangles of the Depression. They agreed that the basic problem had to do not with production but with distribution and consumption. Of the many remedies being mooted at the time, the poet and senator agreed on some and disagreed on others. Pound advocated a shorter working day, public works, stamp scrip, national dividends, and price controls; he opposed old-age pensions, veterans' bonuses, unemployment compensation, and the devaluation of the dollar. Cutting favored a shorter working day, public works, veterans' bonuses, and unemployment compensation; he opposed a large old-age-pension program and remained silent on the questions of stamp scrip and national dividends. The most important point of agreement between the poet and senator derived from Social Credit theory and entailed the nationalization of the banking industry, the elimination of interest charges on deficit financing by the government, and federal control of credit in the public interest. All of these projects were pending before the Congress, hypotheses competing to become experiments. Although most of them failed to clear the final hurdle and win federal funding, their sponsors were informed and responsible American citizens.

II
The Letters

13 Feb. [1934]

EZRA POUND
VIA MARSALA 12-5
RAPALLO

Senator
Bronson Cutting

My Dear Senator

As the old thieves seem to be getting it in the neck, and as the efforts of the press owners to suppress facts about European Economics are not completely successful, even if Bankhead has been scared into the timber, what about a little cultural activity. Now that some Judge has shown himself to be a cut above the yahoo.

ART/ 211. Be amended / to apply only to books or post cards having no literary or artistic merit and whose *sole appeal is* their obscenity. Surgical and medical information and works of recognized or demonstrable literary merit to be free of interference.

Having been brought up to suppose the republican party was THE party etc/ I still don't think that even the infinite and bootlicking patience of the American citoyen CAN be expected to reinstate an organization that has dumped the successive shitpails / Harding Coolidge and Hoover, plus Andy/ and the rest of the gang now looking jail=wards. I don't see why you shd/ go down with that rotten boat.

Or as a matter of fact why a little knowledge of Gesell and C.H. Douglas shdn't penetrate the Senate Chamber, for the improvement etc/ etc.

It's got to come.

patiently yours
Ezra Pound

Notes on Letter 16

(13 Feb. [1934])

Bankhead. On Senator John H. Bankhead and stamp scrip, see the Introduction to Chapter Three, pp. 96–97 above.

some Judge. On 6 December 1933 Judge John M. Woolsey of the United States District Court in the Southern District of New York ruled that James Joyce's *Ulysses* (1922) was not obscene within the meaning of Section 305 of the Smoot-Hawley Tariff Bill of 1930 and could therefore be legally imported into the United States. The change in Section 305 that allowed the case to come into Judge Woolsey's court was largely the work of BC; see Chapter One, pp. 16–19 above. On Article 211 and postal censorship, see the Introduction to Chapter Two, pp. 24–27 above.

Andy. Multimillionaire Andrew William Mellon (1855–1937) was secretary of the treasury from 1921 to 1932 under Presidents Harding, Coolidge, and Hoover. In 1934–35 the government tried unsuccessfully to prosecute Mellon for income tax evasion. See also Letter 17 below.

Gesell. German businessman and monetary reformer Silvio Gesell (1862–1930) developed a theory of paper money or stamp scrip not linked to the value of metals and periodically taxed by means of a stamp purchased and affixed to the money itself. See the Introduction to Chapter Three, pp. 96–97 above, and Letters 27 and 30 below.

17. TL, carbon copy, 2pp., Beinecke Library

[Feb./Mar. 1934?]

My Dear Senator

What you say about Baldwin and Nicolson is O.K.

I take it we agree that Wilson was about the most pungent skunk that ever got to the White House/ Harding what Alice calls him "a slob" and Hoover a crook and cat's paw?

IF you MEAN anything/ the place to unhorse the British god damn scoundrels is ECONOMICS.

IF you can bust the press boycott/ which is run by De Wendel (hell incarnate), Vickers, Rothermere, Deterding, I suppose DuPont or who? Mellon etc.

IF you can (without even putting yourself in danger by professing a given doctrine) but by forcing DISCUSSION of the three questions I have put, you can definitely LET in the decent English, and put out the god damn scoundrels.

The questions ARE, once again:

1. What is an auxiliary currency?

2. When money is rented, who ought to pay the rent, the man who has it when the rent falls due, or some fellow who hasn't??

3. What is the result of every factory, every industry, under present (dog dratted idiotic system) producing prices faster than it emits the power to buy..???

Internal disorder makes war. [Internal disorder reaching for ?]

[rest of page cut off]

THE MEANS of distribution EXIST (are known) just as potent for DISTRIBUTION, as modern productive means are for Production.

Ole Doc/ Warren has got paralysis in his head/ he has debunked one fake, but cant move any further.

And as fer thet Nashnl Commyteeeee/tea party/ with Vanderlip and Gregory/ they dump eight pounds of hooey into this place once a week.

France and England will run like hell from open Econ/ discussion. It is worth 45 navys. and 5000 battleships.

England will always understand Mr Baruch. perfectly.

Damn it, the time is NOW.

Have you ever read any Confucius? I am sending you a little with compliments/ most people are too dumb to understand such simple horse sense. I have known a lot of highbrows (including Bill Yeats (the ghost and fairy poet) who call it platitude. But you can't beat it.

The Bull Moose down in Rome, is the best thing in Europe. Gives 'em what they can understand. Drained the swamps, more grain and better grain,

(got to have ENOUGH first . . . after that distribute

[rest of page cut off]

Notes on Letter 17

([Feb./Mar. 1934?])

My Dear Senator. This letter was addressed to Senator William E. Borah, but a copy was sent to BC as well. Because EP intended it to be read by both recipients, we have treated the letter as part of his correspondence with BC.

What you say. In separate speeches reported by the *New York Times* on 8 February 1934, Stanley Baldwin and Harold Nicolson (see notes below) attacked the U.S. Senate's refusal to ratify the Treaty of Versailles and to join the League of Nations in July 1919. On 9 February the *Times* responded to the speeches in an editorial entitled "Again the Scapegoat" (18). On 15 February, Borah, a staunch opponent of ratification, took up the gauntlet on the floor of the Senate, having read the editorial. His remarks were reported in "Borah Denounces 'Libel' by Britons," *New York Times*, 16 February, p. 4, and in "Borah Denounces British View of U.S., Versailles Pact," *Chicago Tribune* (Paris), 27 February 1934, p. 2. EP learned of the controversy from the second of these articles: "A bitter denunciation of English statesmen who blame the present European crisis on the United States' failure to ratify the Versailles Treaty was voiced in the Senate recently by Senator William E. Borah, Idaho insurgent Republican, former chairman of the Senate Foreign Relations Committee and one of the 'bitter enders' who blocked the treaty's ratification. His remarks were directed at Stanley Baldwin, former British Prime Minister, and Harold Nicolson, member of the British Foreign Office, his text being a recent editorial in an eastern paper in which the Britons were quoted as laying the blame for the present situation on the United States." Borah went on to say that "there has evidently been a break in the hereditary traits of English statesmen. . . . The craven spirit was never an attribute of English statesmen."

Baldwin. Stanley Baldwin (1867–1947) was three times prime minister of the United Kingdom (1923, 1924–29, 1936–37). Speaking in debate on the floor of the House of Commons, Baldwin said, "There was no more reeling blow struck at [the League of Nations] than when the American Senate refused to support Wilson. The security that France, with her wounds still bleeding, thought she had got from Wilson disappeared in a moment. That as much as anything, if not more than anything, has been the one thing that has made things more difficult than anything else in Europe by always bringing up the question of security." See "War Threat Seen by British House," *New York Times*, 8 February 1934, p. 4.

Nicolson. Sir Harold George Nicolson (1886–1968), diplomat, member of Parliament, and man of letters. Nicolson toured the United States in 1933 and published a biography of Dwight Morrow (see Letter 2 above) in 1935. Speaking in Vienna, Nicolson deplored the passing of the "old diplomacy," with its principle that a country was bound in honor by the signature of its accredited spokesmen. The new diplomacy began, according to Nicolson, "when the American Senate refused to ratify the Treaty of Versailles, signed by their fully accredited representative . . . with America's repudiation began an era of diplomacy by statements and conferences—the most undesirable form imaginable." See "Kellogg Pact Scored by Harold Nicholson [*sic*]," *New York Times*, 8 February 1934, p. 5.

Wilson. President Woodrow Wilson (see Letter 6 above) played a major role in the negotiations that produced the Treaty of Versailles at the end of the First World War. In "Bureaucracy: The Flail of Jehovah," *The Exile*, No. 4, (Autumn 1928), EP writes, "Wilson's reign was a period of almost continuous misfortune to the organism of official life in America" (10).

Alice. Alice Roosevelt Longworth (1884–1980) was the daughter of President Theodore Roosevelt, wife of the Speaker of the House of Representatives, and *grande dame* of Washington society for most of the twentieth cen-

108

tury. In her memoir *Crowded Hours* (New York: Charles Scribner's Sons, 1933) the sharp-tongued Mrs. Longworth describes President Harding, with whom she often played poker, as "just a slob" (325).

press boycott. Some of these names appear in EP's Canto 38 (1933), which likewise expounds his vision of a conspiracy of wealthy industrialists and bankers to control and censor the press. See also *The Symposium* 4, 2 (April 1933), 252–56; rpt., *Ezra Pound's Poetry and Prose*, 6: 31–34.

De Wendel. The De Wendel family owned a large iron and steelworking company that manufactured machinery and armaments in France. François de Wendel (1874–1949) became managing director of the company in 1903. He was also president of the Comité des Forges and a director of the National Bank of France. De Wendel was said to control *Le Temps, Le Journal des débats,* and *Echo de Paris.* In "Peace Pathology," *New Democracy* 2, 2–3 (30 March–15 April 1934), 7, EP speaks of "the Baron de Wendel, who is indubitably the most concentrated power for evil on Earth"; rpt., *Ezra Pound's Poetry and Prose*, 6: 147.

Vickers. The Vickers family owned iron and steelworks in Sheffield, England. By 1933 Vickers-Armstrong was Britain's largest manufacturer of armaments. In "The Vickers Firm," *Chicago Tribune* (Paris), 22 April 1933, p. 4, EP asks "how many wars they have deliberately promoted in order to profit by the sale of their well known line of knicknacks?" Rpt., *Ezra Pound's Poetry and Prose*, 6: 35.

Rothermere. Among the English newspapers owned or co-owned by Harold Sidney Harmsworth, Viscount Rothermere (1868–1940) were the *Evening News*, the *Daily Mail,* the *Daily Mirror,* the Sunday *Pictorial* and the *Leeds Mercury.*

Deterding. Sir Henri Deterding (1866–1939) was director-general of the Royal Dutch Petroleum Company, which later merged with the Shell Oil Company.

DuPont. The DuPont family rose to prominence in the United States as manufacturers of gunpowder and other munitions during the First World War. Pierre Samuel DuPont (1870–1954), head of the family in EP's day, was also president of General Motors and influential in both the Republican and the Democratic parties.

Mellon. For Andrew W. Mellon, see Letter 16 above. Reputed to be the second richest man in the United States, Mellon made his fortune principally from the manufacture of aluminum, the extraction of oil, and banking.

three questions. See Letter 15 above.

Warren. On Professor George Frederick Warren (1874–1938), see the Introduction to Chapter Three, pp. 95–96 above.

Vanderlip. Frank Arthur Vanderlip (1864–1937), expert on international finance and former president of the National City Bank of New York, was a prominent member of the Committee for the Nation to Rebuild Prices and Purchasing Power. Formed early in 1933 to combat the Depression, the committee consisted initially of three hundred business and industrial leaders, headed by James H. Rand, Jr., of the Remington Rand Corporation. They were united in support of various inflationary measures. In its *Interim Report and Immediate Recommendations* (1933), for example, the committee advocated abandonment of the gold standard and devaluation of the dollar. Highly effective lobbyists and propagandists, the members of the committee backed their recommendations with a barrage of resolutions, reports, analyses, statistics, letters, and telegrams. EP, who was on the committee's mailing list and corresponded with its officers, conceded that it had "seen a bit of daylight" in some of its pronouncements; but he remained suspicious of it as a "'committee' of magnates" and a "Committee for (diddling) the Nation." It "mixes a lot of twisty education in its propaganda and no weekly column can keep up with it. Isolated quotations from Vanderlip might be Truth herself at the microphone." See "American Notes," *New English Weekly* 6, 25 (4 April 1935), 509–10, and 7, 22 (10 October 1935), 425; rpt., *Ezra Pound's Poetry and Prose*, 6: 274, 328.

Gregory. Sir Theodore Emanuel Gugenheim Gregory (1890–1970) was Sir Ernest Cassel Professor of Economics at the University of London from 1927 to 1937. He was an expert on banking, monetary theory, and international trade and exchange. Among his publications are *The Present Position of Banking in America* (1925), *Select Statutes, Documents and Reports, Relating to British Banking, 1832–1928* (1929), *The Gold Standard and Its Future* (1932), and *Gold, Unemployment and Capitalism* (1933). Gregory was a member of the Macmillan Committee (see Letter 13 above). The committee's report records his lack of sympathy with Social Credit ideas, manifested when C. H. Douglas gave evidence at a hearing in 1930. In EP's Canto 52 (1940), we are told: "Gregory damned, always was damned, obscurantist."

Baruch. Millionaire Bernard M. Baruch (1870–1965) was chairman of the War Industries Board under President Wilson (1918–19) and an influential elder statesman of the Democratic party well into the 1960s. Baruch prescribed higher taxes, reduced federal spending, and balanced budgets as a remedy to the Depression. He opposed abandonment of the gold standard. EP's satire of him, "Very Old Tune," *New Democracy* 1, 11 (1 February 1934), 2 (rpt., *Ezra Pound's Poetry and Prose*, 6: 128), was followed by Edwin Newdick's critique (p. 3) of Baruch's essay "The Dangers of Inflation," *Saturday Evening Post* 206 (25 November 1933), 5–7.

Confucius. EP's translation of *Ta Hio: The Great Learning* was published in Seattle by the University of Washington Book Shop in 1928.

Bill Yeats. For W. B. Yeats, see Letter 11 above. In his writings Yeats often granted at least provisional credence to tales of supernatural phenomena.

Bull Moose. This was the nickname of American President Theodore Roosevelt (1858–1919) and the independent or Progressive party that he led in the presidential election of 1912. The name derived from the fact that Roosevelt had told reporters who inquired about his health that he felt as fit as a bull moose. EP's transfer of the epithet to Mussolini (for whom see Letter 6) was calculated to appeal to Borah and BC, who saw themselves as continuing the progressive or "Bull Moose" tradition of the Republican party. The comparison of Mussolini to Roosevelt was a journalistic commonplace of the time, encouraged by Mussolini himself; see John P. Diggins, *Mussolini and Fascism: The View from America* (Princeton, N.J.: Princeton University Press, 1972), 63, 65, 99, 224, 226. For Mussolini's draining of the Pontine marshes, see Letter 21 below. Another widely publicized fascist project was the planting of enough grain to end Italy's dependence for its daily bread upon foreign imports.

8 Mar. 1934

United States Senate
Committee on Military Affairs

Dear Pound:

Please excuse my negligence in failing to reply to so many communications. All of them were profoundly enjoyed.

I enclose a page of the *Record*, containing my brief remarks on January 27th, for which you ask. I was talking under a ten-minute limit, so could not go into these matters very thoroughly.

I don't know what chance we have of getting on a sound basis in the near future. I fear we are going to continue "experimenting" for another year, at least. Anyway, Major Douglas is expected here in April, and perhaps we can arrange to get him an interview with some of the higher-ups.

In the meanwhile, neither the Administration, nor anyone else, has answered the third question which you propound. I am afraid the reason is that they don't want to ask themselves a question to which the answer is so obvious.

Believe me always

Sincerely yours,
Bronson Cutting

NOTES ON LETTER 18
(8 Mar. 1934)

brief remarks. During the debate on a bill
"to provide for the better use of the monetary gold stock of the United States" (H.R.
6976), BC supported a reduction in the gold
content of the dollar. He also advocated several farther-reaching measures, such as out-
lays for public works and the creation of a
central bank which would absorb the Federal Reserve System and "monopolize the
credit system of the country for the benefit
of the public and not for the benefit of the
bankers." See the *Congressional Record* 78,
2 (27 January 1934), 1476–77, and the Introduction to Chapter Three, pp. 99–101
above.

Major Douglas. See Letter 14 above.

In the meanwhile. EP quotes this paragraph in "The U.S. Social Credit Bill," *New
English Weekly* 4, 25 (5 April 1934),
599–600; rpt., *Ezra Pound's Poetry and
Prose*, 6: 167.

19. TLS, 1p., Library of Congress

8 Mar. [1934]

EZRA POUND
VIA MARSALA 12-5
RAPALLO

Senator Bronson Cutting

My Dear Senator

After Roosevelt's speech on March' 4th, the issue is clear, and one wd. think, unavoidable:

Why shouldn't the increase of purchasing power which he demands, and which [he ?] admits to be necessary; namely why shouldn't the nation's credit be distributed per capita to the citizens instead of being "allocated" by special favour either to banks or to groups of "employers"?

The enormous source of this (the government's) credit lies in the nation's real profits, namely the surplus of the country's production over what it consumes. This is the meaning of "Economic Democracy"

yrs

Ezra Pound

P.S. damnd if I see how he can dodge it.

Notes on Letter 19

(8 Mar. [1934])

Roosevelt's speech. On 5 March 1934, a year and a day after he first took office, President Roosevelt made a major radio speech before a convention of businessmen in Washington. He called for higher wages in order to bring about "an increase in the purchasing power of the people. . . . Millions of persons are still without work, and the purchasing power is thus considerably shrunken. We can increase or maintain this purchasing power only by doing all in our power to keep prices at the lowest level consistent with high wages and an increase in employment. . . . All the information which I possess leads to this inevitable conclusion: we must take immediate action to increase wages and reduce hours of labor." See "Roosevelt Wants Wage Boost," *Chicago Tribune* (Paris), 6 March 1934, pp. 1, 3. EP responded to Roosevelt's speech in "A Retrospect," *Chicago Tribune* (Paris), 14 March 1934, p. 5; rpt., *Ezra Pound's Poetry and Prose,* 6: 141. He pointed out that he himself had called for a shorter working day as early as October 1931 (see the Introduction to Chapter Three, pp. 89–90 above), and he called once more for a national, Social Credit dividend to increase purchasing power: "Is there anything essentially undemocratic in conceiving the citizen as a SHAREHOLDER in the nation, entitled to a small slice of benefits accruing from the nation's improved production? . . . . AS the trouble is now ADMITTED to be shortage of purchasing power. And as the official figures show one sixth of the nation on the government payroll (or in receipt of benefits) and something like 17 million out of work,

wouldn't we save a good deal of discussion by an IMPARTIAL dividend, payable in *jeton money,* and not subject to the whims of bureaucracy or special favors to anyone." EP refers to the president's speech again in "Mr. Roosevelt at the Crossroads," *New Democracy* 2, 7 (15 June 1934), 5; rpt., *Ezra Pound's Poetry and Prose,* 6: 180.

"Economic Democracy". The title of Major C. H. Douglas's principal work (see Letter 14 above), in which he advocates a "national dividend" of the type that EP here proposes.

23 March [1934]

RAPALLO
VIA MARSALA, 12 INT. 5

My Dear Senator

I don't want you to waste time answering my letters IF you've got anything better to do. What the bloody layman finds difficult to onnerstan IZ: can't the honbl/ Senator from XYZ, putt a little insecticide on the fake economists. (Ground hog bill in India, as sample or model).

A BILL

1. That no professor shall be removed from his economic seat, settee, chair, sofa or other curial support for having entered into open and untrammeled debate on Economics.

2. That no professor shall be deemed to be other than an louse ignoramus and/or god damn nuisance UNTIL he have studied a little history AND be ready to face the THREE QUESTIONS asked by E.P.

(I hope some of the Haavud boys have tried 'em on that bloated bullzarse Sprague).

/ / / /

end of A BILL.

/ / / /

Yaas ole Doug/ izza comin. Horstralyia has greeted him. IF FRANKIE don't see him, then Frankie is just a plain god damn fool.

Devaluation of dollar as now practiced/ is fairly near to simple dishonesty. And statement from considerable altitude that "no intelligent man expects the govt. to PAY recently incurred indebtedness" looks like the govt. was trying to be a new Kreuger . . . at least on the plane of ETHICS a little righteousness never did no ruler no *harm*

P.S. Who told Bankhead not to mention stamp scrip *again*?

I suppose, as between gentlemen, an' descending four centimetres from the speech of the CURIA, we may assume that the three preceding INCUMBENTS of the White House were simple godddam shits, and that F.D. is NOT of that category.

Still how CAN Farley be kept on, NOW?

AND is it necessary to have Hull (certainly the most driveling idiot . . . unless the *Chi. Trib.* has misquoted him... that ever sat in the cabinet..not excepting even Woolsome Woodies Mr Colby.

(Quinn's remark re. B.C. "DIPlomat!!!!? Don't want a DIPlomat, wot he want's izza DOORmat.).

Waaal/ sir. You done spoke glorious words an I hope to use 'em in something more likely to be read than the secret archives. Did anybody but *New Democracy* quote that speech? (apart from Orage's citation of it).

Some dirty dog has gone and discriminated against citizens who broaden the mind by travel and foreign contact (vide proposed Soc/ Credit Bill. N.E.W. 22. March p. 532. col. 2. From which I request you to strike OUT the words "voter resident in" and replace 'em with common decency by "citizen of".

This present idiotic administration is already robbing my pore and 74 year aged father of 40% of his pension (god damn 'em) for no reason save that Warren is hick/mind and that Frankie is wandering about picking gooseberries.) & that is *No* reason for the Douglasites to go parochial. Even if I am the only person to notice it.

GOD dam/ woodgrainers of the Concord School/ Mark Twain's cowardice// all that slabsided half/literature of the ottocento. Wilson's foreign information got from Missouri . . . and the need of something to represent the country abroad . . . something OTHER THAN Dicky Washtub Child. (God damn i dont say Child isn't *representative*. . . . but *IF* THAT IS AMERICA fer JHZZ ACHE the country has got to be *MIS=represented* abroad until it is representable. I.E. ameliorated.

Has anybody heard of a guy named BURR . . . mebbe dead by now // but there wuzza guy FIT to be an nambassador. (forget his front name .. he was married to a she/novelist called Amelia . . . I beeleev . . .) Was working on cotton etc. during the war . . . may be dead . . . but if not Frankie needs him.

AN gordammmm/ Wd/ or wdnt/ a WAIL for decent education be timely. ???

Surely the blithering ignorance of the american "educated" and governing classes OUGHT by now to have indicated the need of a little mental life in our "inschtooshunz of learning". Didn(t you once have a noozpaper.. or isn't there some noozpaper that wd/ let me loose. (Even the *London Morning Post* has admitted me to noise column.)

AND; O YESS/ as y're/ a military affairist (at least on yr stationery // Can you tell me how much DuPont or what is it stock Col. MacCormick holds. (the *Chicago Trib.* guy) and WHAT is back of that paper, which has some decent qualities BUT . . . .

E. Pound

Notes on Letter 20

(23 March [1934])

Ground hog bill in India. We have not identified the source or the object of this reference.

Sprague. Oliver Mitchell Wentworth Sprague (1873–1935) was professor of banking and finance in the Graduate School of Business Administration at Harvard University. "Sound Money Sprague," as he was sometimes called, taught President Roosevelt at Harvard and was chief economic adviser to the Bank of England from 1930 to 1933. He resigned from the Roosevelt administration on 21 November 1933 because of his disagreement with the policy of manipulating the international price of gold to devalue the dollar (see the Introduction to Chapter Three, pp. 95–96 above). With the publication of *Recovery and Common Sense* (1934), Sprague became a prominent antagonist of Roosevelt's monetary policies. In "As to Sprague," *New Democracy* 1, 11 (1 February 1934), 3–4 (rpt., *Ezra Pound's Poetry and Prose*, 6: 129), EP vents his hostility toward the influential economist: "There are two possible views as to O. M. W. Sprague: either he is an accomplice of the most evil and dastardly forces in Europe or he is too ineffably stupid to have understood what was going on around him while he sat in with the European armament financiers. . . . If he has ever been conscious of anything, if he is in any way more than a hypnotized rabbit, Sprague stands for the system that made the last war and is doing its utmost to make the next one. The sooner his type of biped is wiped off the American continent the better for all of us." See also Ezra Pound, "Judas Had It," *Outrider* 1, 2 (January 1934), 1, 3; rpt., *Ezra Pound's Poetry and Prose*, 6: 119.

Doug. Major C. H. Douglas (see Letter 14 above) visited Australia, New Zealand, the United States, and Canada in 1934. BC entertained him in Washington (see the Introduction to Chapter Three, p. 101 above, and Letter 24 below).

Frankie. President Franklin D. Roosevelt.

Devaluation of dollar. See the Introduction to Chapter Three, pp. 94–96 above.

Kreuger. Swedish tycoon Ivar Kreuger (1880–1932) committed suicide in Paris on 12 March 1932 when it was discovered that he had forged bonds in a vain attempt to protect his failing investments in real estate, construction, banking, mining, and securities. The collapse of Kreuger's empire cost American investors alone 250 million dollars.

Bankhead. See the Introduction to Chapter Three, pp. 96–97 above.

CURIA. The Curia was the meeting place of the Senate in ancient Rome.

Farley. James A. Farley (1888–1976) of New York was President Roosevelt's campaign manager and, from 1933 to 1940, his postmaster general. On 9 February 1934 Farley cancelled all contracts with domestic carriers of U.S. air mail on the grounds that all but one of the contracts had been obtained by conspiracy or collusion during the Republican ascendancy of 1921–33. Farley claimed that the government had been defrauded of nearly forty-seven million dollars. But in a front-page article entitled "Wall St. Got Airmail Tip," the *Chicago Tribune* (Paris) for 6 March 1934 reported that news of the cancellation had been leaked to Wall Street in advance, thus enabling speculators to sell aircraft stocks short. Sales of such stocks had increased tenfold in January; for example, J. P. Morgan sold forty-five hundred shares of United Aircraft Company two weeks before Farley's cancellation of the contracts. On 7 March, speaking on the floor of the United States Senate, Huey Long accused Farley himself of being the source of the leak; see *Chicago Tribune* (Paris), 8 March 1934, p. 3. Despite EP's incredulity, the postmaster was kept on; he appears in Canto 46 (1936), where his job is again in jeopardy. In 1934 Farley visited New Mexico to help plan the Democratic campaign against BC's reelection; see the Introduction to Chapter Three, p. 87 above. For more on Farley, see the Introduction to Chapter Four, pp. 167–69 below.

Hull. Cordell Hull (1871–1955) of Tennessee was President Roosevelt's secretary of state from 1933 to 1944. On 8 March 1934, Hull asked the House Ways and Means Committee to grant Roosevelt the power to negotiate bilateral tariff treaties for trade with other nations. Domestic prosperity and international peace would follow, Hull argued, if America could dispose of its excess production on foreign markets: "the impossibility of finding markets for products leads to overproduction, attempts at artificial manipulation of internal prices, unemployment, flight of capital and the difficulty of paying money between nations." See "Hull Makes Pleas for Tariff Change to Revive Production," *Chicago Tribune* (Paris), 9 March 1934, pp. 1, 3. In "Mr. Roosevelt at the Crossroads," *New Democracy* 2, 7 (15 June 1934), 5 (rpt., *Ezra Pound's Poetry and Prose*, 6: 180), EP scornfully quotes the first ten words of Hull's statement. For BC's opposition to the changes in the tariff law proposed by Hull, see Richard Lowitt, *Bronson M. Cutting* 265–67.

Colby. Bainbridge Colby (1869–1950) was President Woodrow Wilson's secretary of state in 1920–21 and law partner in 1921–24. Colby opposed the diplomatic recognition of Russia and supported the Treaty of Versailles and the League of Nations.

Quinn. John Quinn (1870–1924) was a wealthy New York lawyer and patron of the arts.

New Democracy. From 1933 to 1936 EP contributed frequently to this Social Credit periodical, which was edited by Gorham Munson and others and published in New York. Excerpts from a Senate speech of 29 January 1934 by BC are quoted in "Consumption Must Be Financed," *New Democracy* 1, 12 (15 February 1934), 6.

Orage. A[lfred]. R[ichard]. Orage (1873–1934) edited the *New Age* from 1907 to 1922 and the *New English Weekly* from 1932 to

1934. His editorial in the *New English Weekly* 4, 18 (15 February 1934), 410, quotes BC's Senate speech of 27 January 1934 (see Letter 18 above). On BC's relations with *New Democracy,* the *New English Weekly,* and Orage, see the Introduction to Chapter Three, p. 100 above, and Letter 21 below.

Soc/ Credit Bill. On the Social Credit bill, see the Introduction to Chapter Three, p. 98 above.

pension. For the impact on Homer Pound's pension of the devaluation of the dollar, see the Introduction to Chapter Three, pp. 95–96 above.

Concord School. In the mid-nineteenth century, Concord, Massachusetts, was the center of the American Transcendentalist movement, which included Ralph Waldo Emerson, Henry David Thoreau, and others. EP's indictment of them and of Mark Twain (Samuel Clemens, 1835–1910) for ignoring contemporary economic facts is repeated in "The U.S. Social Credit Bill," *New English Weekly* 4, 25 (5 April 1934): "The national literature remained either *finto marmo* and *finto legno* [fake marble and fake wood] with the Concord school or ignoble with Mark Twain's avoidance of reality and sticking to vendable copy" (599; rpt., *Ezra Pound's Poetry and Prose,* 6: 167).

Wilson's foreign information. Probably a reference to Champ Clark (1850–1921) of Missouri, who served in the U.S. House of Representatives in 1893–95 and 1897–1921. Clark was Speaker of the House from 1911 to 1919 and a member of the Foreign Affairs Committee. In 1912 he was Woodrow Wilson's chief rival for the Democratic presidential nomination. A former college president, newspaper editor, and prosecuting attorney, Clark was known for his progressive views, his colorful costume and oratory, and his wide acquaintance with classical and other literature.

Child. Novelist, journalist, and editor Richard Washburn Child (1881–1935) was United States Ambassador to Italy from 1921 to 1924. He was an ardent advocate and publicist of Mussolini, and may have ghostwritten much of the autobiography of Il Duce that was serialized in the *Saturday Evening Post* in 1928.

BURR. Dr. Charles H. Burr (1869–1925), whose wife Anna Robeson Burr (1873–1941) published an autobiography in 1909 and many novels during the 1920s and 1930s. In a 1934 letter to EP (Pound Archive), Mrs. Burr writes: "Your letter is interesting and gratifying to me. The 'man named Burr' to whom you refer was my husband who worked in England during most of the Great War and told me of meeting you one day at Miss May Sinclair's. We returned home in 1918 & he died in 1925." Amelia J. Burr, whose name EP confuses with that of Anna Robeson Burr, was a poet of the same period.

London Morning Post. Between 20 March 1934 and 13 September 1935 EP contributed twenty-four items to the *Morning Post.*

Col. MacCormick. The father of Colonel Robert Rutherford MacCormick (1880–1955) was one of three brothers who made fortunes from the invention and manufacture of the MacCormick reaper. MacCormick acquired the *Chicago Tribune* in 1914. EP contributed frequently to the Paris or European edition of the newspaper between February 1921 and April 1934. Early in 1934, five installments of a speech by MacCormick entitled "The Prospect for America" appeared in the Paris *Tribune*, the last of them on 1 March. EP's query may have been prompted by this series.

21. TLS, 1p., Library of Congress

19 April [1934]

E. POUND
RAPALLO
VIA MARSALA 12-5

B. Cutting. u.S.Senate

Dear Senator

Bravo! an welcome to our 'omely' abitat. namely the *N.E.W.*

That's the line. IZ thur anny use *my* workin' on anyone in
particular?

I wdn't say you suggested it (them). What about Teddy Junior?
any good, or just Dick Whitney's latest alias, and Monty Norman's
local representative?

To avoid libel and liability, you cd. put the list in same form
as yr/ earlier list of literates///

Senators or great assets of Republican party, capable of understanding economics, or having sufficient honesty to favour econ/
horse sense . . . or likely to be scared into decency by thinking that
their political future wd. be aided by going Douglasite NOW.?
At any rate, knowledge of nucleus, or possible converts and
convertables, wd. help. I mean I shd. or cd. economise on
postage and typing ribbons.

Oh yes/ RE public works. The line I am taking HERE is that it
is "monstrous that every time the state creates real wealth (as the
new city Sabaudia etc. or new fields that will grow grain) it gets
into debt to particular individuals."

yrs.
E. P.

Notes on Letter 21

(19 April [1934])

the N.E.W. On 19 April 1934 the *New English Weekly* (vol. 5, no. 1, 6–9) reprinted BC's "Is Private Banking Doomed?" from the March 31 issue of the American magazine *Liberty*. In this talk with Santa Fe journalist Frederick C. Painton, BC declared that American Federal Reserve banks should be nationalized because "private control of credit must be abolished." The article also appeared in the *Congressional Record* 78, 8 (4 May 1934), 8051–53. See the Introduction to Chapter Three, pp. 101–102 above.

Teddy Junior. Theodore Roosevelt, Jr. (1887–1944) was active in Republican politics between 1921 and 1933. He was assistant secretary of the navy in 1921–24, candidate for the governorship of New York in 1924, governor of Puerto Rico in 1929–32, and governor-general of the Philippines in 1932–33. After the Democrats came to power, Roosevelt devoted his energies to the American Liberty League. In the summer of 1934, his name was often in the news as the Republicans tried to regroup for congressional elections in November.

Whitney. Richard Whitney (1888–1974) was president of the New York Stock Exchange from 1930 to 1935 and an associate of the banking house of J. P. Morgan (see Letter 29 below). Whitney was later convicted of securities fraud and jailed. In *ABC of Economics* (London: Faber and Faber, 1933), EP writes: "The whinings of a Whitney and the yowls of stock jobbers are no better than any other form of gangster's sobstuff" (108).

Monty Norman. Montagu-Collet Norman (1871–1950) was governor of the Bank of England from 1920 to 1944. In this capacity, he was frequently a target of EP's attacks upon the banking establishment.

public works. On the respective attitudes of EP and BC toward public works projects, see the Introduction to Chapter Three, pp. 90–91 above. The issue of public works was in the news in March 1934 because the Civil Works Administration, which in five months had spent nearly one billion dollars on public-works projects, expired then. Its successor, the Works Progress Administration, was not created until May 1935.

Sabaudia. Named for the ancient province of Savoy, Sabaudia was one of three new cities built in the Pontine marshes of Italy after Mussolini had them drained. Begun in 1931, Sabaudia was inaugurated on 15 April 1934.

22 Apr. [1934]

E. POUND
RAPALLO
VIA MARSALA 12-5

My Dear Senator

HOW the hell can honest men stay on Industrial Advisory Board without pay.?

I mean how the hell can *the one* presumably intelligent man (who ain't rich) stick on it with the bloated ploots. unless he gets his hotel bill.

As an opposition member . . . might be a tactful constructive act to suggest that W.E. Woodward get a salary.

I don't spose they've got any other members with two louse's worth of sense.

EF th KENTRY iz to use men's WORK and all their workin time, it ought to pay 'em.

Yrs
Ez. P.

Notes on Letter 22

(22 Apr. [1934])

My Dear Senator. The generality of EP's salutation was intentional, because this letter was also sent to Senator William Borah (Pound Archive).

W. E. Woodward. Historian, biographer, and journalist William E. Woodward (1874–1950) served on the Industrial Advisory Board, the Business Advisory Council of the Department of Commerce, and the Long Range Planning Council during President Roosevelt's first term of office. EP especially admired two of Woodward's books: *George Washington: The Man and the Image* (1926) and *A New American History* (1936); see *Impact* 256–59 and 270–71. EP corresponded with Woodward from February 1933 to January 1940 (Pound Archive) and quotes him in Canto 86 on the subject of Roosevelt. Some, though not all, of their correspondence is reproduced in Ezra Pound, "Letters to Woodward," *Paideuma* 15 (Spring 1986), [105]–120. In a letter of 9 April 1934 Woodward says, "Then there is the question of money; members of the [Industrial Advisory] Board receive neither salaries nor expenses, and it costs a hundred dollars a week to live at a Washington hotel. I'm poor."

15 May [1934]

E. POUND
RAPALLO
VIA MARSALA 12-5

To the Right Reverend Cutting
U.S. Senate

My dear Senator

Do senators speak to each other, or only to gawd 'n' th' radio publiKKK?

Borah has just sent me copy of his radio// he SEZ th trouble iz distribution BUT he don't SAY what to DO, tho' he ought damn well to know.

"Lavoro" of Genoa mentions new stamp scrip move in Monte Carlo (evidently serious attempt, tho' I dunno that it will get by the bankbuggahs.)

Art. R. Robinson seems a gentle soul (prob. shocked as hell by my langwidge, by now, as I wrote on receipt of his speech and before gettin hiz letter.)

Supreme Court clerk reports that it ain't manners fer the court, wait, wait, it ain't pursuant to applicable rules and statoots" fer them to shoot that bastard Nic Butler.

IZ thur enny stachoots to prewent a "foundation" spending its money on what it AINT founded to spend it for, and neglecting to spend it fer WHAT (in this tube) Andy laid it down there fer 'em to spend it fer??

AND if so, who pinches fat Nicholas, the Rt. Rev Attorney General or some bloke workin in a steal fabrique, to provide Nic. And CO/ with Delmonico dinners at which to fahrt about inter=brotherly= national LOVE ???

I can readily see that a quiet scholardly chap like yrself might in the past have found more congenial companions than Bill Buffalo Borah, but mebbe he is gittin a l'il culture (economic)

On the principle that you can't tell the pubk/ more'n ONE thing at a time. That radio of his not bad. (two paragraphs out of five pages), but ending up on main note.

The great dust cloud will have helped the grasshoppers a bit.

These red programs vide enclosure very scarce/ in fact a collectors' item.

Do send me a list (or partial. I mean call it partial, to avoid idea you are committin' libel.) of senators or living reps/ capable of understanding simple economic arithmetic.

I take it the repub/ pty/ will not arise in 1937?? but still lookin forrard. . . .

From what I hear from a bloke wot met him [in ?] th Ritz. Teethadore Jr/ is NOT the rising sun. Dynastic impulse wont impel THAT.

In fact F.D. as near the light as most of 'em. IF he cd. shed Farley!!! and Hull (OH Hull!!!)

ever
Ezra Pound

Notes on Letter 23

(15 May [1934])

Borah. For Senator William Borah, see Letters 2 and 8 above. In his radio speech of 22 March 1934, published in the *Congressional Record* 78, 5 (23 March 1934), 5218–20, under the title "Some Phases of the Agricultural Problem," Borah contends that "it is our distributing system which has broken down."

"Lavoro." On stamp scrip in Monte Carlo, see the Introduction to Chapter Three, p. 96 above.

Robinson. EP had seen an excerpt from a speech by Senator Arthur R. Robinson in the *Congressional Record* 78, 2 (27 January 1934), 1475–76, in which Robinson proposed a veterans' bonus of two billion dollars; see the Introduction to Chapter Three, p. 93 above. EP's strongly worded letter of protest, dated 22 April, crossed Robinson's letter of 11 April (Pound Archive).

Nic. Butler. Dr. Nicholas Murray Butler (1862–1947) was president of Columbia University from 1901 to 1945, a prominent member of the Republican party, and head of the Carnegie Foundation for International Peace from 1925 to 1945. For his work with the Foundation, which was endowed by Pittsburgh steel magnate Andrew Carnegie (1835–1919), Butler was awarded the Nobel Peace Prize in 1931. In "By All Means Be Patriotic," *New English Weekly* 1, 25 (6 October 1932), EP writes: "Carnegie left a large endowment for peace which could not have fallen into worse hands than those of Nicholas M. Butler, a vain and pretentious seeker after glory. I don't doubt that there are honest men working in the Carnegie foundation, but up to now it has shown no vigorous intention of studying the *causes* of war. . . . Butler is a particularly good example of the murderer's accomplice" (589; rpt., *Ezra Pound's Poetry and Prose*, 5: 377–78). By *"causes"* EP explained that he meant the competition of nations for for-

eign markets and the self-interest of munitions makers. In "Academic," *Chicago Tribune* (Paris), 2 October 1933, p. 2 (rpt., *Ezra Pound's Poetry and Prose*, 6: 81), EP says of Butler, "He was & is friend of every evil fostered from Wilson to Hoover. More than any one man he has impeded & prevented the Carnegie Foundation from investigating international arms rings, Zaharoff, Vicker [*sic*], Creusot, Briey, etc." See also Pound's correspondence with Representative George H. Tinkham on the subject of Butler, in Philip J. Burns, *"Dear Uncle George": Ezra Pound's Letters to Congressman Tinkham of Massachusetts* (Ph.D. diss., Rhode Island, 1988) 43, 44, 47, 48–49, 50.

Attorney General. Homer S. Cummings (1870–1956) was President Roosevelt's attorney general from 1933 to 1939.

dust cloud. The great drought that began in 1933 made a so-called Dust Bowl of 150,000 square miles in Oklahoma, Kansas, Texas, and New Mexico. On 11 May 1934, a cloud of dust fifteen hundred miles long and nine hundred miles wide covered the eastern third of the United States, from Chicago to the Atlantic; see "Colossal Dust Cloud Sweeps U.S.," *Chicago Tribune* (Paris), 12 May 1934, pp. 1, 3. This storm alone removed an estimated 300 million tons of fertile soil from the Great Plains. A massive infestation of grasshoppers was predicted for later in the summer.

red programs. EP sent BC one of the magenta-pink concert programs printed for the 1934 performances of the Amici del Tigullio in Rapallo; it may be seen in Cutting Papers, Box 36. On BC's love of music, see Chapter One, p. 14 above.

Teethadore Jr/. Theodore Roosevelt, Jr.; see Letter 21 above.

F.D. President Franklin D. Roosevelt.

Farley!!! and Hull. See Letter 20 above. In an article published on the same day he wrote this letter, EP calls for "the elimination of Farley and Hull from the cabinet." See "Ahead," *New Democracy* 2, 5 (15 May 1934), 5; rpt., *Ezra Pound's Poetry and Prose*, 6: 175.

24 May 1934

United States Senate
Washington, D.C.

Ezra Pound, Esq.

Those above the line are open-minded. Those below have mostly crank notions of their own, but could perhaps be converted. Most of them were at the party I gave for Douglas, but I am afraid there were few conversions. As an expositor the Major is a little less aggressive than is customary in his partibus infidelium. In haste,

yours.
B.C.

Senators   Reps

Borah   Kvale   Minn
Bone   Wash   Zioncheck   Wash.
La Follette   Goldsborough   Md.
Wagner   N.Y. City   Patman   Tex
Black   Ala.   Lewis   (Md.)
Wheeler   Mont.
Costigan   Col.

Couzens   Mich.   Steagall   Ala.
Thomas   (Okla)   Dies   Tex.
Norris   Nebr.   Sinclair   N. Dak.
Fletcher   Fla.   Hoeppel   Cal.
Nye   N. Dak
Clark   Mo.
Shipstead   Minn.
Frazier   N. Dak.

Notes on Letter 24

(24 May 1934)

Douglas. See Letters 14 and 20 and the Introduction to Chapter Three, p. 101 above. EP summarizes BC's account of the reception in "L'economia ortologica—Il problema centrale," *Rassegna Monetaria* 34, 7–8 (July–August 1937), 711, and in "The Central Problem," *Townsman* 4, 13 (March 1941), 13–17. These articles are reproduced in *Ezra Pound's Poetry and Prose,* 7: 221, and 8: 107–10.

in his partibus infidelium. Latin, "in these lands of the infidels." Abbreviated to *in partibus,* the phrase is used in ecclesiastical titles to designate non-Christian regions. For example, a bishop *in partibus* serves in an area controlled by pagans or heretics and therefore has no practical authority.

Borah. See Letters 2, 8, and 22 above. EP cites many names from this list in "Hidden Govt.," *New Democracy* 4, 4 (15 April 1935), 67; rpt., *Ezra Pound's Poetry and Prose,* 6: 276. He also mentions it in a letter of 27 December 1935 to Representative George H. Tinkham: "Senator Cutting's confidential list of Senators and Congressmen who understood something of the subject was rather BRIEF." See Philip J. Burns, *"Dear Uncle George": Ezra Pound's Letters to Congressman Tinkham of Massachusetts,* 72.

Bone. Republican Homer Truett Bone (1883–1970) represented the state of Washington in the Senate from 1933 to 1945. One of EP's letters to him appears in *Impact,* 274–75.

LaFollette. See Letters 2 and 13 above.

Wagner. Democrat Robert Ferdinand Wagner (1877–1953) represented New York in the Senate from 1927 to 1949.

Black. Hugo L. Black (1886–1976) was Democratic senator from Alabama between 1927 and 1937, when he was appointed to the United States Supreme Court. He played a key role in the 1930 Senate debate over customs censorship; see Chapter One, p. 19 above.

Wheeler. See Letter 2 above.

Costigan. See Letter 13 above.

Kvale. Minnesota Congressman Paul J. Kvale (1896–1960) of the Democratic Farmer-Labor party sat in the House of Representatives from 1929 to 1939.

Zioncheck. Democratic Congressman Marion A. Zioncheck of Washington (1901–1936) was a member of the House from 1933 until his death.

Goldsborough. T. Alan Goldsborough (1877–1951) was Democratic congressman from Maryland in 1921–39. EP corresponded with him in 1934–35 (Pound Archive). On 22 August 1935, Goldsborough introduced a Social Credit Bill (H.R. 9216) into the House of Representatives; see Letter 20 and the Introduction to Chapter Three, p. 98 above.

Patman. Democratic Representative Wright Patman (1893–1976) of Texas served in the House from 1929 to 1967. In 1934, he cosponsored BC's bill to create a Federal Monetary Authority; see the Introduction to Chapter Three, pp. 101–2 above.

Lewis. Democrat David J. Lewis (1869–1952) of Maryland had two periods of service in the House of Representatives. The first ran from 1911 to 1917 and the second from 1931 to 1939.

Couzens. Republican James Couzens (1872–1936) represented Michigan in the Senate from 1922 until his death.

Thomas. Democratic Senator J. W. Elmer Thomas (1876–1965) represented Oklahoma from 1927 to 1951; see Letter 28 below.

Norris. See Letter 2 above.

Fletcher. Democratic Senator Duncan Upshaw Fletcher (1859–1936) of Florida served from 1909 until his death.

Nye. Republican Gerald P. Nye (1892–1971) represented North Dakota in the Senate from 1925 to 1945.

Clark. Bennett Champ Clark (1890–1954), son of Champ Clark (see Letter 20 above), was Democratic senator from Missouri in 1933–45.

Shipstead. Senator Henrik Shipstead (1881–1960) of the Democratic Farmer-Labor party represented Minnesota between

Notes on Letter 24 continue

1923 and 1947. EP corresponded with him in November and December of 1934 (Pound Archive).

Frazier. Republican Lynn J. Frazier (1874–1947) represented North Dakota in the Senate from 1923 to 1941. A member of the Committee on Banking and Currency and a champion of debt-ridden farmers, he cosponsored the Frazier-Lemke Farm Bankruptcy Act of 1934 and the Frazier-Lemke Mortgage Moratorium Act of 1935, which helped destitute farmers to regain their farms from their creditors. Earlier, Frazier had unsuccessfully sponsored a bill to refinance the entire farm mortgage indebtedness of the nation at an interest rate of 1.5 percent by issuing low-rate government bonds or (if the bonds failed to sell) paper money. EP corresponded with Frazier in November and December of 1936; see the Pound Archive and *Impact*, 273.

Steagall. Democratic Representative Henry Bascom Steagall (1873–1943) of Alabama served in the House from 1915 until his death. As chairman of the House Banking Committee, he sponsored much important legislation during the 1930s, including the Glass-Steagall Act of 1 June 1933, which created the Federal Deposit Insurance Corporation and expanded the powers of the Federal Reserve Board.

Dies. Texas Democrat Martin Dies, Jr. (1900–1972), had two periods of service in the House of Representatives. The first ran from 1931 to 1945, the second from 1953 to 1959. Early in 1934, Dies, a leading silverite, sponsored a bill to subsidize the export of U.S. agricultural products by permitting foreign nations to pay for them with silver valued at a premium of 25 percent above its world price. The Dies-Pitmann Silver Purchase Act was signed by President Roosevelt on 30 June.

Sinclair. Republican James Herbert Sinclair (1871–1943) of North Dakota sat in the House from 1919 to 1935.

Hoeppel. John Henry Hoeppel (1881–1976) was Democratic representative from California between 1933 and 1937.

30 May [1934]

E. POUND
RAPALLO
VIA MARSALA 12-5

To the Rt. Reverend Cutting, chaplain to the murkn seenate/

Yer/ rivrince/

The NNNclosed recd/ this a/m/ from the Rt. Rev/ Eliot (T.S.) late Norton Purr/feezer at the idem/ inschooshun. as illystrashun of the effeks of the baboon LAW (211 of the Pea/in/all coda)

This is the kind of silliness an smuttiness fostered in the gt/ centre of onanism at Cambridge Mass/ where they have Sprague to TEACH economics/ or backhousehold saving.

Will you blokes ever START on the risveglio or WAKING UP of american eddykasun/ or do you want yr old age pestered by idiots made WORSE by the present asinine system of obfuscating the young.

yrs/ with ever increasing piety
E.P.

Notes on Letter 25

(30 May [1934])

Eliot. For Eliot's appointment as Norton Professor of Poetry at Harvard, see Letter 11 above. The enclosure has not been identified.

baboon LAW. On Article 211 of the Penal Code, see Letters 1 and 12 and the Introduction to Chapter Two, pp. 24–27 above.

Sprague. See Letter 20 above.

26. TL, carbon with typed greeting and closing, 3pp., Library of Congress

7 June [1934]

E. POUND
RAPALLO
VIA MARSALA 12-5

Dear Senator Cutting/ Herewith carbon of a letter I am sending to Senator Borah/ for reasons that shd/ be apparent in the text.

cordially yrs

My Dear Senator

I have just had a seven page letter from W.E. Woodward complaining that Douglas (C.H.) didn't answer his question ETC.

The whole of W.E.W's muddle arising from his not having grasped the possibility of a FIXED price, let alone of "compensated or adjusted or just" price.

If a man as intelligent as Woodward, as near to the works, hasn't SEEN that yet, there must be "countless millions" needing primary instruction.

You got over the POINT re/ distribution in the radio talk you sent me. Is there any reason why you or Senator Cutting shdnt. go on the air with the simple facts re/ possibility of *FIXING prices* (of necessities, say food stuffs (basic) and even certain qualities of well made textiles TO THE CONSUMER.

You have fixed prices TO THE PRODUCER on wheat etc in the U.S.A.

But the bloody bastardly suppression and distortion, and fundamentally indifferent and unintelligent lack of interest in Italian news has wasted peoples time and they do not REALIZE that here we have the price of meat, bread etc. posted up on the walls of the market etc. and people do NOT have to pay more.

I suggest the utility of the following course of argument on radio.

I. The existence of anything proves that it is POSSIBLE (i;e; that it is possible for it to exist)

II. Prices TO THE CONSUMER were in various countries fixed during and after the war. They are now FIXED by decree in Italy. This don't prove that we ought to change the form of American govt. and turn fascist. It proves that fascism DOES certain things, and if the things it DOES are more intelligent than what the U.S. Govt. is now doing, the U.S. Govt. ought to LEARN.

III. The value of money is WHAT it will BUY. Money is worth what you can GET for it. A system of inflation or deflation or any other damn wangle that TAKES no count of WHAT the money will buy, is a hoax.

IV. Quite obviously DOUGLAS' economics will NOT WORK if you omit one of the chief FACTORS. ANY more than a tripod will stand up if you remove one of its legs.

V. FIXED price is one of Doug's MAIN factors. IT is a special KIND of fixed price; based on JUSTICE that is to say it is based on what the COMMODITY REALLY COSTS to the nation.

The system for computing this cost is no more complicated than the system of computing costs NOW used in any trust or manufacturing company.

VI. All so called arguments against Douglas' which leave out the FIXED (just) price, are NOT arguments against Doug but against the arguer's own muddle and miscomprehension.

I am sending carbon of this to Senator Cutting. IF there is any POSSIBLE obscurity in the above statement I wd/ be grateful to have it pointed out.

cordially

[The following is a postscript to Cutting.]

I'll send details re/ Italian price system if wanted. Prices of some things settled by local authorities/ taking count of local conditions/ reshipments etc. of food stuffs etc.

Obviously the reductions of RENTS here act pretty much as a DIVIDEND.

Just as Muss' grain policy, reduced railway fares, drainage etc. ACT as MATERIAL DIVIDENDS.

The god damn british (including Doug's informal staff, have been cornfed on British press lies etc. and are NOT UP TO DATE in understanding of Italy and what gets done here. (they are quick as mice to yell about what AINT.

Notes on Letter 26

(7 June [1934])

Woodward. For W. E. Woodward, see Letter 22 above. His six-page letter to EP, dated 25 May 1934, complains that, after a speech in New York, C. H. Douglas evaded the following question: "Could Major Douglas give any concrete idea of how his Social Credit plan might be put into actual working?" (Pound Archive).

12 June [1934]

E. POUND
RAPALLO
VIA MARSALA 12-5

B.C. (portentous initials/ Whose Johnny B. are you)

My Dear Senator

Thanks very much/ will have 'em pestered by British pubctns/ if poss/

I spose itz pollyTicks ??? that you didn't make it *clearer* that a NAT/ BANK SHOULD be for the NATION. I mean not merely a NAME, but profits to go to nation.

NOT a radical idea/ As I have printed. The Venetian Senate heard of it in 1260 something/ and *laid it on the table till* 1583/ when it occasioned a banking reform that lasted till Nappy Bonyparty. Banco di Napoli was "reorganized"

THERE IS ONLY ONE bank that has lasted since 1602. And that is the Monte dei Paschi of Siena. The MODEL of Sound Banking See Rota "Storia delle Banche "if you read woptalian.

Otherwise I will send on the facts. Medici knowledge/ no frills/ reconstruction bank/ as distinct from creditor's gangs, organized to bleed debtors.

DAMN IT ALL/ what aren't some murkn/ eddycation ???

Or why the hell aint I putt where I cd/ edderkate some of the bloody bastuds.

STILL imposs/ to print anything serious. (cf/ the brutish huns/ who have just brought out edtn/ of Frobenius new book FIFTEEN THOUSAND copies in first edtn/ 600 pages/ 150 pages illustrations/

Idea of CREDIT OFFICE instead of debt office/ is good.

TAXES are all bloody rot.

Have written Prof/ Soddy/ that something ought to be done to authorize a PRIMER/ I dont care whether they start with my *ABC* or what they start with; could you push idea that some PRIMARY text book of ECON/ ABC/ primer of wottell shd/ be emitted//

Routledge has got round to doing it with my "ABC of READING" (thetz for Kullchuh !!! i;e; refeened licherchoor) but the dithering illiteracy of ALL our generation in ECON/ ought also (or rather MORE) to be tackled.

It is a bleeding crime to leave things like Nic. Butler and the whole gormy REST of 'em/ college profs/ american hackKademy etc/ still there obfuscatin' the nex generation.

If Doug has "raté son coup" [missed the mark] I spose we've got to dig in and prepare for another 30 years war . . .

Could you and/or Borah GET elected in 1936 even if you cd/ cop the nomination from the god damn swine who compose the bulk of the republican rump?

I see Teethadore Second/ has just wits enough to know he is too nearly half witted to try.

ever
E.P.

[The following may or may not be a postscript to Letter 27.]

to lure people into a belief that Hitler cares for the welfare of his subjects.

In the mean time british publishers continue their policy of NOT publishing living books. There is no English edtn. of Frobenius. Gesell's *Natural Economic Order* is published by the Free Economy Pub. Co. 309 Madison St. San Antonio, Texas. at 4.25 and the section dealing with money is, or is about to be printed at 1.75, but normal booksellers have probably no means of finding this out, and it is most unlikely that the "b libraries" will stock it.

obt. svt. or what you will
A. MC L (??)
(E.P. signed or unsigned.

Notes on Letter 27

(12 June [1934])

you didn't make it clearer. BC repeated this criticism in a letter of 7 July 1934 to the American poet H. Phelps Putnam: "Ezra Pound complains that I didn't make it clear that a national bank is really a National Bank—i.e., one which makes dividends for the nation, like the banks of mediaeval Genoa, Venice, and Naples. There again, you can't settle the universe in 18 minutes" (Cutting Papers, Box 11).

radical idea. On 19 May 1934 BC delivered an address before the People's Lobby at the Cosmos Club in Washington. The speech was carried live on NBC radio. In it, Cutting said, "The creation of a national bank which will eventually have a monopoly of the issuance of credit is, to my mind, the most vital issue of the country today." He also noted that one "objection usually made to national banking is that it is a radical idea." The speech was printed in the *Congressional Record* 78, 9 (22 May 1934), 9225–27, 9259–61, and 9795–96; and in *New Democracy* 3, 6 (1 June 1934), 1–3. See also Letters 18 and 21 and the Introduction to Chapter Three, p. 101 above.

Venetian Senate. In *Storia delle Banche* (Milano: Tipografia del Giornale *Il Sole*, 1874), Pietro Rota devotes a chapter (5) to the public banks of Italy in the sixteenth, seventeenth, and eighteenth centuries. There (110–13) he describes the establishment of a public bank by the Venetian Senate on 28 December 1584 (not 1583, as EP has it here). The Banco della Piazza de Rialto was a government monopoly directed by three magistrates, who were forbidden to invest depositors' money for private gain. This principle, Rota emphasizes, was a major departure from the usual practice of private banks, which were run as profit-making businesses. Although the public bank remained public only until April 1587, its policies of stewardship and accountability to depositors influenced the formation in

1619 of the Banco Giro, which lasted until the fall of the Venetian Republic in the time of Napoleon (pp. 113–19).

In a footnote, Rota points out that, as early as 1361 (not "1260 something," as EP has it here), Venice charged five experienced bank directors "to consult on a bank of exchange for the benefit either *of the public* or of designated persons" (*"debeant consulere de banchis cambi tenendi, vel* pro communi *vel pro spetialibus personis"*—Rota's italics). The advisors apparently recommended a private institution, Rota observes, because the idea of founding a public bank was set aside and discussed no more until 1584 ("si mise da parte il pensiero di erigere il Banco pubblico e più non se ne parlò fino al 1584"—p. 111). EP first read Rota at the end of March 1933. He refers to these details of Italian banking history in "Mr. Pound's A.B.C.," *New English Weekly* 3, 1 (20 April 1933), 24; in "The Master of Rapallo Speaks," *Outrider* 1, 1 (1 November 1933), 1; in "Nothing New," *New English Weekly* 4, 9 (14 December 1933), 215; in Canto 40 (1934); in "Mussolini Defines State as 'Spirit of the People,'" *Chicago Tribune* (Paris), 9 April 1934, p. 5; in "Mug's Game?" *Esquire* 3, 2 (February 1935), 148; in "Banking Beneficence and . . ." *New Age* 56, 16 (14 February 1935), 184–85; and in "Bank Money or State Money," *Morning Post* (London), 22 April 1935, p. 7. See *Ezra Pound's Poetry and Prose*, 6: 35, 96, 111, 168, 244, 246, 278. In "Mug's Game?" he speaks of "a measure offered to the Venetian Senate in 1263 [*sic*]," embodying "the idea that banking shd. be a monopoly of the state"; the measure was "laid on the carved walnut table for 320 years." For a fuller discussion of EP's interpretation and use of the material from Rota, see E. P. Walkiewicz and Hugh Witemeyer, "A Public Bank in Canto 40," *Paideuma* 19 (Winter 1990), 90–98.

Monte dei Paschi. See Rota, *Storia delle Banche*, pp. 153–58. EP surveys the history of the Monte dei Paschi in Cantos 42–44, where he correctly gives the date of its founding as 1622, not 1602.

edtn/ of Frobenius. Leo Frobenius (1873–1938) was a German anthropologist who studied the tribal cultures of Africa. His *Erlebte Erdteile: Ergebnisse eines deutschen Forscherlebens* was published in seven volumes in 1925–29 (Frankfurt: Abt Buchverlag). EP met Frobenius in 1927 and was influenced by his conception of cultural ideas in action, or *Paideuma.*

Prof. Soddy. Frederick Soddy (1877–1956) was Professor of Chemistry at Oxford University and winner of the Nobel Prize in chemistry in 1921. He subsequently turned his attention to economics, publishing *Wealth, Virtual Wealth and Debt* (1926) and several other influential booklets.

ABC. EP's *ABC of Economics* was published in London by Faber and Faber on 6 April 1933. His *ABC of Reading* was issued on 24 May 1934 by George Routledge and Sons of London.

Gesell's Natural Economic Order. Silvio Gesell (1862–1930) was a German businessman who imported surgical supplies into Argentina. His theories of economic reform, including the use of stamped paper money or stamp scrip, were formulated in *Die natürliche Wirtschaftsordnung durch Freiland and Freigeld* (1916). This was translated into English as *The Natural Economic Order* by Philip Pye (Berlin: Neo-Verlag, 1929). Pye's translation was reprinted in two volumes by Dr. Hugo Fack (San Antonio, Texas: Free-Economy Publishing Company, 1934–36). EP reviewed the San Antonio edition in the *New English Weekly* 6, 16 (31 January 1935), 331–33; rpt., *Ezra Pound's Poetry and Prose,* 6: 241–42. See also EP's "The Individual in His Milieu: A Study of Relations and Gesell," *Criterion* 15, 58 (October 1935), 30–45 (rpt., Ezra Pound, *Selected Prose 1909–1965,* ed. William Cookson (New York: New Directions, 1973), 272–83, and *Ezra Pound's Poetry and Prose,* 6: 317–27), and the Introduction to Chapter Three, p. 96 above.

A. MC L. Alan McLean was a young American Social Creditor whose parents lived in Rapallo.

[July 1934?]

The Hon' Sen. B.C

Have just recd. copy of Senator Thomas' (Elmer) cable to Harrison. Very lucid. In fact CLEARER than most Douglasite propaganda.

Why the devil cant a dozen senators form some sort of education committee. high brow books shop or whatever to import or have pubd/ the NECESSARY current books, that do NOT get into America quick enough.

McNair Wilson, Brockway; yr/ present god damn correspondent; etc.

Yale Univ. press now says it wants to print all my LITERARY material as it appears.

I have told 'em there is Economics/ (but dont know who owns 'em.)

Thomas strikes me as less woolleeyy and muzzy than most of yr/ confreres.

Cant he be led to Doug as "a FORM of controlled inflation"?

AND gor damn it, when are the Dougs/ going to see the relation to stamp scrip/ which COULD end taxes altogether, and do a lot of the work Doug aims at with adjusted prices.

The thing is much more comprehensible/ and if a bridge is strong enough it dont matter very much if it is a helluva lot TOO STRONG.

They now get scared at idea of how much dividend wd/ be. whereas direct payment of all govt. expenses by s/s/ wd' be less alarming.

Abolition of taxes, is A step toward divs/ and wd/ help bust the idee fixe. re natr/ of money etc.

Thomas' cable has several essential points.

Naow/ honest and confidenshul/ wot about the polite Mr Morgenthau ?? Does he mean it? and if so what? Am I, as a comparatively honest man, supposed to go into opposition, or is the present administration still wondering whether it mightn't better go straight?

The good guys iz I spose republikums (or not ?) but can they at all heave Noo Yok? or do the Morugum boys want to get back on Rookerfeller bad enough to have a *decent* republican in the white house?

tell us, bruvver, fer we are on a far shore,

yrz

Notes on Letter 28

([July 1934?])

Senator Thomas'. Democrat J. W. Elmer Thomas (1876–1965) represented Oklahoma in the Senate from 1927 to 1951. During the Depression he favored the remonetization of silver, a reduction in the gold content of the dollar, and the issuance of up to three billion dollars in paper greenbacks to re-inflate the national economy. In diluted form, these measures were incorporated into the Thomas Amendment to the 1933 farm bill, which passed with administration support during the first hundred days of Roosevelt's presidency. Thomas was a tireless watchdog of the Federal Reserve System, which he blamed for the bank crisis of 1932–33 and for its resistance to his inflationist monetary policies. George L. Harrison, governor of the Federal Reserve Bank of New York, was a particular subject of Thomas's scrutiny because of Harrison's resistance in 1933–34 to Roosevelt's departure from the international gold standard (see Letters 17 and 20 and the Introduction to Chapter Three, p. 95 above). On 8 July 1934, Thomas sent a three-page cablegram to Harrison, urging him not to support a proposal under discussion at an international meeting of bankers in Switzerland "to stabilize our dollar with England's pound or to enter an agreement to tie it to a fixed weight of gold." Thomas told Harrison that "when representing private interests you conduct secret negotiations abroad affecting the gold value of our dollar or discuss tying it to the English pound or any other currency you attempt to assume the powers reserved by the Constitution to the Congress to regulate the value of money." The cablegram was published on 10 July and EP had received a copy by 24 July, when he wrote to thank Thomas for sending it and proposed a senatorial distributing center like the one described here. Their correspondence continued until 26 August 1934 (Pound Archive). On 25 July EP wrote to Dorothy Pound: "Senator Thomas has sent me copy of his cable to Harrison, telling him to quit trying to represent the country without bein authorized // cable much better medium than speech, and Thom/ quite lucid" (Lilly Library, Indiana University).

Wilson. The versatile Robert McNair Wilson (1882–1963) was a surgeon and a writer of history, biography, and fiction. He was medical correspondent of the *Times* from 1914 to 1942, and he was the author of *Promise to Pay: An Inquiry into the Principles and Practice of the Latter-Day Magic Called Sometimes High Finance* (London: George Routledge and Sons, 1934). EP praised this book to readers of the *Chicago Tribune* (Paris) on 6 March 1934, p. 2, and 2 April 1934, p. 2; rpt., *Ezra Pound's Poetry and Prose*, 6: 140, 166. He corresponded with Wilson from March 1934 to April 1958 (Pound Archive).

Brockway. The prominent socialist Archibald Fenner Brockway (1888–1988) was general secretary of the Independent Labour party from 1933 to 1939. He wrote *The Bloody Traffic* (1933), a study of the armaments industry, and *Will Roosevelt Succeed? A Study of Fascist Tendencies in America* (1934).

Yale. The Yale University Press published EP's *ABC of Reading* in September 1934 and *Make It New* in March 1935.

Mr Morgenthau. Henry Morgenthau, Jr. (1891–1967), was President Roosevelt's secretary of the Treasury from 1933 to 1945 (acting secretary in 1933–34). In 1934 Morgenthau unsuccessfully opposed the remonetization of silver. He was also a member of the Farm Credit Administration and an important adviser on agricultural policy. EP corresponded with him from 3 March 1934 to 25 June 1936 (Pound Archive). EP's letter of 7 August 1934 protesting against the intentional destruction of agricultural surpluses is reprinted in *Impact*, 271.

Morugum. Millionaire banker J. P. Morgan, Jr. (1867–1943), was called before a Senate investigating committee in May and

June of 1933. Although he was not accused
of illegal actions, Morgan was embarrassed
by revelations of questionable banking practices and nonpayment of income taxes. Because his business rival John D. Rockefeller,
Jr. (1874–1960), of the Chase National Bank
was thought to have exploited Morgan's dis-
comfiture, there was tension between their
houses.

29. Signed telegram, Beinecke Library

[23 Aug. 1934?]

Ezra Pound

Send em along.

Bronson Cutting

Notes on Letter 29
([23 Aug. 1934?])

Send em along. BC here invites EP to contribute articles to the Santa Fe *New Mexican;* see Letter 30 and the Introduction to Chapter Four, p. 161 below. In a letter to Dorothy Pound of 25 August 1934, EP says that he has received an "unintelligible cable from Cutting, may refer to my doing some econ/ for local papers in New Mexico" (Lilly Library, Indiana University).

[Aug. 1934?]

revered senator/

yr cable firm in tone but not very explicit in detail

I spose refs/ a letter from Mrs H. contents of which were known
to me only in outline, and the lady has now left these shores.

Said you had two papers, which say YES.

I shd/ like to see sample copies of each/ also to know whether I am
supporting a specific Douglas//Cutting BILL, or a state election/ or
Borah/Cutting or C/B or wottell for the next presidential.

OR instructin a prairie infant class in generl/ ECONoMIKKS.

Have already sent you several sheets of this noo stashunary.
Blank was Volitionist questionaire

The papers can use the questionnaire with comment that NO MAN
shd. get PAID for teaching econ/ till he can and WILL say yes or
no, or at any rate answer the 8 items.

We ought to bring in the Gesellites. They've a good paper and are
bringing out G's *New Econ. Order.*

309 Madison St.
San Antonio, Texas.
(Free Econ. Pub. Co.)

I am at moment preaching a blend of Mussolini's horse sense,
plus Doug/via Gesell, and with the divs pd/ in stamp scrip.

If you want just economic tutoring for the pubk/

[rest of page cut off]

[The following may not belong to letter 30]

COULDN'T it be USEFUL? I mean couldn't a useful way be found to publish the FUNDAMENTAL points of agreement between the Nat. Worker paert [party?] AND the advanced economists. ???

Along these lines/

DIFFERENCE between property and capital (vide my *ABC).*

Source of values (Marx "labour" superseded by cultural herit plus a quantity of actual WORK that simply damn well decreases and WILL continue to decrease with increasing rapidity . . . hope this is CLEAR? Corollary/ SUCH value is NOT property of individuals but of the aggregate.

Question of usury (vide McN. Wilson's *Promise to Pay.* stamp/scrip as POSITIVE anti=usury. tax ON THE MONEY itself . . . all other taxes shd/ be ABOLISHED, and cd/ be, either via/ s/s/ or via DOUGLAS.

Infamy that state shd/ get into debt by CREATING material wealth. nation shd/ own and govern its purchasing power.

I don't see what you people have AGAINST this. It seems to me inherent in socialism/Douglas or contemporary econ/ thought, and ALSO in the "idea statale" when that is cut off from Hitler and the parodics . . . however . . . that is MINOR point so far as Eng/ is concerned . . . stupid to waste time on nomenclatures when we all want at least part of the same list of things.

Notes on Letter 30

([Aug. 1934?])

Mrs H. Elizabeth Sage (Mrs. Meredith) Hare of Santa Fe was a friend of BC, an ardent Social Creditor, and a major financial supporter of A. R. Orage's *New English Weekly.* She visited EP in Rapallo in the fourth week of July 1934 and subsequently arranged for him to contribute the "Ez Sez" editorials to the Santa Fe *New Mexican;* see the Introduction to Chapter Four, p. 161 below.

two papers. Since 1912 BC had owned not two but three journals: the Santa Fe *New Mexican*, a daily newspaper; *El Nuevo Mexicano*, a Spanish-language weekly; and the *New Mexico Review*, a weekly. EP began to contribute to the daily on 26 March 1935; see the Introduction to Chapter Four, p. 161 below.

Volitionist questionaire. EP devised a broadside consisting of eight economic principles printed on the left side and space for responses to them on the right; see Noel Stock, *The Life of Ezra Pound: An Expanded Edition* (San Francisco: North Point Press, 1982) 321–22. According to Donald Gallup's *Ezra Pound: A Bibliography* (Charlottesville: University Press of Virginia, 1983), item E2m, EP began on 18 August 1934 to distribute his questionnaire to bankers, politicians, writers, and others all around the world.

G's New Econ Order. See Letter 27 and the Introduction to Chapter Three, p. 96 above.

my ABC. For EP's *ABC of Economics*, see Letter 27 above.

Promise to Pay. For R. McNair Wilson's *Promise to Pay*, see Letter 28 above.

28 Nov. [1934]

E. POUND
RAPALLO
VIA MARSALA 12-5

[illegible words] Senator
Bronson Cutting

My Dear Senator

As none of you blokes can be persuaded to learn ANYthing about economics, what about grabbing the new N.R.A. moment and bashing the baboon law, thereby gittin th jedge out ov hiz embarrassment. (vide encs/ from Paris editions of estabd/ news/ concealers. *Trib.* an *N.Y.herald.*?

2.

I retract, 3% of the above. Bankhead has heard of the XXth century. Cdn't. you moderate it a bit?

3/

When the hell are the old bitches that loved Melon/ Insull Wiggin, and THAT ebotch going to be killed or thrown out of the education system. Jail the saboteur Nic. Butler. And insist on a rudimentary knowledge of history for 43% of the economic "experts". Waaal, why NOT?

Univ. educ. in the U.S. has been a belleeedink farce for as long as you and I can remember.

and so forth. Happy days!

yours
Ezra Pound

Notes on Letter 31

(28 Nov. [1934])

N. R. A. The National Recovery Administration was created during the first hundred days of President Roosevelt's Administration in 1933 to combat the Depression by coordinating the efforts of government, labor, and business according to a national plan. In September 1934, General Hugh Johnson, head of the N. R. A., resigned in the face of charges that his enforcement of regulatory codes had become dictatorial; he was replaced by a five-member board of directors. EP's allusion to a "new N. R. A. moment" probably refers to the political climate in Washington immediately following the mid-term congressional elections of November 1934, in which the voters appeared to endorse Roosevelt's policies by increasing the Democratic majorities in both the Senate and the House of Representatives. The legislation passed by the new Congress in 1935 is sometimes labeled "the second New Deal." Among the pending bills was one to renew the authority of the N.R.A. itself.

the jedge. Upon her arrival from London, customs officers at the port of New York searched the luggage of Mrs. Hazel Moore, legislative secretary of Margaret Sanger's National Committee on Federal Legislation for Birth Control. Acting upon the authority of Section 305 of the Smoot-Hawley Tariff Act of 1930, the officers confiscated not only Mrs. Sanger's *The Medical and Biological Aspects of Birth Control* but also a book entitled *The Rhythm* by Dr. Leo J. Latz, a proponent of the natural or "rhythmic" method of birth control. The incident was reported in the *New York Times,* 12 October 1934, p. 23, and in the *Chicago Tribune* (Paris), 22 October 1934, p. 3. The latter article is mockingly entitled "Even Natural Birth Control Can't Get By N. Y. Customs."

Bankhead. See Letter 16 and the Introduction to Chapter Three, pp. 96–97 above.

Melon. Andrew Mellon; see Letter 17 above.

Insull. At the height of his career, English-born utilities magnate Samuel Insull (1859–1938) was on the boards of sixty-five American companies worth two billion dollars. His empire collapsed dramatically in 1932, and he was indicted for mail fraud. He was tried in October–November 1934 and acquitted on 24 November.

Wiggin. Albert Henry Wiggin (1868–1951) was president and chairman of the Board of Chase National Bank, the world's largest, from 1911 to 1930. A 1933 Senate investigation into Wall Street practices revealed that Wiggin had profited from selling short the stock of his own bank and evading income taxes.

Nic. Butler. See Letter 23 above.

2 Jan. [1935]

E. POUND
RAPALLO
VIA MARSALA 12-5

[illegible word]

B. Cutting

My Dear Senator

There is a bastid named Van Mises telling the young Leg of
Nations blokes in geneva that money is a commodity. An I hear
there is a boom on, for selling the U.S. to the god damn league.

I dont spose Yr/ hon/ colleague Mr Pope MEANS that. and what I
wrote him this a/m: will prob/ shock his mountainy sensibilities.
(Not heard from his Idaho colleague since I was impelled to make
a few remarks on Herbie the burbie the HOO/HOveh . . .

I wd/ appreciate report on the general barometric sensitivity
(verbal) of the senate/ statistics for compilation of the record. In
other words which words shock (oh horribly) those senators
familiar with the sound (of) but not the appearance of?

/ /

Seriously, the Dean of Canterbury has done damn good pamphlet
on WHY Pov/ amid Plent/ with a few notes of Japan/ li'l brown
peepul, wot are using Soc/ Cr/ fer dominion instead of domestic
uplift and help the 'elpless.

/ / /

Another very dangerous point/ not for diffusion// does anyone
know how far the American masons know ANYthing about the
Grand Orient or how likely they are to be diddled by it?

The kicking Wall St/ if done for benefit of international banks DONT, in my never sufficiently humbl opinyum, show enlightened pathriotism. But wd/ Wyoming EVER know there was a bombproof cellar under Mishthr RoTTschild's house in Paris, vhere ahl hiss aht voiks coes vhen Rohtty/ goes avay vrum Paris? news from a lady not lunched.

Hell, why dont you spend yr/ vacations abroad, in years NOT preceding elections.

German company (5 cos.) director sez it is lookin UP UP/ "Freiwirtschaft?" "Oh no no no NO, Weltwirtschaft".

and thass thaaat.

Townsend plan is the pewk? (correct me if in error).

Best advrt/ matter for Doug/ is prob/ Japan, a practical peepul.

Incidentally Crate Larkin seems to have something INSIDE his skull.

And, as I think I wrote, Gesell's *N.E.O.* looks to me a useful vol/ for anyone ever likely to get into a argymint. Doug constructed. didn't think much about fools, and left-overs; but Gesell has cut up Marx etc. etc./ besides the bk/ is amusin.

[ever yr ?]

EZ P'O

Notes on Letter 32

(2 Jan. [1935])

Van Mises. The conservative Austrian economist Ludwig Edler von Mises (1881–1973) was Professor of International Economic Relations in the Graduate Institute of International Studies at Geneva from 1934 to 1940, when he emigrated to New York. With F. A. von Hayek, he later became a founder of the Libertarian movement in the United States. In the *New English Weekly* for 5 September 1935, EP alleged that "Van Mises, who spouts at Geneva, in favour of lies, superstition and infamy, has never heard of the modern world, and possibly a potent source of evil, is least [*sic*] in a position to poison the minds of students" (326; rpt., *Ezra Pound's Poetry and Prose*, 6: 312).

Mr Pope. James Pinckney Pope (1884–1966) was Democratic senator from Idaho between 1933 and 1939; he later became a director of the Tennessee Valley Authority. EP corresponded with Pope from July 1934 to May 1936 (Pound Archive). On 2 January [1935] EP wrote, "Dr/ Sen/ You abs/ must NOT jam us into the Leag/ of Nats/ as long as they are preaching the lie that money is a commodity, in Geneva." What had probably alarmed EP was an article entitled "America and the League," published in the *Times* of London for 31 December 1934, p. 12. According to this report, Senator Pope had announced on 29 December that he would lay before the Congress a joint resolution authorizing U.S. entry into the League of Nations. On 10 January 1935 Pope spoke in favor of U.S. membership in a national radio broadcast. Pope's "Idaho colleague," and a staunch opponent of League membership, was Senator William E. Borah.

Dean of Canterbury. Hewlett Johnson (1874–1966), Dean of Canterbury Cathedral from 1931 to 1963, was known as the "Red Dean" because of his radical writings and social actions. His pamphlet *Social Credit and the War on Poverty* (London: Stanley Nott, 1935) mentions Japan on p. 12, but EP seems to be alluding to a Social Credit aspect of Japanese expansionist policy that Hewlett does not mention and we have not been able to identify.

the Grand Orient. Freemasonic lodges in France, Italy, Spain, and South America are known as Grand Orients. They have traditionally been more anticlerical, radical, and open to Jews than the lodges of Germany, England, and the United States. In late nineteenth-century France, many religious, social, economic, and political ills were blamed upon a Jewish-Masonic conspiracy, supposedly centered in the Grand Orient of Paris, to destroy Christianity and rule the world. The existence of such a conspiracy was reaffirmed by *The Protocols of the Elders of Zion,* by much German journalism of the Weimar period, by Hitler's *Mein Kampf,* and by Fascist propaganda of the 1930s. Both Hitler and Mussolini suppressed the Masonic movement as incompatible with fascist allegiance.

RoTTschild's house. In a review of "John Buchan's 'Cromwell,'" *New English Weekly* 7, 8 (6 June 1935), 149 (rpt., *Selected Prose,* 235, and *Ezra Pound's Poetry and Prose,* 6: 295–96), EP wrote, "The manifest arc from light to black festering darkness can be measured in the material facts:—I. The church of St. Hilaire in Poitiers. II. The bomb proof, gas-proof cellar beneath the Rothschild private palace in Paris, whereto the works of art (as having commercial VALUE, monetary worth) are transported when the great chief usurer leaves that fatal and mentally foetid city. The latter is the objective and material register of progressive human degradation, as result of mental obtuseness." EP also mentions this cellar in three lines of Canto 52 (1940) that were blacked out as possibly slanderous in printings before 1986: "specialité of the Stinkschuld/ bomb-proof under their house in Paris/ where they cd/ store aht voiks." See, too, "100% Money," *New English Weekly* 7, 17 (5 September 1935), 326– 27; rpt., *Ezra Pound's Poetry and Prose,* 6: 311–12.

Freiwirtschaft. Free Economy was a central concept of Gesellite economics and the title of a number of books and articles published in the 1920s by Philip Pye, Rolf Engert, Theophil Christian, and others.

Townsend plan. For EP's opinion of the old-age pension plan of Dr. Francis Everett Townsend (1867–1960), see the Introduction to Chapter Three, p. 92 above.

Crate Larkin. In 1934 businessman and monetary reformer James Crate Larkin (1878–1947) published *From Debt to Prosperity: An Introduction to the Proposals of Social Credit* (New York: The Economics Group of New York). By 1935 the book had gone through two editions, six printings, and a French translation. EP corresponded with Larkin from 14 October 1934 to 16 November 1935 (Pound Archive, Beinecke Library). In "American Notes," *New English Weekly* 6, 15 (24 January 1935), 310–11 (rpt., *Ezra Pound's Poetry and Prose* 6: 240), EP wrote, "Crate Larkin, president of the Larkin Co. of Buffalo, N. Y., one of America's clearest Social Credit writers, has published a series of 13 articles . . . in the 'Buffalo Times.' The Larkin Co. is one of those which asserted the ancient right of Industrial Companies to issue their own money. This the Larkin Co. did in the form of 'merchandise bonds,' emitted three days before the famous 'bank holiday,' in denominations from 25 cents to 2.50 dollars. This money was good money and functioned, until it was outlawed by political intrigue." EP's report was based upon a letter to him from Larkin dated 19 November 1934. Larkin's articles are summarized by John Drummond in "'J. Crate Larkin Contends,'" *New English Weekly* 6, 18 (14 February 1935), 370–71. See also J. Crate Larkin, "Larkin's Merchandise Bonds," *New English Weekly* 7, 8 (6 June 1935), 158.

Gesell's N. E. O. For Silvio Gesell and his book *The Natural Economic Order,* see Letters 27 and 30 and the Introduction to Chapter Three, p. 96 above.

4 Apr. [1935]

E. POUND
RAPALLO
VIA MARSALA 12-5

To the Hon/ the Strong an Silent, The Cutting:

Sorr:

I keep a/pee/rusin' the *Santa Fé N.mxkn.* I dunno who sends it,
but it comes to guide me/

Naow about yer frien' Huey the Kingfish: is he going to see
MONEY? is he going to cut out the silly idea of dividing what he
peels off where it AINT?

I am quoting the *S.F.N.Mex* editorial when Mairet gets caught up
with about two bales of my stuff.

Coughlin seems to know more than he did, but where does it get
TO?

My "Jefferson and/or Mussolini" is at last in galley proofs (so is my
second econ/ outbreak. "Impact." Nott and Co. series.) second half
of the J/M ought to be useful. Two years old but naobuddy aint
caught up with it yet.

NOBODY will print my li'l poEMS about F.D.R. (who protekks
him?)

I had the tip about Huey being edderkated sometime ago, before
you people started boostin him in N/Mex.

I dunno if you take trouble to see the *Criterion?*

Odon Por is now writing regularly in *Critica Fascista,* and in
Cultura Fascista/ both official organs. Por full of sound sense.

Forget whether I said the London *Morning Post* printed a series of my letters., almost complete nut shell course in econ/ finally sub/edtr/ found they couldn't attack the banks (article on history of early banking, finally pubd. in *New Age*. was too much for *Post*. (at least just before the 5 full page reports of the brit/ Big Five banks.

Wallace seems to have wilted.

Wish I cd/ persuade you to keep me a bit more INFORMED.

I suppose DeKruif pulls some weight as publicity? even if I don't YET.

I seem to have several readers that I didn't us/ter. and even "Esquire" prints a spare copy nown again.

[ever ?]

Ez. P'o.
trustin you note the
chinese significance

Notes on Letter 33

(4 Apr. [1935])

Huey the Kingfish. Huey P. ("Kingfish") Long (1893–1935) was nicknamed for a character on the "Amos 'n' Andy" radio show. For Long's "Share Our Wealth" plan and his relationships with EP and BC, see the Introduction to Chapter Three, pp. 93–94 above.

Mairet. Philip Mairet was an editor of the *New English Weekly*.

Coughlin. In 1934 the popular radio orator Father Charles Edward Coughlin (1891–1979) had his own network and an estimated audience of ten million listeners. In November of 1934, when EP began to correspond with him, Coughlin founded the National Union for Social Justice. The goals of the Union included the nationalization of banking, credit, and currency; abolition of the Federal Reserve System, and a just annual wage. During 1935 Coughlin became increasingly critical of President Roosevelt and the New Deal. By 1938, he began to preach against an international conspiracy of Jewish bankers and to advocate a political order which bore some resemblances to Fascist corporatism in Italy. EP mentioned Coughlin frequently in the *New English Weekly* at this time and corresponded with him until July 1937 (Pound Archive). See, for example, "American Notes," *New English Weekly* 7, 12 (4 July 1935), 225–26; rpt., *Ezra Pound's Poetry and Prose*, 6: 300–301.

"Jefferson and/or Mussolini." EP's book of this title was published in London by Stanley Nott in July 1935. In May, Nott published EP's pamphlet *Social Credit: An Impact*.

Criterion. This London quarterly was edited by T. S. Eliot and published from 1922 to 1939. It carried EP's "1934 In the Autumn" in the issue for January 1935 (vol. 15, pp. 297–304) and his "In the Wounds (Memoriam A. R. Orage)" in the issue for April 1935 (pp. 391–407); rpt., *Ezra Pound's Poetry and Prose*, 6: 227–31, 262–73.

Odon Por. From 1923 on, Hungarian-Italian economist Odon Por (1883–?) wrote many books and articles about the guild and corporate structure of Mussolini's Italy. His column entitled "Cronaca della 'Nuova Economia'" appeared in seven issues of *Civiltà* (not *Cultura*) *Fascista* during 1935. EP translated Por's "Systems of Compensation" for the third number of the *British Union Quarterly* (July/September 1937; rpt., *Ezra Pound's Poetry and Prose*, 7: 197–214) and his *Italy's Policy of Social Economics 1939/1940* (Bergamo: Istituto italiano dei arti grafici [1941]). The latter appears in EP's Canto 78 as "Odon's neat little volume."

article. EP's "Banking Beneficence and . . ." appeared in the *New Age* 16 (14 February 1935), 184–85; rpt., *Ezra Pound's Poetry and Prose*, 6: 246–47.

Wallace. Henry Agard Wallace (1888–1965) of Iowa was an agricultural scientist, journalist, and businessman who served as President Roosevelt's secretary of agriculture from 1933 to 1940 and as his vice president from 1941 to 1945. EP corresponded with Wallace from January 1935 to July 1940 (Pound Archive) and met him in Washington in 1939.

De Kruif. Paul Henry de Kruif (1890–1971) was a bacteriologist, pathologist, and writer of popular books and essays about medical science. His articles appeared regularly in the widely read magazines of the Curtis Publishing Company, including the *Ladies' Home Journal,* the *Saturday Evening Post,* and *Country Gentleman.* EP reviewed de Kruif's *Hunger Fighters* (1928) in the *New English Weekly* for 22 February 1934, pp. 451–52 (rpt., *Impact,* 228–29, and *Ezra Pound's Poetry and Prose,* 6: 132–33). He corresponded with de Kruif from August 1933 to July 1940 (Pound Archive), and converted him to Social Credit early in 1934. De Kruif was acquainted with Henry A.

Wallace, to whom he introduced EP in 1939, and with President Roosevelt, of whose Infantile Paralysis Prevention Research Commission de Kruif was secretary.

"Esquire." Between August 1934 and November 1957, EP contributed nine items to *Esquire* magazine; see the Introduction to Chapter Four, p. 162 below.

the Chinese significance. Spelled in this way, EP's name recalls that of the Chinese poet, Li Po, and also the character *P 'o*3.5 (M. 5354, "sincere . . . substance of things").

4

"Ez Sez"

I
INTRODUCTION

In his 23 March 1934 letter to Cutting, Pound asked the senator, "Didn(t [*sic*] you once have a noozpaper.. or isn't there some noozpaper that wd/ let me loose." (See Letter 20, p. 117 above.) The newspaper in question was the Santa Fe *New Mexican,* which Cutting had purchased in 1912 and still owned, and which served to help maintain his political power base in northern New Mexico.[1] Mrs. Meredith Hare, a prominent Social Creditor, seems to have suggested to the senator that he open the pages of the *New Mexican* to Pound. In response to a telegram from Cutting (Letter 29, p. 144 above), Gorham Munson, acting for Pound, sent the senator three short pieces by the poet "to fill the gap until" his "copy" should begin "to arrive from Italy."[2] None of the pieces, however, found its way into print, and in December Pound began receiving copies of the paper, apparently accompanied by a note from its editor inquiring, in Pound's words, "as to why I dont contribute." Pound responded, probably early in 1935, and declared himself open to persuasion of both the verbal and monetary kinds. "If you want anything more from me you'll have to say so, and state rates," he wrote, adding that he did not "expect 'Esquire' prices from a daily paper, unless syndicated." (See Letter reproduced p. 184 below.) As a result of the ensuing negotiations, if any, the *New Mexican* for a time ran on its editorial page "Ez Sez, Being Some Pithy Promulgations by Ezra Pound." In all, Pound contributed seventeen items in the series, the first appearing on 26 March 1935, the last on 4 October of that year.

The editor of the *New Mexican,* E. Dana Johnson, was born in West Virginia on 15 June 1879 and came to New Mexico in 1902. He worked for the *Albuquerque Journal* and *Albuquerque Herald* before Cutting hired him in 1913. Tall, handsome, courtly, he was a popular figure in Santa Fe and an active preservationist. He wrote light verse and was considered a master of witty, sarcastic invective. His editorial column was for a time entitled "Jabs in the Solar Plexus." Thus, he may have been receptive to, or even have had a hand in shaping, the tone and format of Pound's own "jabs" at politicians and economists.

It is not necessary to invoke Johnson to account for "Ez Sez," however, for the column brings to mind at least two other possible antecedents. Its title and the "crackerbarrel" voice Pound often affected in it both suggest he may have been playing off or emulating Will Rogers's own "Will Rogers Says."[3] In addition, "Ez Sez" seems to owe some of its information, if not a stylistic debt, to George Durno's "The National Whirligig." In 1934–35, Durno's daily column, to which Pound refers in his piece for 28 March, offered tidbits about the inner workings of the Roosevelt administration, the latest exploits of Senator Huey Long, or other capitol gossip, some of which may have helped form or reinforce the judgments expressed in "Ez Sez." "The National Whirligig" was widely syndicated and was carried by the *New Mexican.*

The folksy, didactic "Ole Ez" persona, of course, is one Pound perfected and employed frequently in the 1930s. Moreover, the rhetorical strategies and contents of the "Ez Sez" items sometimes bear significant similarity to some of his contemporaneous contributions to other periodicals. Many of the 1935 entries in Pound's "American Notes" column in the *New English Weekly,* for instance, replicate, expand on, or clarify references in "Ez Sez." In mentioning "'Esquire' prices" to Johnson, he may have been alluding to the series of pieces he placed with Arnold Gingrich's magazine beginning in 1934.[4] The five of these which appeared in 1935 again often cover the same general territory as the *New Mexican* items. Indeed, Pound, through cross-references, twice calls attention to the connections between the two concurrent series; in "Ez Sez" for 8 August, he reminds his readers of what he told them about Upton Sinclair in one of the *Esquire* essays,[5] while he alludes in one of the magazine pieces to the "valentine" for Secretary of Labor Perkins that appeared in the column on 28 March.[6] Such references create the impression that he thought of all of his periodical publications as constituting a larger text, a kind of continuing "epissl" to the "murkn peepul". Whether or not any contemporary readers actually followed him in both the *New Mexican* and *Esquire* (even Pound seems to have had his doubts about this), it is illuminating to read the two series together, while in a larger context the examination of Pound's neglected political journalism and correspondences of the 1930s can cast light on once cryptic passages in the Cantos he composed during the decade.[7]

An examination of the "Ez Sez" typescripts housed in the Pound Archive (Series 43, Box 89) shows that he wrote more editorials than the *New Mexican* published. In addition to the seventeen items that appeared in the newspaper, the Archive contains thirty-three unpublished, undated editorials, all but one of which appear to belong to the "Ez Sez" series.[8] The material is so extensive, and would require so much annotation to be fully intelligible, that we have decided not to include it in the present edition. Considerations of length and proportion determined our decision.

Fifteen of the thirty-three unpublished editorials survive as original typescripts with carbon copies, whereas eighteen exist as carbon copies only. This may mean that the fifteen duplicated items were never sent to Santa Fe but held in reserve, whereas the other eighteen columns were sent but not accepted for publication. (The editorials that *were* published exist in the Archive only in carbon-copy form.) In short, Pound may have submitted twice as many texts as were printed, and may have written nearly three times as many.

The editors of the *New Mexican* thus played an active role in shaping the "Ez Sez" series. They probably selected the pieces they printed from a considerably larger sample that Pound had provided. In one instance (25 May 1935), they combined two separate typescripts into a single editorial. In other cases, they deleted portions of Pound's text that seemed unnecessary or redundant. They also edited for propriety, removing profane and blasphemous expressions, and deleting or altering potentially offensive or slanderous remarks. Occasionally they added language to Pound's typescripts, usually for the sake of clarity or grammatical correctness, but sometimes for no apparent reason. They reduced many, but by no means all, of Pound's emphatic capitalizations to conventional lower-case typography. They corrected numerous irregularities of grammar, spelling, punctuation, capitalization, and typography; but they (or their printers and proofreaders) also introduced a few typographical errors and inadvertent omissions. Finally, they provided closing signatures and datelines where Pound had not already done so. Many of these textual variants are given in the explanatory notes that follow the editorials in the present edition. (The principles governing our selection of variants are stated in the Editors' Preface.)

Three of the published "Ez Sez" pieces contain direct references to Cutting. On 25 May Pound "blasts" Sinclair, then "blesses" his patron in a postscript: "Bronson Cutting could at least teach him something." The 3 August column serves as a eulogy for the man who, in the poet's opinion, possessed "the best mind in the senate." Here, and again on 16 August (as well as in his 16 July letter to Johnson), Pound claims the senator "was finally for Social Credit," was enthusiastic about it despite the less than stirring performance of C. H. Douglas in America. As has been mentioned before (see Introduction to Chapter Three, p. 100 above), there is no evidence to support such contentions. Whether or not Pound believed these claims, he displayed no compunction about publicly testifying for the deceased senator, putting words into his mouth, or enlisting his memory in the service of the cause.

"Ez Sez" mentions many of the same issues and figures that dominate the correspondence, in particular its later phase. Banking reform, child labor, make-work, Huey Long and Father Coughlin all turn up at least once. The main didactic purposes of the column were clearly to promote and denigrate: to promote the Social Credit program and its prophets, as well as amateur economists of the fringe who in Pound's view had displayed some degree of enlightenment; to denigrate the "so-called" experts, especially economics professors, those he calls in an *Esquire* essay "the learned gentry that have Purrfesser in front of their names and X.C.B., Dr. Xot. P.B. and so forth trailin'."[9] He reserves particularly acidic criticism for those who were "misguidedly" offering alternative programs for economic reform, including members of the Roosevelt administration and Upton Sinclair.

A.
"THE LEFT WING NEW STEALERS"

By early 1935, Pound was taking every opportunity to excoriate many of FDR's advisers (see Introduction to Chapter Three, p. 84 above). He had clearly become impatient with what he saw as the failure of the administration to implement innovative economic programs, or to heed the advice of such lay "experts" as himself and Major Douglas. In the second "Ez Sez" entry, for instance, he states, "More chance of educating Kingfish and Coughlin, than of educating the 'left wing new stealers,'" later clarifying this with "Whatza use of peepul callin' 'emselves PROgressives and then dishing up all the old stuff that has been proved nonsense in England?" (28 March 1935). His use of "stealers" indicates that he is adding corruption to the charges of ignorance and incompetence, and he seems to have routinely canvassed newspaper reports and columns, including Durno's "Whirligig," looking for whiffs or outright accusations of impropriety or scandal.

1.
"Sister Perkins"

Frances Perkins (1880–1965), secretary of labor from 1933 until 1945, was the first woman ever to serve as a cabinet member. Pound's sniping at her was undoubtedly lost in the general barrage; during her tenure she came under increasing fire from Congress until her resignation in 1945. A number of Pound's other responses to her statements are of the ad hominem variety and perhaps even less polite than his "valentine" in "Ez Sez." Elsewhere he asserts "Perkins and Hull can be judged by public utterance and found a peril to the nation" and: "Perkins's ignorance is on a par with Upton Sinclair's. Any group of high school boys could understand that work is not a commodity, and that money is not a commodity."[10] Through his attacks on her, however, he was also targeting the policies for which she was spokesperson, in particular a reliance on public-works programs, which he viewed as a temporary and debt-creating expedient.[11]

If he was accusing Secretary Perkins in "Ez Sez" of exhibiting insensitivity to the actual plight of working people (as well as indolence), she was concerned with portraying herself and the administration as quite the opposite. The conclusion of her book *People at Work*, published in 1934, contains the following lines, including, interestingly, a statement that, though in a different context to be sure, sounds much like Pound's own "work is not a commodity":

> The Department of Labor which this nation has set up to promote human welfare, has a conscious and deliberate dedication to human needs—to understand if it can and to listen with a concentrated ear to what people need and hope. *The labor of the human being is not a commodity*, nor an article of commerce, and the world does not consist of buying power and efficiency and sound investment.[12]

2.
"Tugwell . . . no better than Moley"

Having served as Columbia University professors prior to their appointments to key positions in the administration, Rexford Guy Tugwell (1891–1979) and Raymond Moley (1886–1975) were almost bound to draw

Pound's fire. A professor of economics and member of FDR's "Brain Trust" (1932–33), Tugwell wore several official hats, including those of assistant secretary of agriculture (1933–36), undersecretary of agriculture to Henry Wallace (1934–36), and head of the Resettlement Administration (1935–36). Tugwell resigned from government service effective 31 December 1936, although he later returned to it as governor of Puerto Rico from 1941 to 1946.

In writing that "Tugwell always was Sat. Eve. Post balony, and blah" ("Ez Sez," 28 March), Pound may be responding to the assessments of others. Father Coughlin, for example, was extremely critical of Tugwell's approach in directing the Resettlement Administration. Under Tugwell, the agency "tried to put families back on the land, a measure which Odon Por had praised when Mussolini attempted it too."[13] Felt by some to be one of the most radical members of the Roosevelt administration, Tugwell created a design for a planned economy: "Profits would have been limited and their uses regulated, prices controlled, gains eliminated. . . . When industry is government and government is industry, the dual conflict in our modern institutions will be abated."[14]

Moley, a political scientist, was officially assistant secretary of state to Cordell Hull, unofficially for a time the chief member of FDR's "Brain Trust." A correspondent for the *Chicago Tribune*[15] described Moley's role in the administration as follows:

> He occupies a suite of offices at the State Department surrounded by a bevy of attractive young women secretaries, including honor students of one of his political science classes at Barnard College. Altho [*sic*] he is vested with the title of Assistant Secretary of State, an administrative office, State Department administration is the least of his duties. He is concerned with the whole reach of governmental policies from foreign relations to fiscal affairs, from industrial integration to the incidence of taxation. He is reputed to be the closest adviser of the president.

Moley played these roles, however, for but a brief period (March–September 1933). He resigned both his official and unofficial positions and later wrote a biting criticism of the New Deal, *After Seven Years* (1937).

The fact that Moley was, in Pound's eyes, "a tame cat lapping out of Astor's saucer"[16] was enough, certainly, to inscribe his name with the "blasted," but one of the more immediate things that probably was arousing "Ez's" ire in late March 1935 was Moley's criticism of Long and Coughlin. A few weeks later Pound defended those very outspoken critics of the administration as follows: "The cry of demagogy against either the Kingfish (Long) or against Father Coughlin don't hold *if measured by* the ballyhoo of their opponents.

No cheaper ballyhoo than that of Johnson, Astor, Moley has ever ramped in America."[17] Upton Sinclair accused FDR's chief adviser of participating in the sabotaging of his gubernatorial campaign (see below).

3.
"FATTY JIM"

In the pages of the *New Mexican*, Pound continued to excoriate the behavior of James Farley, the postmaster general, whose actions he had alluded to in letters to Senator Cutting the previous year. In the piece for 25 May, he served up this bit of sarcastic praise for FDR's patronage chief:

> Waaal I will hand it to Farley (Mr. Farley the secretary and member of the cabinet). For two years I have thought Farley was no dam good. I mean I listed him with Nic Butler, and Andy Mellon and Herbie Hoover as people that would be more use to their fellow citizens in a cannibal country than in an highly industrialized one like our own, but Farley has proved one thing (at least some of his colleagues have helped, but in the main it's fatty Jim who has proved it). He has proved that the ONLY way for a country to spend its money without boodling, pork-barreling and undue favors to rather unpleasant citizens is BY A NATIONAL DIVIDEND paid per capita, each citizen getting exactly the same amount.

In associating Farley with various improprieties, Pound is again echoing the accusations of others.

In addition to the alleged leaking of inside information hinted at in Pound's letters to Cutting, other Farley activities had by the spring of 1935 come under increasing fire from a variety of quarters. Late in 1934, for instance, stamp collectors had denounced his practice of distributing to friends and associates special imperforate sheets of stamps, said "gifts," by one estimate, having been valued at 150,000 to 5,000,000 dollars.[18] In February 1935, an inflamed Huey Long asked the Senate to investigate "general and specific charges of misconduct, irregularity, dishonesty, and other activity" on the part of the postmaster general," citing in particular the relationship between the James A. Farley Holding Co. and General Builders Supply, a concern that had sold supplies to companies constructing public buildings, including the New York Postoffice Annex.[19] Farley was also being pressured to resign from either his cabinet post or his political positions as chairman of the Democratic National Committee and New York State Democratic party chairman.[20] Long styled

Farley "The Prime Minister, James Aloysius Farley, the Nabob of New York."[21]

Farley again drew Pound's attention a month later for "pushing a bill for keeping scientific information out of the mails. Anything to take the public mind off honest economics." The man some called "Big Jim" had now "shown himself as something worse than a mere good natured boodle-favourer,"[22] for the bill in question was an attempt to amend existing law "to permit prosecution for the transmission of 'obscene,' including contraceptive, literature at the place of receipt as well as origin," in short, an effort to strengthen the "baboon" laws that had first impelled Pound to contact the senator from New Mexico. The bill was introduced by "Senator Hayden and Representative Higgins, as presented by the Postoffice Department, and 'at the request of the Postmaster General.'" According to postal officials, the intent of the bill "was more effective control over the activities of a group of New York publishers" who could no longer be successfully prosecuted "since the Woolsey decision permitting the entry of *Ulysses*." "Conceding that complaints might be filed against doctors, nurses, and other medical and scientific authorities which would lead to their prosecution in other than their own jurisdictions, and the imposition of penalties not included in the present laws, postal officials nevertheless contended that such action would be highly unlikely, as it was not, and is not, their desire or intention to proceed against 'such people.'" The bill as presented was opposed by Senator La Follette, among others.[23]

Farley's particular "crimes" notwithstanding, by spring of 1935 he had become for Pound only the most visible embodiment of a corruption permeating the administration, an illness that was the inevitable consequence of doing "business as usual": "Farleyism is, perhaps, Roosevelt's incurable disease. Having tolerated the 'ragione di stato,' the political exigency long enough to become President, it is difficult, etc., etc., to be the 'greatest President' of the republic. and only a year and a bit to go."[24]

4.
ICKES

Pound did not tar all the president's men and women with the labels incompetent or criminal. In "Ez Sez" (28 March), he places the secretary of the interior in a different category: "Ickes seems the only one of the cab. worth a damn. How did HE get there?" Harold LeClaire Ickes (1874–1952) served as secretary of the interior (1933–1946) and also as administrator of the Public Works Administration. Huey Long once referred to him as "The Lord High Chamberlain, Harold Ickes, the chinch bug of Chicago."[25] Ickes, however, had a reputation for integrity and incorruptibility; one of his nicknames was "Honest Harold." He vigorously effected the administration's strategy of making work and was a vocal castigator of anti-Semites.[26] Despite this, Pound seems to have felt that the University of Chicago graduate was, like Cutting, a literate and educable statesman. He corresponded with him, about poetry as well as politics.[27] He reiterated his opinion in "American Notes": "Ickes is possibly the only man in the cabinet who will escape the contempt of future historians."[28] And in *Guide to Kulchur* he again singled him out: "Roosevelt's cabinet, with the exception of Ickes, has not the necessary acumen to consider these questions with the seriousness you wd. find in any european seminar outside of England."[29] Ickes did not share his opinions of Long and Coughlin, deriding the former's Share Our Wealth plan and the latter's radio "poetry" and deeming them "contemptible" men "of crooked intellect" who "deliberately" set out "to fool the underprivileged" with "fantastic" schemes.[30]

5.
"Marriner Ec"

Pound's equivocal approval of Marriner Stoddard Eccles (1890–1977) was not nearly as lasting. Eccles was appointed governor of the Federal Reserve Board on 10 November 1934 and headed the Federal Reserve System from 1936 to 1948. In "Ez Sez" Pound wonders about placing him among the at least minimally enlightened:

> Wot, he sez, interrogative, is Marriner Ec (however he spells it) spekles gettin' a faint antelucanal glimmer of the risin' fact that the nation has credit, and don't need to go out an' hire it from Barney Baruch and his friends? . . . Marriner, has Frank Vanderlipp heard you say that? (29 May)

A comment in the *New English Weekly* helps to clarify the statement: "Governor Eccles, of the Federal Reserve Board, recently said, before the House Banking and Currency Committee, 'Our problem is one of distribution. By distribution we mean not the distribution of existing wealth, but the distribution of the wealth as it is currently produced. . . .' Governor Eccles appeared before the Banking Committee of Congress for eleven consecutive days, and talked a good deal of Social Credit philosophy."[31]

Eccles, who wanted to reform the entire Federal Reserve System, was testifying in support of a banking reform bill that he and FDR were trying to push through Congress. According to Earle Davis, the bill in question was intended to effect three major changes: "(1) Power over open-market operations was given to the National Open Market Committee of the Federal Reserve Board in Washington. This made the supply of reserves and volume of money and credit subject to a national, not regional, credit policy. (2) Separate offices of chairman and governor of the Federal Reserve Boards were abolished. This made the Federal Reserve appointees the men who actually ran the banks and supposedly stopped local bankers from doing pretty much as they pleased in issuing credit. (3) 'Eligible paper' used as backing for credit was changed to 'sound assets,' so that much more credit could be easily released if the national authority thought it necessary to promote distribution or ward off depression."[32]

Although in the *New Mexican* Pound seems somewhat supportive of Eccles, and though he made positive comments about the bill elsewhere,[33] he also referred to the Federal Reserve head as a "bank tout" and soon changed his mind about the effectiveness of the legislation.[34] By fall of the following year, he was writing in the following manner of the limitations of Eccles' efforts:

> Report (certainly sincere, and direct enough) that Eccles of Federal Reserve is trying to do good by increasing coverage. This diminishes bank power to create money, but does nothing toward getting it directly into the hands of those who most need it. The Nude Eel is still squirming about in the stabilization problem and doing its soft-headed damndest to avoid looking at money.[35]

According to the *New York Times,* the major opponents of the Eccles proposal had leveled the following accusations:

> (1) That it is a scheme to get partisan political control of the nation's credit, which means its citizens' money. (2) That it puts private wealth, now and in the future, at the mercy of whatever dangerous radical or demagogue may be in political power in Washington. (3) That it is a concealed pathway to inflation. (4) That it creates a central bank which, like the Reichsbank of the Nineteen Twenties in Germany, will impose policies which will soon require people to pay for their purchases with basketfuls of paper currency.[36]

Frank Vanderlip (see note on Letter 17) had indeed been paying attention. As the *Times* reported, on 2 May he claimed "that a 'reign of terror exists among bankers' and that none of them dared to speak out against the Eccles bill," adding that "seventy members of Congress" had confided that "they were voting as they were told rather than as they felt."[37] (See Introduction to Chapter Three, pp. 101–02 above for Cutting's alternative proposals.)

B.
"Bro. Aberhart"

In August 1935 events in Alberta, Canada, for a brief time allowed Pound to hope that an alternative to New Deal economics based on Social Credit principles might find grassroots support in North America. In that month, William Aberhart's Social Credit forces swept the Alberta legislative elections. Aberhart, or "Bible Bill" as he was called by some, was a lay preacher who promulgated "charismatic" doctrines. He served as principal of Crescent Heights High School, Calgary, later became dean of Calgary Prophetic Bible Institute, and launched a series of very popular radio broadcasts. In 1929 he founded his own sect, the Bible Institute Baptist Church. Aberhart first encountered Social Credit in 1932 in a book by Maurice Colbourne (see note on "Ez Sez," 13 August) and referred to it often in his radio broadcasts. By 1939 over nine thousand children were "enrolled" in his "Radio Sunday School." His Social Credit party won a stunning victory on 22 August 1935, winning fifty-six of sixty-three seats in the legislature and making it possible for him to assume the office of premier. Following Douglas, Aberhart promised a dividend of "$25 a month to every man, $25 for his wife, from $5 to $20 for each of his children." Adapting Douglas's program, he also proposed "a 'just' or 'compensating' price, to be fixed by a commission." Aberhart used the skills he had honed in the classroom and on the air to make "social credit a revealed religion to his followers, unchallengeable because unarguable."[38] But, according to Gorham Munson, Aberhart's own resolve wavered when it came to implementing the doctrine. The

outgoing government had already signed Major Douglas to a two year contract "to advise and give directions upon all questions and problems of or arising in relation to the present financial and economic condition of the said Province of Alberta," and it was thought that Douglas would immediately sail from England to set Aberhart straight in the first months of his Premiership. This Douglas did not do, revealing his unpreparedness to seize an historic opportunity; he advised Aberhart through the slow mails, thus permitting the bankers to get to the new Premier "firstest with the mostest," and when Aberhart was bamboozled into appointing an orthodox financier, R. J. Magor, to be his economic adviser, Douglas resigned. For a year and a half the Aberhart government drifted along orthodox lines.

Visiting Edmonton in 1937, John Hargrave, leader of the Social Credit party of Great Britain, "inspired a revolt in the Alberta Social Credit Party which insisted that Aberhart at least take steps to implement Social Credit." But "Aberhart suffered continuous repulses as the higher courts declared piece after piece of legislation *ultra vires* and Dominion authorities disallowed other acts. All Aberhart was permitted to accomplish," Munson feels, "was a kind of provincial 'new deal,' some amelioration of the lot of the debtor. He was not allowed to take the smallest step in installing Social Credit, and therefore," in Munson's view, "the widespread notion that Social Credit was tried and failed in Alberta is erroneous; what failed was a bungling attempt to introduce Social Credit."[39]

As the reference in "Ez Sez" suggests, in writing about "Brother Aberhart," Pound also began on the defensive. In "Alberta and the British Press," he asserted that the "English attacks on Aberhard's [*sic*] victory reduce themselves to saying that Aberhard will NOT BE ALLOWED to put his ideas—or Douglas' ideas—into practice."[40] In "Hands Off Alberta," he himself seems to accept this prognostication, predicting the inevitable employment of "EVERY known and inventable sabotage," while criticizing the "Quakers" in the Social Credit movement, those "calm and inactive people who do not believe in disorder." Seeming to take for granted eventual defeat in Alberta, he argues that the "stoppage or failure of ANY possible 'experiment' wd. not OF NECESSITY prove anything save the existence of legal obstacles."[41]

C.
"CALIFORNY"

On a number of occasions during the rather short life span of the column, "Ez" directed his readers' attention farther down the West Coast. "Californy" or "Kallyforny," as it becomes when Pound is trying to seem "folksy," was in the 1930s affected by many of the economic ills debilitating the rest of the nation, while bearing the additional burden of having to assimilate the droves of migrant workers fleeing the Dust Bowl conditions in the Plains. Then, as in the 1960s, California sprouted scores of "fringe" or "avant-garde" doctrines, saviors, and pseudoscientists. As always, in apprising the readers of the *New Mexican* of events west of them, Pound "blasts" and "blesses," catalogues ideas and separates false prophets, such as Upton Sinclair, from true believers (usually in Social Credit) into what are for him clearly defined categories. When, for instance, he tells them that "Mr. Bannister . . . [l]ives out in Californy (with woodentop Upton)" the intended contrast is obvious.

1.
"WOODENTOP UPTON"

In referring to and ridiculing Upton Sinclair in "Ez Sez," "American Notes," and, most extensively, *Esquire,* Pound was responding to three things: Sinclair's EPIC program, his published account of the 1934 California gubernatorial campaign, and a "debate" with George E. Sokolsky that appeared in Gingrich's magazine in August 1935 and for which Pound was the "invited referee." Perhaps best known as a muckraking social realist and the author of *The Jungle,* Sinclair (1878–1968), a longtime socialist, in September 1933 ended his affiliation with the Socialist party and became a Democratic candidate for governor of California. His program to End Poverty in California was spelled out in a pamphlet written from the perspective of an imagined future and entitled *I, Governor of California and How I Ended Poverty.* The EPIC plan, styled "the beginning of a crusade,"[42] consisted of twelve points, "chief of which," as summarized by one historian,

> were the proposals for state land colonies where the unemployed might farm under the guidance of experts, similar operation of idle factories, and a state distribution system for the exchange of these several products—all to be financed by state-issued scrip. It proposed repeal of the sales tax, enactment of a steeply graduated income tax, and increases in inheritance and public utility corporation taxes. It contained a proposal for tax exemption on homes occupied by the owners and on ranches cultivated by the owners, provided the assessed value did not exceed $3,000. There was a Georgian proposal for a ten-per-cent tax on unimproved building lots and on agricultural land not under cultivation. Finally, there was a provision for fifty-dollar-a-month pensions to the aged needy, to the physically incapacitated, and to widows with dependent children.[43]

Underlying and central to the EPIC reforms was the concept of "production for use." Believing that unemployment was "the result of the profit system" and a "permanent condition in a profit system society," Sinclair essayed to do away with it once and for all by means that some termed "radical." His system of "land colonies and factories for the unemployed" "would become self-sufficient," "self-governing and independent of the capitalist system." The "unemployed would produce goods for their own consumption"; "surplus produce from the colonies and factories would be exchanged between them"; and "a separate medium of exchange" for use in the system would be created.[44] In the primary election Sinclair received more votes "than any other candidate, Republican, Democratic or Progressive," but he lost the general election to the Republican incumbent, Frank Merriam. The margin was only 259,063 votes, despite the fact that Sinclair ended up running without the support of a single "major citizens' group, party, or press."[45]

Early in the next year, Pound in "American Notes" offered his reaction to the result of the election:

> The California Election is to be tolerated. Whether Merriam meant it or not, the scare thrown into the worst elements of California society, namely those licking Hoover's boots and upholding every known form of corruption, was such, that a Republican candidate went Social Credit during the last pre-election flurry.

The retention of Merriam, who may or may not have sincerely voiced something like Social Credit doctrine, and who by most accounts was a mediocre governor and a scheming politico, was, it seems, preferable to change if that change was to come through implementing a competing program, one, according to Pound, consisting of "a prize collection of old scrap iron, dead and heteroclite ideas dating from the 'eighties' of the last century."[46]

It is impossible, of course, to judge how much of Pound's attitude toward Sinclair was the result of sincere evaluation of the merits of his platform and how much the product of professional jealousy—Sinclair, after all, was a writer who definitely *had* made political waves. Whatever the case, however, that attitude is loudly and clearly expressed in "Ez Sez" as elsewhere. Sinclair is a doltish, unregenerate purveyor of outmoded ideas that have been repackaged to deceive the unwary consumer. The only difference between him and "the left wing new stealers" is a "Difference of age," for his ideas are even more tired:

> Science goes on. But pore ole Upton just doesn't. Back in 1888 there wuz a lot of ideas, and back in 1898 there was a early model of Oldsmobile. Do you use 'em?

EZRA POUND AND SENATOR CUTTING

Would you call a fellow a LEADER if he insisted in drivin' one of them things?

For the past 15 years economic thought has gone on, just like thought in any other study or science. Now wouldn't you think a man who was setting himself up as a leader would try to find out what had happened since he got out of knee breeches? Or do they get that way out in Californy?

I'ma askin'. (25 May)

Others did not judge the candidate to be quite such an anachronistic buffoon. In *The New Republic,* for instance, Carey Williams noted that Sinclair had "managed to build an effective organization" on practically nothing, had "revealed unexpected political talent," and had become both a threat to the national administration and a target for those conservatives trying to take advantage of the "great wave of reactionary sentiment" generated in California by the general strike that began in May 1934.[47] Linking him with La Follette and Cutting, *The Nation* claimed that Sinclair's "candidacy has quickened the political life of the State in an amazing way. He has made the electorate face the economic issues of the day." Endorsing him along with the senators from Wisconsin and New Mexico, the journal asserted that "if Sinclair is elected, the cause of social and economic justice will be advanced. If he loses, the forces of privilege and black reaction will be heartened the country over."[48]

In August 1935, Pound used "Ez Sez" to jab at Sinclair again: "if any of you friends remember like how I told the wealthy readers of Brother Gingrich's paper ESquire how ole Upton went down to Washington and got TRUSTFUL, you will be pleased to hear that this is a Californian habit." What he was "reminding" his readers about was the following passage from "A Matter of Modesty":

And the mos' discouragin' thing about the Administration has just been printed by Uppie Sinclair. Ghees!! wotter book he has written! "What a kind man," he sez. "What a luvvable man!" he sez. And he tells deh WOIL' wotter luvvybl man is the President, and inna few weeks he is out yellin: "His bassarly friens double X'd me!!"

But thet ain't the harf ov it deerie, what is DEEpressin' (Are we ter beeleev' it? I hope not) but WOT iz depressin' is Upton's story of hoe he wandered all about and around in them orfices down thaaar by the POtomack, and everybody listen'd to Upton, and everybody said "Yes, Sir," to Upton, and treated him as a light of intelligence.

The book very loosely paraphrased here is Sinclair's *I, Candidate for Governor: And How I Got Licked.*[49]

In his account of the campaign, Sinclair describes a trip to Washington in

September 1934 during which he consulted with the president and members of the "Brain Trust" and was assured that he "should have Administration support, that the pretense otherwise was all 'the bunk'" (83–84). Moreover, he claims, FDR himself was familiar with, understood, and supported his economic theories and reforms:

> I found that he had read my book and knew the EPIC Plan. I told him our situation regarding unemployment. I told him my firm conviction that he had ten million permanently unemployed men and their families to care for. To keep them on the dole would pile up the public debt and drive the nation into bankruptcy. There was only one possible solution, to put them at productive labor and let them/ produce what they were going to consume. He understood all that clearly, and after we discussed it at length he said about as follows:

> "My advisers tell me that I have to talk to the people again over the radio and explain to them what I am doing. I am going to give that talk in two sections. The first will deal with general problems, and the second will deal with unemployment. I am coming out in favor of production for use."

> To that I said: "If you do that, Mr. President, it will elect me."

> He said, "That is what I am going to do. It will be somewhere about the 25th of October." (76–77)

At times, Sinclair does express the kind of unqualified respect for Roosevelt that Pound parodies:

> I had a formula about the President which I had been repeating all over the State. I repeated it to him when we met. "I might have joined the Republican party, but I saw that it was the party of Herbert Hoover, and I thought Mr. Hoover might be unhappy if I joined his party. I looked at the Democratic party and saw that it had given us in the White House a man who has not merely a kind heart but also an open mind." There would be applause at this; and I would add: "That is a rare combination in a statesman, and it's a lot better luck than you deserve." (65–66)

In other places, however, his assessment is more equivocal:

> I must explain my attitude toward Franklin D. Roosevelt. I do not think I have ever been more curious about any man in my life. . . . There were two possibilities: he might be blindly groping; or he might be a wise man, letting the people have their own way and learn by their own blunders. (74)

Whether or not Sinclair was as naive as Pound suggests, by most accounts he had reason to complain that he had been betrayed. His campaign began to founder seriously in the final weeks after the results of a poll, which

176

some have suggested was rigged, appeared in *Literary Digest*. It predicted that Merriam would win "sixty-two percent of the total vote and thus undoubtedly influenced many wavering Californians to throw their support to the popular candidate."[50] Sinclair's forces had published a letter of support written by Postmaster Farley. After the *Digest* poll, however,

> the weather changed suddenly. There came stories out of Washington to the effect that the letter had been mailed through an accident; it was one of those blunders which stenographers commit whenever their chiefs alter their minds suddenly; it was a mere form letter, and signed with a rubber stamp. (175)

Professor Moley "came out with a denunciation of the EPIC Plan and its candidate" (176), and the speech given by the president on 23 October contained no mention of "production for use" and no statement of support for Sinclair (183). Many factors contributed to the defeat of the EPIC crusade. Conservatives played to fears of the "Red Menace" by suggesting Sinclair was a Soviet puppet.[51] The socialists "denounced him as a deserter and opportunist," and many Democrats were troubled by his lack of experience and the radical nature of his proposed economic experiment. But, undoubtedly, "President Roosevelt's noncommital attitude and the failure of most of the leaders of the New Deal to give him unqualified support cost Sinclair many Democratic votes."[52]

It clearly irked Pound that eleven months after the election Sinclair was still being asked to share his expertise. His side of the August 1935 *Esquire* "debate" with Sokolsky was entitled "We Choose Our Future" and was built about the thesis that "Capitalism has used up all markets and must turn to war, fascism, or collectivism."[53] Sokolsky, on the other hand, argued from the position that "Capitalism constantly creates new markets through raising the standard of living."[54] "Referee" Pound, of course, rebutted both in November, concluding that "Upton's fault is a fault of blindness," whereas "Sokolsky's fault is a root fault of volition," and offering Douglas, Gesell, and "Bannister the California postmaster" as correctives.[55]

2.
BROTHER BANNISTER

Instead of "Upton's" pamphlets or *Esquire* article, Pound would have his readers consult the writings of "brother Bannister," whose profession that he was following some kind of "scientific" methodology quite probably made him even more appealing to Pound, who was often attracted to pseudoscientists, particularly when their species of pseudoscience reinforced his preconceptions and prejudices.[56] Louis Herbert Bannister was postmaster at Al Tahoe, California, for almost fourteen years. He published by himself the book that Pound somewhat inaccurately cites in "Ez Sez": *When We Become Scientific*.[57] The first part of the book consists of a reprint of a piece by J. W. Bennett on "The Cause of Financial Panics" (*The Arena*, March 1884), focusing on the injustice of land rent and interest taking (37) and citing as part of its evidence the "prejudice against Jews for interest taking and the views of Mediaeval Christians on the subject" as "set forth in the pages of Shakespeare" (36). In the second part, Bannister, endeavoring to appear as "scientific" as possible, presents charts and numerous quotations in offering his remedy, the basic elements of which he summarizes as follows:

> I would first declare a moratorium of all interest bearing debts in this country,—then, repeal all laws relating to our present financial system, and establish in its place a Scientific System for conducting the exchange of products, in which *Exchange Checks* [emphasis Bannister's] would become our Legal Tender Money, and would bear a definite Relation to Service in exchanging products. They would go into service for products sold through the National Exchange, and when brought to the National Exchange for redemption in products, they must be cancelled. This would be a Scientific and Balanced Currency, and would function with the same Scientific Order that obtains in our Postal System. (80–81)

This curious document closes with what appears to be an advertisement encouraging Bannister's readers to visit his "resort property" in the "delightful" Lake Tahoe region.

At about the same time as the "Ez Sez" entry, Pound quoted Bannister in the "American Notes" column:

> Amid the overwhelming soup of stupidities and in the utter decay and squalor of the American professoriate Mr. L. H. Bannister's "When we become Scientific" is a rope to a sinking swimmer. . . . Mr. Bannister was a postmaster. He had *seen* a postage stamp cancelled . . . "Were we as absurdly foolish in conducting our Postal System as we are our distribution of commodities, that also would require large warehouses in which to store several classes of mail." "No more necessity of having interest-bearing bonds back of National Exchange cheques than back of every issue of postage stamps." "Promising to pay interest for a medium of exchange every time it goes into circulation is wrong in principle."[58]

A month later, Pound employed the California postmaster in an attack on FDR: "The present system, as Brother Banister [*sic*] noted, is aimed at creating interest bearing debt. In this, President Roosevelt is the most determined Conservative that ever sat in the White House. The taint of this infamy is on every New Deal measure."[59] Finally, Pound used Bannister as follows to rebut Sokolsky:

> Bannister the California postmaster had seen postage stamps cancelled. He has pulled several fast ones on Sokolsky's system of happiness, such AZ:
>
> "If the postal system was as looney as the monetary system, we wd. have to build huge warehouses to contain the vast stacks of UNDELIVERED MAIL."
>
> meaning in words of almost exclusively one syllable that the mail would not be delivered FAST ENOUGH.
>
> but not meaning that a part of it mightn't get delivered AFTER A TIME (t, i, m, e, TIME).[60]

3.
CONTROVERSY

As "Ez" saw it, the other good news out of "Californy" was the founding of a periodical called *Controversy*. This Social Credit organ, begun in Carmel, California, by Harold Lewis Mack, published twenty-three issues between 25 October 1934 and 15 July 1935. The first nine were edited by W. K. Bassett; contributors included Lincoln Steffens, Yvor Winters, William Saroyan, and Langston Hughes. After 1 January 1935, the magazine was published semimonthly in San Francisco under the editorship of Elliott Taylor. In "The Credit Forum" of *The New English Weekly*, Pound described Mack's background:

> A week or so back I announced that the founder of a new United States group was a former banker, Colonel Harold L. Mack, who writes vigorously for Social Credit in the new "Controversy," and who is now President of the newly born California State Social Credit Association, is founder and partner in the brokerage house of McDonnell and Co. Colonel Mack is held in high esteem by the entire business community of the Pacific Coast. A recognized expert in orthodox finance, he gave up two years to the cause of mastering Social Credit, and having done so, is for it to the hundred per cent. of offering to lead the distinguished men and women who already constitute, and will increasingly constitute, the Californian movement.[61]

Mack wrote regularly on economic theory for *Controversy*, and was also the author of *"Something for Nothing": An honest monetary system is vital to true Democracy* (1936) and *The Problem of the Jews* (193?). In general, however, *Controversy* seemed to go out of its way to repudiate the anti-Semitic strain of some Social Credit thought.

Mack's magazine was receptive to Pound's work, quoting from his pamphlet *Social Credit: An Impact* soon after its publication in May 1935, and publishing a letter from him in the following issue.[62] Mack also paid close attention to the activities of Cutting. He wrote at least twice to the senator, offering to help him "inject Social Credit theories into politics by having it adopted as the basic plank of one of the major parties."[63] The periodical described Cutting as "interested in Social Credit," praised his bill to establish a Federal Monetary Authority, and quoted him for the benefit of its readers.[64] After his death, it ran an extremely laudatory eulogy:

> In the death of Senator Cutting, America's loss is irreparable. Here was a man in high political place who was not treating a deadly disease with shin plasters; here was a man who knew the major cause of our dire malady and who had the courage to move to extirpate it. By voice and by pen he had powerfully advocated that fundamental financial reform which would speedily end this depression and would inhibit future ones. Realizing the worth of Senator Cutting and the present vital need in the nation of such high intelligence and fine courage, it is difficult not to quarrel with the verdict of a fate which cuts him down and yet allows the Farleys, the Longs, the General Johnsons and their ilk to live and thrive.[65]

D.
"CARRY ON THIS CRUSADE"

For a time Pound himself quarreled with that verdict. "Ez Sez" continued to appear for five months after the senator's demise, and in the column he attempted to continue to use Cutting's name to advance the cause of Social Credit, composing for the dead senator a "farewell letter" (8 August) made up of items from Pound's own agenda. He tried, as well, to designate an "heir." At the end of his "eulogy" for Cutting, for instance, he asserts: "There is no man who could carry on this crusade with greater affection from the people than could Senator Hiram Johnson." And he began to tout Long as a possible successor during the few months the "Kingfish" remained alive.[66] It is hard, however, to miss the hint of an elegiac tone that permeates the 8 August entry as well as the piece in which Pound rationalizes the failure of the reception Cutting hosted for Douglas (16 August). Both manifest undertones of a sense of loss, the loss not only of the "best mind in the senate," but of promising opportunities, of what might have been had Pound's wildest dreams been realized.

Malcolm Cowley credits Gertrude Stein with having said of Pound that he was "a village explainer, excellent if you were a village, but if you were not, not."[67] Santa Fe in 1935 may have been cosmopolitan in certain ways (or certain circles), but in others it was still not far from a village; and while there may have been some sophisticates who fully absorbed "Ez Sez," one must assume it perplexed the majority of the local villagers.[68] The problem with "specialists" in economics, Pound wrote in late 1934, is that "they have no idea when their explanations are comprehensible and when they are 'above the heads' and 'beyond the grasp' of the average reader of good will."[69] Ironically, at about the same time, he himself was becoming increasingly guilty of a similar kind of misjudgment. In attempting to win American converts, "apostle" Pound, to be sure, makes an effort to accommodate his readers by referring to local issues and by often limiting his focus to the western states and the nation's capital. But many New Mexicans must still have found a good number of the things in the column to be "above their heads" or "beyond their grasp," if only because the pieces frequently assume a familiarity with things Pound has read or written elsewhere or because they refer in other ways to matters so specialized as to fall into the category of personal rather than public knowledge. Losing his sense of audience, leaving more and more of his readers behind, Pound was already headed toward the obscurantism of much of the later Cantos.

II
THE EDITORIALS

TL, carbon copy, 1 p., Beinecke Library

[Early 1935?]

Private

Edtr/ S/F/N/mexcn/

Recd/ large roll of copies. Also enquiry as to why I dont
contribute. If *you* have asked me, the letter hasn't arrived.

Your Washington news is good/ better than in such N/Y/ papers as
I have seen. ratio of the distance bein' equivalent to % of facts
printable.

I am doing American Notes in *New English Weekly,* and can
therefore relay anything that ought to reach U.S. via London . . . it
is the only route possible in many cases.

If you want anything more from me you'll have to say so, and state
rates. I want National Dividends, and dont mind workin' for 'em,
but I cant believe in the seriousness of all/any/ and every edtr/ jus
because I hear from their friends.

I don't expect "Esquire" prices from a daily paper, unless
syndicated.

and so forth

If you keep on sending me the paper, I will cite it by name when
possible in *N/E/W/*

26 March 1935   [C1171]

Belated Valentine:

The failure to stop child labor in New Mexico makes rotten reading
for the foreign observer. But the whole failure of America to think
straight makes equally rotten copy.

Work is not edible. Meaning you can't eat it. Money is not edible.
The day when Americans will ask themselves what they want and
then ask for it, instead of asking for something else, seems further
from earth than ever.

Do you want work? No. You mostly do not. You want something
else, and you think work is a necessary means to getting it.

A lot of things, such as capacity for playing the violin, require
work. Nobody can get 'em without working. Nobody has yet been
born with a capacity to paint like Velasquez at the age of six.

A lot of other things like watermelons and bison have to be worked
for sometimes. Sometimes you can't get them at all. Sometimes you
can buy 'em if you have money.

None of these statements ought to be incomprehensible to a
university graduate, or a Kentucky mountaineer.

But the nature of necessity has been regarded as mysterious since
the beginning of time.

You want work? What is it? Seventeen burly bishops got together
in London and decided that work ain't the same as employment.
They said work is work, but employment implies the sale of your
energy, SALE, sale of energy, usually under economic pressure.
That required some thinkin'. Charlie Hughes would never have
done it.

Of course British bishops wear aprons, etc., and deans wear gaiters up to the knee and look bloody funny, and England is a funny old country, but bigob they just went ahead and said it. Some wise crack. And they said the Holy Book don't anywhere say anything 'bout employment as a means of shinin' up the Xtn's little soul.

Child's Guide to Politics for 1935: Mistrust any man no matter how high in office who tries to block inquiry into the nature of money, its source of issue, and the ratio of the whole people's power to buy, to the price of what the whole people produces.

Second lesson: Shoot any blighter who tries to get you off discussion of America's own home affairs, by talking about foreign relations.

EZRA POUND

P.S. (I've been in Europe some time. There is nobody over here who can help the inhabitants of New Mexico to govern New Mexico.)

E.P.

Rapallo, Italy

Notes on "Ez Sez"

26 March 1935

Variants

(1) eat : EAT (2) Money is not : Money is NOT (3) what they want : WHAT THEY WANT (4) something else : something ELSE (5) Do you want : Do YOU want (6) No. You mostly do not : NO. You mostly do NOT (7) you think work : you think WORK (8) require work : require WORK (9) watermelons: watermellows (10) for sometimes : for SOMETIMES (11) get them:get 'em (12) None of these : Now none of these (13) implies the sale : implies the *sale* (14) Some wise crack : SOME wise crack (15) Child's Guide to Politics : CHILD4S GUIDE TO POLITICS (16) the whole people's power : the WHOLE' PO PEOPLES' power (17) whole people produces : WHOLE prople produces.

child labor in New Mexico. See Introduction to Chapter Three, pp. 88–89 above, and note on Letter 7, p. 53 above. EP is likely responding to coverage in the Santa Fe *New Mexican* of the fate of the proposed child labor amendment to the United States Constitution. On 5 February, the paper reported "that ratification was defeated in the house by one vote" and that "its permanent relegation" for that session "was accomplished by two votes." Opponents of the amendment saw it as an incursion of the federal government into the home, claimed too many people were already on relief, and argued that it would be better to have children working than "loafing in the streets" ("State Turns Thumbs Down on Amendment to End Child Labor," Santa Fe *New Mexican,* 5 February 1935, p. 1). Three days later the *New Mexican* claimed that "the child labor amendment is as dead as King Tut insofar as the state senate is concerned—and the legislature, the house having buried it so deeply that not even an 'X' can be found to mark the spot" ("Child Labor Bill Ordered to Graveyard," Santa Fe *New Mexican,* 8 February 1935, p. 1). Finally, this was placed in a national context at the end of the month, when the newspaper ran a wire-service report as-

serting that "Hope for ratification of the child labor amendment this year by all of the required 36 states virtually" had "been abandoned by some of its chief sponsors" ("No Hope for Child Work Act," Santa Fe *New Mexican,* 26 February 1935, p. 1). See also "Child Labor Measure Dead," Santa Fe *New Mexican,* 7 February 1935, p. 1.

Seventeen burly bishops. EP paraphrases report C. A. 484A of the Church of England Assembly, "Interim Report of the Social and Industrial Commission on Unemployment" (London: J. B. Nichols and Son, 1935). Signed by eight bishops (not seventeen as EP has it), eight other clergymen and twelve laymen, the commission's report makes "a distinction between 'work' and 'employment.'" Work, defined as Christian vocation, "only becomes employment in the economic sense when a person is in relationship with another person or body of persons who give him a claim on wealth (*i.e.* goods) in return for his labour." Thus, although it is a sin not to work, "'unemployment' is not necessarily an evil." "To be unemployed is not necessarily morally wrong" (3–6). The report goes on to devote three pages (9–11) to a summary of Major C. H. Douglas's theory of Social Credit as an alternative to both capitalism and socialism. After a widely publicized debate, the church assembly granted the commission's report an ambiguous acceptance in the second week of February 1935. Social Creditors followed these events with great interest; see the "Notes" of "Pontifex" in the *New English Weekly* 6, 17, 18 (7, 14 February 1935), 347–48, 366, and see also EP's "American Notes," *New English Weekly* 6, 24 (28 March 1935), 490, and "Towards Orthology," *New English Weekly* 6, 26 (11 April 1935), 534; rpt., *Ezra Pound's Poetry and Prose,* 6: 246, 247, 259, 275–76. T. S. Eliot, however, warned against reading too much into the assembly's acceptance of the commission's report; see "Douglas in the Church Assembly," *New English Weekly* 6, 18 (14 February 1935), 382–83.

Charlie Hughes. Charles Evans Hughes (1862–1948), chief justice of the United States Supreme Court (1930–1941).

28 March 1935   [C1175]

RE DURNO'S REMARKS ON EVAPORATED MYTHS

Wallace too soft to be any use. Tugwell always was Sat. Eve. Post
balony, and blah, no better than Moley.

Only way is to keep hammering on a few ideas so simple that
even the Chavezes will have to admit 'em in time.

Money is NOT a commodity.

Work is not a commodity.

More chance of educating Kingfish and Coughlin, than of
educating the "left wing new stealers"; what difference between
them and Upton?

Difference of age . . . yes . . .

Any information available re/ the attorney general?
(reactionary but not a crook?)

Ickes seems the only one of the cab. worth a damn.
How did HE get there?

Whatza use of peepul callin' 'emselves PROgressives and
then dishing up all the old stuff that has been proved nonsense
in England?

"All the unemployed will have WORK for 25 years."
—Sec. Perkins.

Everybody works but Perkins,
She sits round all day
A-sayin' what she can say.

All the old i-de-ahs
That grandpap layed away
In an attic trunk with mothballs,
Hooray! HOO-ray!
    Can you EAT it?

Work, work, work*,
    Can you eat it?
Work, work, work,
    Can you eat it?
She sits round all day.
Oh fry your work,
    Oh, boil it!
Oh serve it up with cheese!
Work, work, work,
    Can you wear it?
Oh FREEZE, gol darn you, freeze!

—EZRA POUND.
Rapallo, Italy

---

*Footnote: Work is not a commodity.

NOTES ON "EZ SEZ"

28 March 1935

Variants

(1) RE DURNO'S REMARKS ON EVAPO-
RATED MYTHS : Re/ Durno's remarks on
epaporated myths (2) Only way : ONLY way
(3) the Chavezes : the Chavez (4) what difference : what dif/ (5) of the cab. worth a
damn : of cab/ worth a god damn (6) use of
peepul : use peepul (7) old stuff : old crap
(8) that has been : that have been (9) "All
the unemployed : [from this point to the end
there is no surviving typescript]

DURNO. George Durno, columnist. See
Introduction to this chapter, p. 162 above.
Having perused "The National Whirligig" for
the period September 1934 through March
1935, we have been unable to discover a specific reference to "EVAPORATED MYTHS."
In a letter to Paul de Kruif, however, EP wrote:
"Have just read/ 'two myths evaporate. 1 consumer protection/ 2 that Wallace and Tugwell
have retained any power in new deal' " (Ezra
Pound to Paul de Kruif, 9 March 1935, Pound
Archive). The column often contained items,
including "inside information" and criticism,
about visible members of the Roosevelt administration. References to Wallace and
Moley appeared, for instance, on 25 February 1935, to Tugwell on 27 February, to Ickes
on 9 February, 23 February, 5 March, and 13
March.

Wallace. See note on Letter 33, p. 156.

Tugwell. Rexford Guy Tugwell, member
of FDR's "Brain Trust" (1932–33). See Introduction to this chapter, pp. 165–66 above.

Moley. Raymond Moley, chief member of
FDR's "Brain Trust," assistant secretary of
state to Cordell Hull. See Introduction to this
chapter, pp. 165–67 above.

the Chavezes. Dennis Chavez (1888–
1962); member Democratic National Committee (1933–1936); Democratic Representative

to Congress (1931–35); unsuccessful candidate for U.S. Senate vs. BC, 1934; appointed
U.S. Senator 11 May 1935, filling the vacancy
brought about by death of BC; reelected 1940,
1946, 1952, 1958, serving until his own
death. See Introduction to Chapter Three, p.
88 above.

Kingfish. Huey Long. See Introduction to
Chapter Three, pp. 93–94 above, and note
on Letter 33, p. 156 above. For an extended
treatment of Long and Coughlin, see Alan
Brinkley, *Voices of Protest: Huey Long, Father Coughlin, and the Great Depression* (New
York: Knopf, 1982).

Coughlin. See note on Letter 33, p. 156
above, and Introduction to Chapter Three, p.
91 above.

Upton. Upton Sinclair (1878–1968), social realist and political reformer. See Introduction to this chapter, pp. 173–77 above.

the attorney general. Homer S. Cumming
(1870–1956), attorney general, 1933–39. In
"American Notes," EP writes, "The only two
members of the cabinet deserving any respect,
as such, are Ickes and the Attorney General"
(*New English Weekly* 6, 24 [28 March 1935],
490; rpt., *Ezra Pound's Poetry and Prose*, 6:
259).

Ickes. Harold LeClaire Ickes (1874–
1952); secretary of the interior (1933–1946);
administrator of the Public Works Administration. See Introduction to this chapter, pp.
168–69 above.

Sec. Perkins. Frances Perkins (1880–
1965), secretary of labor (1933–1945). We
have been unable to locate the source of the
quotation EP attributes to her. The statement
may have been a party line among New Deal
relief reformers. Harry Hopkins, the Federal
Relief Administrator, said virtually the same
thing when he visited Paris in August 1934:
"America's unemployment crisis must be
solved by giving work to the unemployed for
the next 25 years. Estimates as to the number of unemployed today vary greatly, but I
should say that 10,000,000 represents a fairly
accurate figure" ("U. S. Jobless Get Jobs, Not
Dole, Says Harry L. Hopkins, Visiting Paris,"

Chicago Tribune [Paris], 15 August 1934, p. 1). In "Hickory—Old and New," after referring to his "valentine" for Perkins, Pound writes, "Work for 25 million peepul. And WHAT OF IT! Any damn fool can work. He can go out and start breakin' pavin' stone and taking up the street to put it down again. But it won't feed him or clothe him, or get him nice woolley coverlets, or them silk sheets that brother Howard Baer puts in his pictures" (*Esquire* 3, 6 [June 1935], 40; rpt., *Ezra Pound's Poetry and Prose* 6: 292). See Introduction to this chapter, p. 165 above.

Work, work, work. EP may be parodying Thomas Hood's "The Song of the Shirt," which employs repetition of the line "Work—work—work!" The poem, recounting the "enslavement" of a seamstress, contains passages such as the following:

'Work—work—work!
My labour never flags;
And what are its wages? A bed of straw,
A crust of bread—and rags.'

20 May 1935   [C1196]

There is no damder imbecility than trying to make work when people want food and clothing.

Any government not run by plain dam fols would make money.

The unemployed, and a great lot of people that aren't unemployed, want money.

Anything above the status of an ape knows that you can make money with a printing press, and that it is good just as long as there is something to back it.

You can back money with the hogs and grain, that Hank Wallace destroys. You can back money with anything that people want. You can even back it, to a limited extent with services. (We used street car tickets for small change in Toulouse during the armistice).

Anybody that lets Frankie kid 'em and Farley lead 'em any further up the garden lane, deserves to get work and not food.

Nothing makes me gladder than to hear the administration finds trouble in making work. Soon it won't need any work to make 'em trouble.

—EZRA POUND
Rapallo, Italy.

Notes on "Ez Sez"

20 May 1935

Variants

(1) damder imbecility : god damnder IMBECILITY (2) work : WORK (3) food : FOOD (4) [deleted after "clothing'] : A government that tries to make WORK deserves a rope. (5) Any government : A government (6) dam fools : god damn fools (7) make money : make MONEY (8) want money : want MONEY (9) it is good : it is GOOD (10) to back it : to BACK it (11) work and not food : WORK and not FOOD.

Hank Wallace. See note on Letter 33, p. 156 above.

Toulouse. The city served as the Pounds' home base for journeys to parts of France from May to September 1919.

Frankie. FDR.

Farley. See Introduction to Chapter Three, p. 86 above, Introduction to this chapter, pp. 167–68 above, and note on Letter 20, pp. 118–9 above.

24 May 1935 [C1199]

Can a man or a country borrow itself out of debt? Ask Me!

Ole Bill Yeats used to know a theosophist who always started teachin' his disciples that the world was hollow (spherical but hollow) and that we were living inside it. Once he got 'em to believe that, they'd believe anything whatever he told 'em.

Can a nation borrow itself out of debt?

There's a bright Chink general has just collected all the taxes in his district up till 1981. That at least isn't selling the children into slavery and making 'em responsible for the kussedness of their idiot fathers.

Can a nation borrow itself out of debt!!

"To keep up prices! Nuts!! Are prices paid in money?

What is money?

Are you folks going on paying 897 professors of economics who can't or won't tell you what money is? Who makes it? How does it get there?

Ever seen any paper money?

How much does it cost to make it?

Has the U. S. A. any credit?

If so why does it go out and rent it from blokes who haven't?

Several people have been asking that question. A congressman asked it a couple of months ago. Don't go and forget Mr. Goldsborough. That fellow is useful.

And what about Senator Bankhead? Speaking of radio transmission, it was three years, or was it two years ago, that Bankhead said something bright in the senate? And to think people go and forget it! To think some blinkin' expatriate has to go dig it up, and ask has anybody over there seen Bankhead (Tallulah's uncle, they tell me . . . but I haven't looked up his pedigree.) What became of th' fellow?

—EZRA POUND

NOTES ON "EZ SEZ"
24 May 1935

Variants

(1) Ask Me! : ASK ME! (2) was hollow : was a hollow (3) anything whatever he : anything he (4) Can a nation : CAN a nation (5) of debt : of DEBT (6) Can a nation : CAN a nation (7) "To keep up prices! Nuts!! : "To KEEPP UP PRICES" ! NUTS !! (8) or won't : or WONT (9) paper money : PAPER MONEY (10) Has the : HAS the (11) If so : IF SO (12) Don't go and forget : DONT GO AND FORGET (13) the senate : the Senate (14) there seen Bankhead : THERE heard of Bankhead (15) became : become.

a theosophist. We have been unable to identify the particular individual to whom EP refers. EP tells a somewhat similar anecdote about G. R. S. Mead in *Guide to Kulchur* (225–26).

a bright Chink general. We have been unable to locate the subject of this racist allusion.

Mr. Goldsborough. Congressman T. Alan Goldsborough. See Introduction to Chapter Three, p. 98 above, and note on Letter 24, p. 129 above. EP also praised the representative in "American Notes": "There are several honourable mentions awaiting spare space in this chronicle, but the FIRST place this week goes to Representative GOLDSBOROUGH for pointing out that 'the Government borrows from the bank, money it doesn't have, pays interest on the credit thus established on Government books in the banks' favour, and finally pays back to the bank money it never received'" (*New English Weekly* 7, 3 [2 May 1935], 45).

Senator Bankhead. John Hollis Bank-head; see Introduction to Chapter Three, pp. 96–97 above, and note 41, p. 244. In "A Matter of Modesty" Pound again "praised" Bankhead's prior efforts to pass a stamp–scrip bill and wondered what had happened to him: "Haz anybody here seen BANK-HEAD? An nif not, who told him to hide? Bet it wasn't Tallulah! 'Virgin huntress chaste and fair' or however that beautiful poEM runs. . . . That a man anna SenAtor from Allybarmer shd/have an idea, or shd/ emit an idea before it wuz worn out and chucked in the dust-bin is NOOZ to the rest of the continent . . ." (*Esquire* 3, 5 [May 1935], 31; rpt., *Ezra Pound's Poetry and Prose*, 6: 279).

Tallulah. Tallulah Bankhead (1903–1968), the actress. Her father was William Brockman Bankhead, Speaker of the House of Representatives and brother of John Hollis Bankhead II (EP's "Senator Bankhead"). She made her New York stage debut in 1918, her London debut in 1923. In February 1935 she began portraying Sadie Thompson in *Rain*, the first of her most memorable roles.

25 May 1935   [C1200]

Waaal I will hand it to Farley (Mr. Farley the secretary and
member of the cabinet). For two years I have thought Farley
was no dam good. I mean I listed him with Nic Butler, and
Andy Mellon and Herbie Hoover as people that would be more
use to their fellow citizens in a cannibal country than in an highly
industrialized one like our own, but Farley has proved one thing
(at least some of his colleagues have helped, but in the main it's
fatty Jim who has proved it). He has proved that the ONLY way for
a country to spend its money without boodling, pork-barreling and
undue favors to rather unpleasant citizens is BY A NATIONAL
DIVIDEND paid per capita, each citizen getting exactly the
same amount.

Now Jim has gone and been educative. He sure has put up an
unconscious fight for the national dividend.

Science goes on. But pore ole Upton just doesn't. Back in 1888
there wuz a lot of ideas, and back in 1898 there was a early model
of Oldsmobile. Do you use 'em?

Would you call a fellow a LEADER if he insisted in drivin' one
of them things?

For the past 15 years economic thought has gone on, just like
thought in any other study or science. Now wouldn't you think a
man who was setting himself up as a leader would try to find out
what had happened since he got out of knee breeches? Or do they
get that way out in Californy?

I'ma askin'.

—Ezra Pound

P.S.—Bronson Cutting could at least teach him something.

Rapallo, Italy

Notes on "Ez Sez"

25 May 1935

Variants

(1) no dam good : no damn good (2) as people : as animals (3) one like : nation like (4) undue favors to rather unpleasant citizens : bribery to influence next elections (5) [deleted after "amount"] : When I selct that list, I don't say that canibals are very choosy. Like gipsies they are supposed to be able to deal with lean meat and fat meat. I've long had a 84 cent reward for for any bright school boy or professor who can find any other use for those four men, AND Farley. (6) Science goes on : [In the typescripts, a new "Ez Sez" begins here; the *New Mexican* has combined two editorials into one.] (7) Do you : DO you (8) For the past 15 years : FOR 15 years (9) economic thought : ECONOMIC thought (10) since : SINCE.

Farley. James Farley, the postmaster general. See Introduction to Chapter Three, p. 86 above, note on Letter 20, pp. 118–19 above, and Introduction to this chapter, pp. 167–68 above.

Andy Mellon. See notes on Letters 16, 17, pp. 105 and 109 above. Andrew Mellon became ambassador to Great Britain in February 1932. He resigned in March 1933, shortly after FDR and the Democrats took control of the government.

Herbie Hoover. Herbert Clark Hoover (1874–1964), president of the U.S. (1929–1933). See Letter 9 above.

Upton. See "Ez Sez" for 28 March, and Introduction to this chapter, pp. 173–77 above. In his 1934 campaign for the governorship of California, Upton Sinclair proposed that the state take over defunct businesses and bankrupt farms, and reorganize them as cooperative enterprises run by unemployed workers. Furthermore, Sinclair proposed to abolish the tax on all incomes under five thousand dollars a year and to impose a tax of 50 percent on all incomes over fifty thousand dollars a year. Pound called for Sinclair to "modernize" his ideas in "$0.87 for Sinclair," among other places (*Chicago Tribune* [Paris], 16 April 1934, p. 5; rpt., *Ezra Pound's Poetry and Prose,* 6: 169).

28 May 1935   [C1201]

The appointment of Chavez just don't surprise him at all seein zwhoo run it.

But it dew seem zif a large segment of New Mexico opinion wd/ remain unrepresented in the upper chamber fer some years to come.

EZRA POUND.

Notes on "Ez Sez"
28 May 1935

Variants

(1) run it : dun it (2) [deleted after "come"]: Perhaps the rattlesnakes like it.

Chavez. See note on "Ez Sez" for 28 March, p. 190 above.

29 May 1935   [C1202]

Wot, he sez, interrogative, is Marriner Ec (however he spells it)
spekles gettin' a faint antelucanal glimmer of the risin' fact that
the nation has credit, and don't need to go out an' hire it from
Barney Baruch and his friends?

Marriner wot of the night?

Marriner, has Frank Vanderlipp heard you say that?

EZRA POUND.

Notes on "Ez Sez"
29 May 1935

Variants

(1) sez, interrogative, is : sez, is (2) nation :
NATION (3) has Frank : have Frank.

Marriner Ec. Marriner Stoddard Eccles
(1890–1977). See note on Letter 31, p. 148
above, and Introduction to this chapter, pp.
169–71 above.

Barney Baruch. See note on Letter 17,
p. 110 above.

Marriner wot of the night? EP here paraphrases Isaiah 21.11: "Watchman, what of
the night?"

Frank Vanderlipp. Frank Arthur
Vanderlip. See note on Letter 17, p. 109
above, and Introduction to this chapter, pp.
169–71 above.

The English hide is thicker than bull's hide, and the English skull
is resistant to a degree almost unknown outside the American
communist party, but brother Long, the Kingfish sure has got
under that hide.

Our English "cousins" (wot oh!) normally think America can sink
or swim, preferably sink, without England's worritin about it.

America is the home of Hollywood, and a place any half (note the
half) educated British meowler can go and take it off the palukas
by lecturin'. The half cooked soup of a English lecturer can get
money for in America, just would not get taken in if the bloke was
local. Violent examples keep cropping up in the fancy subjects.
An American university will let an englender tell it that water ain't
wet, that Quincy Adams never existed, a noted lecturer (from
England) completely forgot the war of 1812. (fergot" by courtesy,
he just never heard of the dam thing.)

The last case was in Florida. And we take it. It's only culture. So I
haff ter laff to see all the British bank-buzzard boys out a weepin'
over the kingfish. It ain't only the papers obviously run by the
London banks with offices in Noo York and the vice (NY) versa
(with, in London) offices that are weepin' one column tears, two
column tears by the barrel. Sez the "Times": Senator Huey Long's
"machinations."

Ain't that a lovely word. Mac-in-a-tions. Machination. Says the "Post" "sin-is-ter," it says Huey is "sinister," and it ain't only the London papers. I saw a long piece from way up in Yorkshire, where the relish gets its name from,

Kind of a Yorkshire relish for
My
Li'lle Yorkshi' Rose!

Telling what a danger is Huey

Of course I keep on suggestin' that they use more moderate langwidge. But its funny how tender the British beef heart has got all of a sudden for Mr. Baruch, Mr. Vanderlip, Mr. Mellon, whom they openarmedly received as ambassador when some folks wished he was home.

However, and this may be nooz, there wuz one tough paper that laughed like L when Huey got off that wise crack about "doin' a ramsey."

Devotedly Yourn

Ole EZ. P.

Notes on "Ez Sez"

1 June 1935

Variants

(1) Long : LONG (2) that hide : that HIDE (3) the half : the HALF (4) lecturin' : LECTURIN' (5) The half : Gheez, the half (6) soup of an English : soap a henglish (7) money : MONEY (8) would not get : would get (9) fergot" : "fergot (10) dam thing : damn thing (11) we : WE (12) [deleted after "take it."] : hell yes. (13) the British bank-buzzard : the bank=buzzard (14) weepin' : WEEPIN (15) It ain't : Gheez it ain't (16) obviously : OBviously (17) one column tears, two column tears : one column tears, half column tears, two column tears (18) "Times" : "TIMES" (19) "machinations" : "MACHINATIONS" (20) Machination : Machinations (21) "sinister" : "SINISTER" (22) relish gets : *relish* gets (23) relish for : relish FOR (24) my : MY (25) Huey : HUEY (26) nooz : NOOZ (27) like L : like hell (28) [deleted after "like L"] : I mean it was a paper where they know the British Slime Minister, they just lafft like hell.

brother Long. Huey Long; see Introduction to Chapter Three, pp. 93–94 above, note on Letter 33, p. 156 above, and Introduction to this chapter, p. 180 above.

a noted lecturer. We have been unable to identify this reference.

Quincy Adams. John Quincy Adams (1767–1848), sixth president of the United States (1825–29). *The Cantos* contains a number of allusions to him, with cantos 34 and 37 drawing on his diary. Pound's Adams was a proponent of free international commerce, an opponent of banks, the Bank, and speculation in paper currency. In *Guide to Kulchur,* Pound asserts that the "history of the United States was ill recorded. It now begins to emerge in historians already mentioned. Not only our American history but our literature in the correspondence of J. Adams, Jefferson, J. Q. Adams, Van Buren" (264). Continuing an assault on the blind-ness of historians and intellectuals in general, EP goes on to note, "Only in March 1937 had I got a man on the American communist fringe (not a party member but a Marxist) to notice that Quincy Adams was a communist (of a sort)" (265).

The last case was in Florida. We have been unable to identify the case.

Sez the "Times." We have not found the word "machinations" in any London *Times* report on Senator Long during the first half of 1935. In "An American Dictator: The Activities of Huey Long" (25 April 1935, p. 13), the *Times* speaks of his political machine but not specifically of machinations. The word "sinister" *is* used, however: "A further law provides that all deputy sheriffs must henceforth be approved by the State Bureau of Criminal Investigation before they can hold office. This body is the most sinister of all Huey Long's instruments."

Sez the "Post." In "'King Clown' Eyes the White House: Senator 'Huey' Long as Public Nightmare No. 1," *The Morning Post* correspondent Deny Smith writes: "The Administration have ceased to regard Huey Long as a clown who will some day trip over his own feet. They realise that he has become a sinister force which must be reckoned with" (11 April 1935, p. 12). EP responded to Smith's report in a letter to the editor entitled "Senator Long and Father Coughlin": "If the author of your article on Senator Long will perhaps withdraw the term 'sinister' from his remarks on the gentleman from Louisiana.... I am not offering Senator Long as a specialist in economics, but you might note that his programme contains nothing so blatantly idiotic as the idea that you can *borrow* yourself out of debt" (*The Morning Post,* 17 April 1935, p. 14; rpt., in *Ezra Pound's Poetry and Prose* 6: 277).

a long piece from way up in Yorkshire. This "piece" remains unidentified. It does not appear to have been a news report or editorial in any of the major Yorkshire newspapers.

Kind of a ... Yorkshi' Rose. EP quotes fairly accurately two lines from the music hall song "Yorkshire Girl," published in 1908 by C. W. Murphy and Dan Lipton. A version of the part of the song containing these lines appears in the "Wandering Rocks" chapter of Joyce's *Ulysses.* "Yorkshire relish" plays on the brand name of a kind of spicy sauce.

Mr. Baruch. See note on Letter 17, p. 110 above.

Mr. Vanderlip. Frank Arthur Vanderlip. See note on Letter 17, p. 109 above, and Introduction to this chapter, pp. 169–71 above.

Mr. Mellon. See notes on Letters 16, 17, pp. 105 and 109 above, and note on "Ez Sez" for 25 May, p. 197 above.

ramsey. Probably a reference to James Ramsay MacDonald, first Labour Party prime minister (1924) and head of a coalition cabinet in 1931–35.

3 June 1935   [C1210]

IF they has got all that money fer eddykashun, IZ they going
to buy any up to date tex books?

IZ eddykashun to be restricted to grammar and what Geo.
Washmtum said to the cherry tree, or are they goin' ter USE any
NEW BOOKS?

Pussnly I'd buy 'em a set of Douglas (C.H.) and pay Doc. Fack of
San Antonio (TexAS) for a new edition of the "Natural Economic
Order."

If the guvvymint is spendin' that money they might as well spend
it on something USEFUL. Hell! In my young days we was all
eddykated up IGGURUNT. We wuz told a lot of HOOEY and
none of the useful facts.

WHY not eddikate the kids to know that MONEY is largely
stamped paper, AND THAT A NATION CAN OWN ITS OWN
MONEY?

What's the harm in tellin' 'em that? Are you eddicatin yer kids,
or merely trying to bring them up in a fog, like we was riz up and
given DIPLoMAHS?

(Yes, I got degrees. Anyone WANT 'em?)

EZRA POUND
Rapallo, Italy

Notes on "Ez Sez"

3 June 1935

Variants

(1) they has got : the Gentleman from New Mexico has got (2) of HOOEY : of gol damn HOOEY (3) in a fog : in a gold damn fog (4) (Yes, I got : (Hell, yes, I got.

Douglas (C. H.). See Chapter One, pp. 6–7; notes on Letters 14, 19, 20, 24, pp. 77, 114, 118, and 129 above and Introduction to Chapter Three, p. 97 above.

Doc Fack. Dr. Hugo R. Fack, German-American who helped spread the word of Gesell in the United States, editing and publishing the official Gesellite organ, *The Way Out.* EP corresponded with him (Pound Archive and Charles Norman, *Ezra Pound* [London: Macdonald, 1969], 347). Fack founded the original Gesell group in New York in 1923, remaining a supporter even after some of the other members dropped out when Hitler rose to power in Germany. Investigated by the FBI, Fack "was shown to have compromised himself in correspondence with the Silver Shirts, an anti-Semitic group led by William Dudley Pelley, and proceedings were instituted against him in 1942 to revoke the citizenship granted him in 1931, but in 1946 he was still active, running a paper called *Freedom and Plenty*" (Mike Weaver, *William Carlos Williams: The American Background* [Cambridge: Cambridge University Press, 1971], 110). See also Introduction to Chapter Three, p. 91 above, and note on Letter 30, p. 147 above.

3 August 1935 [C1234]

CUTTING'S MIND WAS BEST IN THE SENATE

The man who wrote we have lost a President by the death of Bronson Cutting, may be a bit of an optimist. But it seems very probable that we lost the best mind in the senate.

I first came into correspondence with Cutting over a cultural question when he was dealing with the abominable Blease of South Carolina.

I also put it to men who knew Senator Cutting intimately that he had a clearer perception of economic fact than any other man in the senate, and that he was finally for Social Credit. That is, he saw the nation owns its own credit, and that the whole people should benefit by this fact, and that the whole people should be able to buy what the whole people produces.

I don't think he cared a bit more than I do what particular mechanism is used to that end; I think he had an equal contempt for criminals who are trying to sabotage honest effort to this goal, though he would doubtless have used gentler language, and had more compassion on average human slowness and stupidity.

Had he had time to leave us a farewell letter I have no doubt whatever that he would have left us this legacy and injunction:

1. To fight for a national dividend, paid from the nation's credit, and not collected by creation of interest bearing.

Or put it another way: To end poverty by use of congress' power to regulate the currency.

(There is time enough to debate the details. The first great move is to will a sane monetary and credit system.)

Gesell's criteria for what a monetary system should do are the same as the criteria of C.H. Douglas.

There is no man who could carry on this crusade with greater affection from the people than could Senator Hiram Johnson.

—EZRA POUND
Rapallo, Italy

Notes on "Ez Sez"

3 August 1935

Variants

(1) Blease of South Carolina : Bleese, the S. Carolina bully who was finally eliminated from the senate, for the good of his state and the nation. (2) for Social : FOR Social (3) saw the nation owns : SAW that the nations OWNS (4) the whole people should be able to buy : WHOLE PEOPLE shd. be able to BUY (5) end; I think he had : endm but I think he has (6) interest bearing. : interest bearing debt. (7) to will : to WILL (8) for what : for WHAT.

Blease. See Chapter One, pp. 18–19, and notes on Letters 1, 7, pp. 39 and 53 above.

Gesell. See Introduction to Chapter Three, p. 96, and notes on Letters 16, 27, pp. 105 and 139 above.

C. H. Douglas. See Chapter One, pp. 6–7; notes on Letters 14, 19, 20, 24, pp. 77, 114, 118, and 129 above, and Introduction to Chapter Three, p. 97 above.

Senator Hiram Johnson. See note on Letter 2, p. 41 above.

5 August 1935   [C1235]

He sez: "Gee ! !—why can't you home folks like intelligence when it grows like lilacs RIGHT in your door yard.

Ain't it funny that I have to tell his neighbors about Mr. Bannister. Lives out in Californy (with woodentop Upton) and of course SOME of the neighbors know their once postmaster wrote a book. And now here I am readin' it right in the historic background, these lovely Venetian sunsets. Waal, brother Bannister sez (a book called WHEN we git Scientific and he had, nacherly to print himself) he sez:

"Ef the post office system was as loony as the FYnancial system, we wd. have to be building great store houses to hold undelivered mail."

That's TALKIN'.

He sez this here financial system "exists to create INTEREST BEARING DEBT."

That's talkin. Brother Bannister didn't have to go to a library to be told economics by a hired and endowed nitwit. He looked at the postage STAMP.

EZRA POUND
Rapallo, Italy

Notes on "Ez Sez"

5 August 1935

Variants

(1) "Gee : GHEES (2) why can't : why don't (3) background, these lovely Venetian sunsets : background (4) as the FYnancial : as the god damn (I putt that in) FYnancial (5) library : liary.

lilacs RIGHT in your door yard. A somewhat odd allusion to Walt Whitman's dirge for Lincoln, "When Lilacs Last in the Dooryard Bloom'd."

brother Bannister sez. Louis Herbert Bannister, postmaster at Al Tahoe, California, for almost fourteen years. EP is citing his *When We Become Scientific: This book gives the cause of financial panics, and offers a Scientific Remedy* (Pasadena, Calif.: L. H. Bannister, 1933). See Introduction to this chapter, pp. 177–79 above.

Upton. Upton Sinclair. See notes on "Ez Sez" for 28 March, 25 May, pp. 190 and 197 above, and Introduction to this chapter, pp. 173–77 above.

8 August 1935 [C1236]

This IS the nex. episll. An if any of you friends remember like how I told the wealthy readers of Brother Gingrich's paper ESquire how ole Upton went down to Washington and got TRUSTful, you will be pleased to hear that this is a Californian habit. I hear another bright lad from Frisco or them parts seen the Presumdent, and everything was just plush and velvet and the president don't like them bad bankers, and wants all sweetness and light.

Waaal, I HOPE, my hope of land and glory, I hope that bloke understands Franklin better'n I do.

I WOULD like to see Franklin run straight fer the people, and plug fer a honest dollar issued against the REAL resources of the country, NOT against some buzzard's monopoly. And I would like to see CONGRESS wake up and run straight and USE ITS CONSTITUTIONAL right to control the currency FOR THE PEOPLE.

And nothing was ever as wobbly as GOLD or any other damn metal measured BY what people eat.

EZRA POUND.
Rapallo, Italy

Notes on "Ez Sez"
8 August 1935

Variants

(1) This IS : This iz (2) readers : reader (3) I WOULD : Cause bi Xt I WOULD.

This IS the nex. episll. EP alludes to the New Testament epistles of Paul, casting himself as an apostle to the American people.

Brother Gingrich's paper ESquire. Arnold Gingrich was editor of *Esquire.* EP refers to the five articles he contributed to the magazine in 1935. See Introduction to this chapter, p. 162 above.

how ole Upton went down. The reference is to Upton Sinclair's visit to Washington in September 1934. See Introduction to this chapter, pp. 175–76 above.

13 August 1935   [C1238]

Speakin' of the culchurl HERITAGE there iz a lot of honest men
writin' horse sense about MONEY. Just as there is a lot of shifty
palukas trying to keep the public from thinking about this subject.

The trype you git in your highbrow muggyzeens is ter nauseate.

If you had sense and WANTED to know, you wd. read C. H.
Douglas and S. Gesell. And if you wanted to know more there
is Stan Nott (69 Grafton St., London W. 1.) printin' a series of
intelligent booklets. AND there is the Social Credit Secretariat,
163 a. Strand, London W. C. 2 printin' books and a paper, and
there is the New English Weekly, where yr. deevoted svt. writes
early and often, and there is New Democracy in N. Yok and
Controversy in Kallyforny, all a pourin' out the true doctrine
(with no end of famly rows, rucktions and backbiting, but tellin' it
all the same) and Johnnie Hargrave leadin' his Troops and callin'
LLard George and Norman a pair of uncrusted liars.

And there is Jeff Mark, and McNair Wilson, and there is M.
Colbourne and Mont Webb, and a few more all a puttin' down
chapter and verse and makin the hired purrfessors look more
and more silly every day every hour.

And WHEN is the American intelligensiariat going to set up
and take notice.

—EZRA POUND
Rapallo, Italy.

Notes on "Ez Sez"

13 August 1935

Variants

(1) of shifty : of god damn shifty (2) The trype : Jheez. the trype (3) muggyzeens : muggyzeen (4) Colbourne and Mont Webb, and a few : Colboure and a few (5) purrfessors : purrfessor (6) more silly : more god damn silly.

C. H. Douglas. See Chapter One, pp. 6–7; notes on Letters 14, 19, 20, 24, pp. 77, 114, 118, and 129 above, and Introduction to Chapter Three, p. 97 above.

S. Gesell. See Introduction to Chapter Three, p. 96 above, and notes on Letters 16, 27, pp. 105 and 139 above.

Stan Nott. Stanley Nott, Ltd., London publisher of numerous Social Credit works, as well as EP's *Alfred Venison's Poems* (1935), *Social Credit: An Impact* (1935), and the English editions of his *Jefferson and/or Mussolini* (1935) and *Ta Hio: The Great Learning* (1936). See entry on M. Colbourne below.

Social Credit Secretariat. In June 1934, C. H. Douglas became chairman of this recently created English organization. Within two years, most Social Credit supporters had turned their backs on him and the secretariat in disagreement with, and response to the failure of, his tactics. In 1938 an ineffective attempt was made to reform the secretariat, which by then had fallen into a state of near total disunity. See Gorham Munson, *Aladdin's Lamp: The Wealth of the American People* (New York: Creative Age Press, 1945), 202–7.

New English Weekly. Publication founded by A. R. Orage. EP's "American Notes" ran in it from January 1935 to April 1936. See note on Letter 21, p. 122 above.

New Democracy. Review founded in 1934 by American supporters of Douglas and Social Credit. In addition to publishing pieces on economics by such notables as EP and William Carlos Williams, "it also

gave space to James Laughlin's first editorial efforts; *New Directions* was born in the pages of *New Democracy* and so named by Munson" (Mike Weaver, *William Carlos Williams: The American Background* [Cambridge: Cambridge University Press, 1971], 104). See note on Letter 20, p. 119 above.

Controversy. A periodical founded in Carmel, California, by Colonel H. L. Mack. See Introduction to this chapter, pp. 179–80 above.

Hargrave. John Hargrave (1894–1982), novelist, cartoonist, inventor, soldier, and most prominent Social Credit advocate in Britain. The leader of the Social Credit party of Great Britain (earlier called the "Green Shirt Movement for Social Credit"), he proposed that Social Credit could become the "Third Resolvent Factor" to the "Left-Right Conflict." As a tactician, he was more effective and militant than Douglas, with whom he broke in 1938. He and EP engaged in a colorful and fruitful correspondence, but it ended in 1939 because Hargrave could not tolerate EP's involvement with fascism and Mussolini. See Munson, *Aladdin's Lamp,* 198–201, 206–9, and Wendy Stallard Flory, *The American Ezra Pound* (New Haven: Yale University Press, 1989), 73–78, 112–13.

Llard George. David Lloyd George (1863–1945), First Earl of Dwyfor; Member of Parliament 1890–1944; prime minister 1916–1922; one of the "Big Four" at the 1919 Paris Peace Conference. In 1931 Lloyd George had broken with the Liberal party, refusing to join the party leadership in supporting Ramsay MacDonald's programs. In January 1935, Lloyd George attempted a political comeback by devising a plan for recovering from the Depression. His proposals were rejected by the government, but Lloyd George was harshly criticized by radicals and young Liberals for allegedly selling out to the Tories.

Norman. Montagu Collet Norman, governor of the Bank of England. See note on Letter 21, p. 122 above.

Jeff Mark. Jeffrey Mark was author of *The Modern Idolatry* (London: Chatto and

Windus, 1934), of *Analysis of Usury* (London: J. M. Dent and Sons, 1935), and, with J. Madison Hewlett, of *Where Is the Money to Come From? With an Account of the Monetary Experiments of Guernsey, Schwanenkuchen, and Wörgl* (London: Free-Economy Federation of Great Britain, 1931). In his review of *The Modern Idolatry*, R. L. Northridge argues that the book confirms the principles of Social Credit, even though its author explicitly disagrees with Major Douglas (*New English Weekly* 6, 15 [24 January 1935], 316–17).

McNair Wilson. Robert McNair Wilson; see note on Letter 28, p. 142 above.

M. Colbourne. Maurice Colbourne was author of *Economic Nationalism* (London: Figurehead, 1933), later revised as *The Meaning of Social Credit* (London: Figurehead, 1935), and of *The Sanity of Social Credit* (London: Stanley Nott, 1935), one of a series entitled "Pamphlets on the New Economics." The pamphlet was reviewed by Montgomery Butchart in the *New English Weekly* 7, 17 (5 September 1935), 335–36.

Mont Webb. Sir Montague de Pomeroy Webb was the author of *India's Plight*, 5th ed. (London: P. S. King and Son, 1934), a study of the economic situation in India, with special reference to the currency problem. In a letter of 28 April 1935 to e. e. cummings, EP writes, "Sir. Monty Webb is quotin me in free silver paper in Karachi" (Pound Archive).

NOTES ON "EZ SEZ"

14 August 1935

Variants

(1) git aboard : git about.

father Coughlin. See note on Letter 33, p. 156 above, and Introduction to Chapter Three, p. 91 above.

Huey. Huey Long; see Introduction to Chapter Three, pp. 93–94 above, note on Letter 33, p. 156 above, and note on "Ez Sez" for 1 June 1935.

Frank. FDR.

Douglas or Gesell. For C. H. Douglas, see Chapter One, pp.. 6–7, notes on Letters 14, 19, 20, 24, pp. 77, 114, 118, and 129 above, and Introduction to Chapter Three, p. 97 above; for Silvio Gesell, Introduction to Chapter Three, p. 96 above, and notes on Letters 16, 27 pp. 105 and 139 above.

Bankhead. See Introduction to Chapter Three, pp. 96–97 above, note 41 on p. 244 below, and note on "Ez Sez" for 24 May 1935.

14 August 1935   [C1239]

SURE, I read father Coughlin. He knows more. I mean more'n he did, but not quite enough. Not YET.

An' I hear about Huey, who is up a tree since Frank said: "Yes, of Course."

Not meanin' a word of it, but allowin' it wd. kid the troops along during the hot spell.

Waal, Huey, you now ain't got nowhere to go save SANE and decent and up to date economics. Douglas or Gesell or a tasty blend of the two of 'em.

Frankie has caught you up and said: "TAG." You got to move on out into real economics. None of this cut up the cow to increase the milk supply hooey.

You're a gone coon, Huey, unless you git aboard NATIONAL DIVIDEND.

Putt on a nice bright Saturday morning smile and run over to see brother Bankhead.

EZRA POUND.
Rapallo, Italy.

16 August 1935   [C1240]

About that party Bronson Cutting gave for Douglas (Maj. C.H. Douglas, the author of Social Credit) I may know a few things that weren't apparent even to the Senators who attended the party, in as much as I had been in correspondence with Senator Cutting about Social Credit, and that he wrote me after the party.

Firstly he had intended to introduce Douglas to the most intelligent men in Washington. Secondly, he and Douglas had never met before. Thirdly, Cutting was indubitably disappointed with results which were no one's fault. Douglas did not put it over.

Will the kind reader stop and remember that when Britons aren't bumptious they are bashful, and that a Scot is six times as "reserved" as an Englishman.

Douglas is highly human and has a devastating sense of humour which he is much too Scotch to trot out as prelude. He is also an engineer. Douglas, if I know anything about him after sixteen years friendship, expected people to ask him questions. All this occurred before the senators and congressmen were ready to ask him any questions.

Cutting was full of enthusiasm. Social Credit is worth enthusiasm. Some people still have it after 16 years ramming their effort against very thick barriers of stupidity. Douglas still has it. It don't Moley. No one in his wildest frenzy cd. call Doug. a back-slapper. He has, after all, stood solid for certain kinds of honesty for a long time.

The only man who ever cracked a joke about this was Ed. Dulac, who said: "Douglas? I thought that meant Fair Banks."

The fact that Doug didn't rush in and sell the idea to the gentlemen present may be regrettable. It may have preserved a whale of a lot of poverty for months longer than there is any real need for, but it is emphatically NOT a bad mark against the root idea that the WHOLE PEOPLE SHOULD BE ABLE TO BUY WHAT THE WHOLE PEOPLE PRODUCES.

In my next billy I shall turn my mind to a difference between stable governments.

EZRA POUND.
Rapallo, Italy.

Footnote. Every factory, every big manufacturing concern CREATES PRICES FASTER than it emits (distributes) the power to buy. Look it up in Dexter Kimball, look at the books of ANY going concern. That being so, how CAN the aggregate of production under the present system of credit (creation of usury bearing debts) ever give the WHOLE people, enough cash and credit to buy what the whole people produces? Cutting began thinking about that several years ago. Try a think on your own.

Notes on "Ez Sez"

16 August 1935

Variants

(1) Secondly, he : Secondly that he (2) Thirdly, Cutting : Thirdly, that Cutting (3) to ask him any : to ask any (4) Social Credit : After all Social Credit (5) 16 years : 86 years (6) it. It don't : it, but its not Tigwell bally hoo. It dont (7) [deleted after "time"] : Good wine needs no bush.

that party. The reception BC held for C. H. Douglas in Washington in the spring of 1934. Douglas had already visited Australia, New Zealand, and Alberta and Ottawa, Canada, and in April he had delivered a speech at the New School for Social Research in New York (Munson, *Aladdin's Lamp,* 202). See Introduction to Chapter Three, p. 101, and notes on Letters 14, 20, and 24. Many found Douglas uninspiring in person and a less than astute and dynamic leader. In the opinion of Munson, for example, "Douglas turned out to have neither the psychological insight nor the finesse in dealing with men that are required to forge a human instrument for working a political miracle.... instead of arousing the zeal of his followers, his methods caused resentment and discouragement" (202). See section on "Bro. Aberhart," Introduction to this chapter, pp. 171–72 above.

after 16 years. Pound first encountered C. H. Douglas in the London offices of *New Age* and was converted to Social Credit in 1919–20.

Moley. Raymond Moley, member of FDR's "Brain Trust." See Introduction to this chapter, pp. 165–67 above.

Ed. Dulac. Edmund Dulac (1882–1953), French illustrator and painter. He and EP had been neighbors in Kensington, and he had designed the masks and costumes for W. B. Yeats's *At the Hawk's Well.* (See Humphrey Carpenter, *A Serious Character: The Life of Ezra Pound* [Boston:

Houghton Mifflin, 1988], 307–8.) EP makes several anecdotal references to him in Canto 80.

Fair Banks. Douglas Fairbanks, Sr. (1883–1939), swashbuckling star of such films as *The Mark of Zorro, The Three Musketeers,* and *The Thief of Bagdad.*

Dexter Kimball. American engineer; see note on Letter 9, p. 60 above.

Notes on "Ez Sez"

17 August 1935

Variants

(1) Even in : Gheew even in (2) down a rope ladder : down on a rope ladder (3) work? He : work. Gheez. He (4) EZRA POUND : sez EZ.

Father Coughlin. See note on Letter 33, p. 156 above, and Introduction to Chapter Three, p. 91 above.

Eben Selters. We have been unable to identify this individual. Perhaps the anecdote was related to EP by his paternal grandfather, Thaddeus Coleman Pound.

17 August 1935   [C1241]

SEEreeYously DID any of you fellows ever buy a necktie or pants
with a piece of WORK? Cause I didn't, when I go into a
habbydashy and want a shirt or a undervest I have to pay MONEY.

I want peepul to think about this. Father Coughlin got round to it
after a while. Even in grandpap's time they had ways of makin'
more work, there was Eben Selters, he tuk the chain offn the well
bucket and used to crawl down a rope ladder fer every bucket of
water.

Aint that a good way to make work? He put in many an hour of
work in that well hole.

EZRA POUND.
Rapallo, Italy.

Thur is a kenukk been rootin round. Kenukk by th' name of
Butchart, an he dug up the Nevady archives an' found trail ov a
bloke named STEWART (W. M.) anybody here seen STEWART,
I mean anybody old enough in New Mexico to remember Senator
Stewart? And if not, WHY not?

"Justice between debtor and creditor" wrote Stewart "and equal
opportunities for all, are only obtainable by a volume of money
which will always be SUFFICIENT in QUANTITY to bear a
constant or stable relation between ALL the property for sale
and all the money in circulation."

Waal naow, I might ha' wrote thet myself.

"IF production is not checked by contraction, the surplus over
consumption will add enormously to the general wealth of the
nation."

"The contention that an adequate supply of money promotes
internal trade and stimulates business at home, has never been
successfully questioned."

"An inadequate supply of MONEY retards production and adds
to its cost, while an adequate supply of money adds to production
and reduces the expense."

Course nobuddy in Noo Mexico ever looked to see sense in
Nevady. BUT why in the sam hill when it HAPPENS, don't
some bright gheezer lamp it?

Goll DRAT it, the murkn peepul spends millyums a year on eddykashun and don't never learn nothin' useful. When BUTCH takes the trouble to PUTT the solid horse sense of three centuries into a book called MONEY, why don't the school people USE IT?

Here bigob is a book by a man what is so modest he don't write but a two page preface he just goes ahead and putts down what Hume said, what Berkeley, Swift, Ricardo, Stuart Mill, Locke, Solly, Cobbett, and 170 hard headed practical men have SEEN as hard facts of sane economics. That book ought to be in the SCHOOLS. Why don't you putt it in YOUR schools, without waitin' fer Noo York nitwits to run before you.

AND git over the idea that Bro. Aberhart is a feather head, and dig down into Butchart.

Call this a buk review if you like to. The book is printed by Stan Nott (69 Grafton St. London W. 1., which is over in England. If the Noo York publishers wd. rake the hair oil out of their whiskers there might be a U. S. edition.

EZRA POUND

Notes on "Ez Sez"

4 October 1935

Variants

(1) SUFFICIENT in QUANTITY : sufficient in quantity (2) When BUTCH : Why the hell when BUTCH (3) to run before you : to preced you (4) AND git : Git (5) EZRA POUND : yrz EZ P'O.

kenukk. Canadian.

Butchart, STEWART (W. M.). In his anthology *Money: Selected Passages Presenting the Concepts of Money in the English Tradition 1640–1935* (London: Stanley Nott, 1935), Montgomery Butchart includes five pages of excerpts from W. M. Stewart's *Analysis of the Functions of Money* (1898). The four passages quoted by EP occur on pp. 280, 280, 281–82, and 282, respectively; the capitalizations are EP's. William Morris Stewart (1827–1909) was a Republican senator from Nevada (1864–1875, 1887–1905).

two page preface. In the preface to *Money*, Butchart thanks "Ezra Pound, who first aroused my interest in economics and whose suggestions have been a constant provocation to clarity" (5). The book also contains an introduction, in which Butchart suggests that if the passages he has chosen for inclusion "illustrate anything it is the broad and negative thesis that in the history of English writings on the nature and function of money there has been from earliest times to the present no observable advance" (17). In a bibliographical note at the end, he guides the reader to *History of Monetary Systems* (1903) and *Money and Civilization* (1886) by Alexander Del Mar, whose works figure prominently in EP's later Cantos.

Hume. David Hume (1711–1776), Scottish philosopher and historian. An empiricist and skepticist, Hume was an opponent of mercantilism. He produced, among other works, *A Treatise of Human Nature* (1737–40) and *An Enquiry Concerning Human Understanding* (1748), the former later influencing the ideas of Adam Smith. In *Money,* Butchart presents excerpts from *Political Discourses* (1752).

Berkeley. George Berkeley (1685?–1753), Irish bishop and philosopher; best known for his arguments denying the existence of material objects. In addition to more strictly philosophical works, he published *The Querist* (1735–37), a consideration of social and economic reforms. Butchart reprints a passage from the 1750 edition of that work.

Swift. Jonathan Swift (1667–1745), English clergyman and satirist, born in Dublin; author of many pamphlets on economic and political topics, including "A Proposal for the Universal Use of Irish Manufacture" (1720) and "A Modest Proposal" (1729). *Money* contains a short selection from one of his contributions to *The Examiner* (1710).

Ricardo. David Ricardo (1772–1823), English economist, born of Dutch-Jewish parents; author of *On the Principles of Political Economy and Taxation* (1817). Butchart's book includes several passages from his *Works.*

Stuart Mill. John Stuart Mill (1806–1873), English philosopher and economist. Although he later modified his views, Mill early on embraced Benthamism, founding the Utilitarian Society and editing Bentham's *Treatise upon Evidence.* His writings include *Utilitarianism* (1861) and *Principles of Political Economy* (1848), the work excerpted in *Money.*

Locke. John Locke (1632–1704), English philosopher, father of modern empiricism and philosophical liberalism. In addition to *Essay concerning Human Understanding* (1690) and *Treatises on Government* (1690), he produced works on interest rates and the value of money. Butchart provides part of Locke's "Letter to W. Molyneaux, 16 November, 1695" and "Some Considerations of the Consequences of the Lowering of Interests and Raising the Value of Money" (1692).

Solly. Edward Solly (of Curzon Street), London economist. Butchart supplies passages from Solly's "On Free Trade, in Relation to the Present Distress" (1830), "The Present Distress, in Relation to the Theory of Money" (1830), and "Considerations on Political Economy" (1821). Solly also authored "On the Mutual Relations of Trade and Manufacture" (1855).

Cobbett. William Cobbett (1763–1835), self-educated English activist, exiled to America for a period to avoid prosecution for theft. Cobbett became increasingly radical with time, founding *Cobbett's Political Register* and publishing *The Life and Adventures of Peter Porcupine* (1796) and numerous works on economics, including *Paper against Gold* (1815), from which Butchart extracts two brief passages.

Bro. Aberhart. William Aberhart (1878–1943), Canadian politician, schoolteacher, and radio evangelist, premier of Alberta, 1935–43 (died in office). See Introduction to this chapter, pp. 171–72 above.

Stan Nott. See note on "Ez Sez," 13 August 1935, above.

16 July [1935?]

319 San Gregorio
VENEZIA
Italy

Edit. S.F. N.MeXN.

Sorr: this is Private.

I have it straight that B.C. was ready to push social credit and to finance campaign.

I may take this more seriously than you do. I honestly think I cd. help IF I cd. break into syndicate (any syndicate)

no use my repeating and repeating. There is a limit to my energy.

I'll cooperate, or take advice whenever I get it.

:: there was slow up in *S.F.N.M.*, I mean a whole month has just reached me here in one packet.

[May 1935?]

BRONSON CUTTING, IN MEMORIAM

Senator Cutting's death at this time is fatal in the sense that it
was result of sudden calamity, fatal in the sense that it must have
results beyond anyone's power to foresee for the moment.

It throws increased weight on every man in American public life
who cares a damn for honest money, for honest monetary reform.
It throws double weight on every senator or representative who
looked forward to a third party as a means to this end.

The senate is not rich in men who read the classics for pleasure,
in men who have minds sufficiently multifarious to bridge the gap
from Huey to Borah. Who indeed can NOW get any real economic
light in to the Kingfish?

It might be noted that Cutting resisted the New Deal ballyhoo
from the start. He wanted a real eagle, not a blue one. Costigan,
Wagner, Wheeler, who will take over the leadership, meaning the
intellectual economic leadership of the senate if that term have
any reality? In the House: Kvale; Goldsborough, Zioncheck, D. J.
Lewis of Maryland, heaven knows it is a small enough nucleus.

5

The Senator and the Poet

The correspondence of Cutting and Pound illuminates the careers of both men. The interests of each provide an unusual perspective upon those of the other. The senator's cultural concerns and his leadership on national economic and cultural issues loom larger in his communications with the poet than they might in another context. By the same token, the poet's political advocacy seems less eccentric, in the context of his communications with the senator, than it might if viewed in isolation. The more one learns about the complex and fascinating figure of Cutting, the more difficult it is to understand why he has not attracted more attention from biographers and historians of the American Progressive movement. The more one learns about Pound's positions on the issues of the day, the more difficult it is to dismiss them as bizarre, unpatriotic, or ignorant.

I
A Neglected Senator

The name of Bronson M. Cutting deserves a more prominent place than it usually finds on the honor roll of American Progressive leaders. To be sure, Cutting was less visible and less active than some of his colleagues, such as Senators Borah, Norris, LaFollette, and Johnson. Yet he exercised bold initiatives on selected issues and was widely considered to be one of the most able and promising young men in Washington. The first full-scale biography of him, Richard Lowitt's *Bronson M. Cutting: Progressive Politician* (1992), shows him to be a complex and fascinating figure, who amply rewards investigation.

In that biography, Lowitt stresses the New Mexican aspects of Cutting's work: his electoral battles against the Republican old guard, his sustained and successful effort to bring Hispanic voters into the political process, his efforts on behalf of veterans and underprivileged citizens in his adopted state. His correspondence with Pound complements this emphasis by highlighting Cutting's activities on the national scene: his leadership on cultural issues such as customs and postal censorship and his advocacy of federal relief and welfare measures to alleviate the effects of the Depression. From

Pound's vantage point, the reforms Cutting sought in Washington were even more important than those he tried to bring about in Santa Fe.

In Washington, Cutting first identified himself with the venerable Progressive cause of electoral reform. Born into a patrician tradition of *noblesse oblige*, he later came to support a number of measures to help the poor and the powerless, including veterans' benefits, old-age pensions, the regulation of child labor, unemployment compensation, and federal support for public education in rural districts. A distributionist in economics, Cutting favored public works, a shorter working day, and the nationalization of the banking industry. In foreign policy, he cosponsored the bill for Philippine independence and advocated the diplomatic recognition of the Soviet Union. Although he endorsed Franklin D. Roosevelt for the presidency in 1932, by 1934–35 Cutting's program had many points in common with the programs of other dissenters from the New Deal, among them the Social Creditors with whom Pound was also affiliated.

Above all, Cutting carved a special niche for himself as a national champion of Progressive cultural reforms, such as the elimination of federal censorship regulations and the adherence of the United States to the international copyright convention. He became the principal congressional spokesman for artists, writers, editors, and educators throughout the country, and he acquired the reputation of being the best educated, most cultivated member of the nation's legislature. A political cartoon of the time reflects the popular conception of Cutting as an intellectual leader. The caricature shows him reading a large book in preparation for a speech on the Senate floor, and the caption reads, "Bronson Cutting, U.S. Senator from New Mexico, goes in for heavy literature. While most of his colleagues are content to quote from a leaflet or a clipping, Senator Cutting selects a tome which would challenge a weight lifter."

Cutting's heavyweight reputation for Progressive leadership on cultural issues first prompted Pound to contact him. Cutting had already demonstrated his receptivity to the concerns of artists by attacking customs censorship at the instigation of his friends in the Witter Bynner circle. He responded to Pound's overtures by entrusting him with a potentially sensitive list of senators' names. Although their correspondence was clearly more important to the poet than to the senator, Cutting nevertheless valued it enough to continue it for four and a half years.

Syndicated caricature of Senator Cutting by Malone, April 1934.

He did so not because he was indulging the whims of an eminent crank but because he, too, benefited from the exchange. To begin with, he could number a major American poet among his correspondents. He answered Pound's letters in a collegial manner and spoke respectfully of Pound in at least one letter to a third party. In a major foreign policy speech, Cutting used a quotation provided by Pound, and he almost certainly read some of the Social Credit tracts that Pound recommended to him. He was sympathetic to many aspects of Social Credit thought, hosted C. H. Douglas in Washington, and opened the editorial columns of his newspaper to the Douglasite pronouncements of "Ez Sez." In these ways Cutting, like other prominent men in Washington during the early 1930s, granted Pound's views a respectful hearing.

II
A MISJUDGED POET

Viewed in the context of his correspondences with Cutting and others, Pound's politics look far less eccentric, unpatriotic, and uninformed than they can seem when viewed in isolation. In an era of crisis, the American public was willing to entertain a wide variety of experimental solutions. Many of the measures Pound supported were well within the pale of national debate. Stamp scrip, national dividends, the shorter working day, and governmental control of banking, all had influential sponsors in Washington and were pending before the Congress as concrete legislative proposals. Given the nature and scope of discussion at the time, Pound's program seemed no more radical and no less patriotic than many others.

Nor was Pound perceived as a fascist crackpot or anti-Semite by those with whom he corresponded in Washington in the early 1930s. Cutting and others did not refuse to answer Pound's letters, nor did they treat him as an obsessive nuisance.[1] He was regarded in congressional offices as a concerned American citizen lobbying for the good, not of a foreign power but of his native country. His goal—a healthy society, in which life's material and cultural goods circulate freely within a mixed economy guided by political leaders who keep the public interest clearly in view—was shared by many Americans. Pound may have seemed naive and quixotic in believing that he could influence national policy by post from Rapallo; but no one, at this stage, saw him as unpatriotic or demented.

Another common judgment about Pound is that, having lived in Europe since 1908, he was out of touch with American political reality. This conclusion, too, needs revision in the light of the writings in the present volume. His correspondence with Cutting and the "Ez Sez" editorials suggest that, on the contrary, Pound was remarkably well informed about events in the American capital. He could discuss legislation pending before the Congress, the doings of individual congressmen and cabinet members, and the activities of lobbies and pressure groups. He stayed abreast of stateside developments by means of his personal contacts with visitors, his extensive transatlantic correspondence, and his assiduous reading of periodicals available to Americans living abroad. Second-hand reports are no substitute for being on the spot, to be sure; but they helped Pound to maintain at least a partial contact with the trends and moods of his native land.

Of the channels open to him, newspapers and reviews were probably the most important. Pound's letters to Cutting and his "Ez Sez" pieces cite a variety of journals as sources of current political information. He appears to have had reasonably regular access to the following American periodicals: the Paris editions of the *New York Herald* and the *Chicago Tribune*, the New York *World*, the Santa Fe *New Mexican*, the *Congressional Record*, the *Saturday Evening Post*, the *New Republic, Esquire, New Democracy*, and *Controversy*. His British sources included the *Times*, the *Morning Post*, the *New English Weekly*, and *Criterion*. He also read a number of Italian publications; his letters to Cutting mention the *Corriere della Sera, Lavoro, Critica Fascista*, and *Civiltà Fascista*. From his correspondence with Representative Tinkham of Massachusetts, we know that he saw several French newspapers as well, including *Le Temps* and *Le Matin*.[2] Deeply engaged with current events, Pound evidently devoted a significant portion of his resources to maintaining a network of information about the countries he cared for outside Italy.

Pound, then, had knowledgeable suggestions to make about a variety of issues. With some of these suggestions, Senator Cutting agreed wholeheartedly. In Cutting, Pound thought he had found a Social Credit leader of presidential caliber, who might run against Roosevelt in 1936 as a Republican or a third-party candidate and, if elected, heed advice from Rapallo. "I should like to see you go to the White House," Pound told the senator quite frankly (9 October 1931).[3] These hopes made Cutting's sudden death in the air crash of 6 May 1935 all the harder to take. The event had both personal and political repercussions upon Pound's life.

Not since the young French sculptor Henri Gaudier-Brzeska was shot in the trenches of France in 1915 had a death affected Pound as Cutting's did. High hopes of a cultural renaissance perished with both victims. Pound's first attempt at an obituary on Cutting stammered badly.

> Senator Cutting's death at this time is fatal in the sense that it was result of sudden calamity, fatal in the sense that it must have results beyond anyone's power to foresee for the moment.[4]

A few weeks later, blind shock had given way to bitter rage. Pound was more articulate but scarcely more coherent.

> The sadists and the men so in conceit with their own inherited ideas that they would rather preserve them than interfere with the malnutrition of the public, can rejoice in Senator Cutting's death.[5]

It was hard to know whom to blame.

For a few months, as we have seen, Huey Long replaced Cutting as Pound's principal candidate for a Social Credit president. But Long's assassination in September 1935 produced a vacuum of leadership. "The senate . . . has lost two men recently," Pound told readers of the *New English Weekly*, "neither of 'em adorers of USURY. . . . With Cutting gone, and The Kingfish murdered, the American people will have to do its own saving of itself."[6]

With the deaths of Cutting and Long in 1935, the story of Pound's relationship with America and his American audience comes to its denouement, for in that year it all began rapidly to unravel. Pound's attempts to justify and rally support for Italy's indefensible invasion of Abyssinia in October 1935 lost him many American acquaintances and strained an already tenuous link with Senator Borah.[7] Having now quite publicly thrown his lot with the fascists, Pound renewed his efforts to become a personal confidant of Mussolini.[8] American Social Credit activists, into whose ranks Pound had tried to recruit Cutting, began to grow disgusted with Pound's anti-Semitism and ties to fascism, and the movement itself unwound as Douglas's own increasingly conspicuous anti-Semitism divided the fold.[9] From mid-1935 on, ugly and irrational statements about President Roosevelt and the Jews began to appear in Pound's public writings.[10]

By the time Pound made a last-ditch visit to Washington in 1939 to lobby personally for peace and economic reform, his interactions with American leaders were merely perfunctory. Hoping to use the maximum efficiency of one-to-one communication to his advantage, he found that few were prepared to listen to him. As the grandson of a congressman, he was treated with courtesy by a number of senators, representatives, and at least one cabinet member; but the president refused to see him, and Pound himself conveys the tone of the visit in Canto 84, where he quotes Borah as saying: "am sure I don't know what a man like you/ would find to *do* here."[11]

Postal and personal lobbying having failed, Pound turned in 1941 to radio, the medium that Roosevelt, Long, and Coughlin had used so successfully to communicate their messages to the American people. In a sense, the Rome Radio broadcasts were an expanded version of "Ez Sez." But they were not much more successful in reaching a large audience, because they were heard by few and understood by even fewer. Pound must have mentioned Cutting in one of the early, unmonitored speeches; for, in the broadcast of 19 April 1942, Pound says, "I have told you of Senator Cutting's hope and his disappointment."[12] Perhaps Ez told his listeners of Cutting's plan to nationalize America's banks.

Clearly, by dying when he did, Cutting had become a permanent ally in Pound's memory. Had Cutting lived beyond May 1935, he would probably have received from Rapallo letters very different in tone from those Pound sent before that date. How Cutting would have responded, we shall never know; but, no matter what his disagreements with the president might have been, it is hard to imagine that Cutting would have stomached Pound's Rome-Radio invective against "Rosenfeld" and "Franklin D. Frankfurter Jewsfeld."[13]

The senator leads a curious afterlife in Pound's *Cantos.* He appears three times, always in connection with the confidential list of literate colleagues which he entrusted to Pound in his very first letter to Rapallo. This list became, for Pound, one of those "luminous details" that reveal a great deal about a nation at a given moment in its history.[14] Cutting had written: "As for 'literacy', I don't suppose you are interested in people like Moses & Bingham & Dave Reed who sin against the light. That leaves Borah & Norris & La Follette & Hiram Johnson & Tydings & Wheeler & Walsh of Montana & I suppose Dwight Morrow, & not much else. But don't say that I said so" (9 December 1930). In Canto 86 (1955) Pound paraphrases the passage as follows:

> Eleven literates
> 　　　　　　and I suppose Dwight L. Morrow"
> re Senate enrollment
> 　　　　　　Br . . . C. . . . g
> question? about '32[15]

Considering that Pound was writing in St. Elizabeths Hospital, without Cutting's letter at hand, it is hardly surprising that his memory of the passage contains a few minor inaccuracies. (*Ten* names precede that of Dwight W. Morrow in Cutting's letter of *1930*.) Nevertheless, the anecdote pointedly illustrates Pound's dim view of the United States government in the decade of the Depression.

In Canto 98 (1958) Pound repeats the motif in a context that emphasizes not the deficiencies of Cutting's colleagues so much as the superiority of the senator himself. The passage aligns Cutting with other ideal rulers celebrated in *Thrones*.

> "Eleven literates" wrote Senator Cutting,
> > "and, I suppose, Dwight L. Morrow"[16]

Perhaps because the focus is now upon the satirist's positive norms of leadership, Cutting's surname appears in full for the first and only time in the poem.

In Canto 102 (1959) Pound's attention has shifted back to the Senate, and Cutting's name does not appear at all.

> This I had from Kalupso
> > who had it from Hermes
> "eleven literates and, I suppose,
> > Dwight L. Morrow"
> the body elected,
> > residence required, not as in England[17]

The source of the anecdote is humorously Hellenized, and Pound's Odyssean speaker receives the list as gossip from Olympus, insider tattle about the gods from one of their number. The classical allusion is an oblique tribute to Cutting's literacy; for, as Pound reminds us in his 1935 obituary, "the senate is not rich in men who read the classics for pleasure."[18]

While it lasted, the correspondence of the literate senator and the political poet revealed interesting aspects of both men. Cutting's leadership on national economic and cultural issues made him Pound's bright hope. Pound's informed and provocative letters on the problems confronting the Congress and the nation made him Cutting's valued interlocutor. The correspondence is a tribute to the versatility of both men and to a catholicity of interests and knowledge that has grown increasingly rare in American public life.

NOTES

Chapter One

1. The extant texts of the broadcasts have been published in *"Ezra Pound Speaking": Radio Speeches of World War II*, ed. Leonard W. Doob (Westport, Conn.: Greenwood Press, 1978).
2. Pound's congressional correspondences are briefly mentioned in the most authoritative recent biography, Humphrey Carpenter's *A Serious Character: The Life of Ezra Pound* (Boston: Houghton Mifflin, 1988), 521–22, 527. Carpenter wrongly says that Representative George H. Tinkham was "the only American politician willing to pay serious attention to Pound's letters" (527). The correspondences receive more attention in John Tytell's *Ezra Pound: The Solitary Volcano* (New York: Doubleday Anchor, 1987), 221, 227, 230, 237, 240–41, 250–51, 254; but Tytell reads them chiefly as "letters full of invective and hatred" (206). Two studies that treat the correspondences in greater depth are Daniel Pearlman, "Fighting the World: The Letters of Ezra Pound to Senator William E. Borah of Idaho," *Paideuma* 12, 2–3 (Fall–Winter 1983), 419–26, and Philip J. Burns, "'Dear Uncle George': The Pound-Tinkham Letters," *Paideuma* 18, 1–2 (Spring–Fall 1989), 35–65. Burns's edition of the Pound-Tinkham correspondence, entitled "'Dear Uncle George': Ezra Pound's Letters to Congressman Tinkham of Massachusetts" (Ph.D. diss., Rhode Island, 1988), has been announced for publication by the National Poetry Foundation of Orono, Maine. As noted in the Editors' Preface above, Richard Lowitt and Tim Redman have made good use of the Pound-Cutting letters in their recent studies, *Bronson M. Cutting: Progressive Politician* (1992) and *Ezra Pound and Italian Fascism* (1991).
3. See especially J. J. Wilhelm, *The American Roots of Ezra Pound* (New York: Garland, 1985), and Wendy S. Flory, *The American Ezra Pound* (New Haven, Conn.: Yale University Press, 1989).
4. Ezra Pound, "Indiscretions" (1920), in *Pavannes and Divagations* (London: Peter Owen, 1960), 7.
5. See Wilhelm, *American Roots of Ezra Pound*, Chapters One to Three, and Flory, *American Ezra Pound*, Chapter 1.
6. Tytell, *Ezra Pound*, 13.
7. Wilhelm, *American Roots of Ezra Pound*, 20.
8. Wilhelm, ibid., 26.
9. Ezra Pound, "A Visiting Card" (1942), in *Selected Prose 1909–1965*, ed. William Cookson (New York: New Directions, 1973), 325, quoted by Wilhelm, *American Roots of Ezra Pound*, 19, and Tytell, *Ezra Pound*, 13, and repeated in Canto 97. EP may also have been imitating Thaddeus, the renowned orator, when he began to broadcast over Rome Radio in 1936.
10. Richard Hofstadter, *The Age of Reform: From Bryan to F. D. R.* (1955; rpt., New York: Alfred A. Knopf, 1965), 12. Hofstadter's analysis of the development and the limitations of the Populist-Progressive tradition illuminates the politics of EP, who is mentioned on p. 81 in connection with Populist anti-Semitism. Other elements of the tradition present

in EP's thought include an obsession with money and credit, a conspiracy theory of history, and a Yankee-Protestant distrust of immigrant populations.

11. Keith Tuma, "Ezra Pound, Progressive," *Paideuma* 19, 1–2 (Spring–Fall 1990), 80, 84.

12. For more detailed summaries of Social Credit, see Flory, *American Ezra Pound*, Chapter 2, and Earle Davis, *Vision Fugitive: Ezra Pound and Economics* (Lawrence: University Press of Kansas, 1968), Chapters 4 and 5.

13. Ezra Pound, *Personae: The Shorter Poems*, ed. Lea Baechler and A. Walton Litz (New York: New Directions, 1990), 188.

14. See Redman, *Ezra Pound and American Fascism;* Flory, *American Ezra Pound;* and Ezra Pound, *Jefferson and/or Mussolini* (London: Stanley Nott, 1935).

15. Ezra Pound, "Open Letter to Tretyakow, kolchoznik," *Front* 1, 2 (February 1931), 126; rpt., *Ezra Pound's Poetry and Prose*, 5: 274.

16. See Donald Gallup, *Ezra Pound: A Bibliography* (Charlottesville: University Press of Virginia, 1983), 277–321.

17. See E. P. Walkiewicz and Hugh Witemeyer, "Ezra Pound's Contributions to New Mexican Periodicals and His Relationship with Senator Bronson Cutting," *Paideuma* 9, 3 (Winter 1980), 441– 59.

18. On the Tinkham and Borah correspondences, see Pearlman, "Fighting the World," and Burns, "'Dear Uncle George': The Pound–Tinkham Letters."

19. Carpenter, *A Serious Character*, 493, 498, 542.

20. Flory, *American Ezra Pound*, 6. See also Sacvan Bercovitch, *The American Jeremiad* (Madison: University of Wisconsin Press, 1987).

21. See, for instance, Sacvan Bercovitch, "The Rites of Assent: Rhetoric, Ritual, and the Ideology of American Consensus," in *The American Self: Myth, Ideology, and Popular Culture*, ed. Sam B. Girgus (Albuquerque: University of New Mexico Press, 1981), 5–42.

22. Ezra Pound, "Reflexshuns on Iggurunce," *Esquire* 3, 1 (January 1935), 55; rpt., *Ezra Pound's Poetry and Prose*, 6: 232.

23. Carpenter, *A Serious Character*, 489–91. Pound first wrote to Mussolini's private secretary in April 1932 and finally met Il Duce in January 1933.

24. The first full-scale biography of BC is Richard Lowitt's *Bronson M. Cutting: Progressive Politician* (Albuquerque: University of New Mexico Press, 1992). Henry Steele Commager nearly undertook a biography in the late 1930s, but abandoned the project. Our account of BC and his family is indebted to Lowitt and to the following sources: the Bronson M. Cutting Papers, Manuscript Division, Library of Congress (hereafter cited as Cutting Papers); New Mexico State Records Center and Archives, Historic File 47; *Dictionary of American Biography* (New York: Charles Scribner's Sons), 2 (1929): 68–69, 11 (1933): 318–19, and 21 (Supplement One, 1944): 215–16; Jonathan R. Cunningham, "Bronson Cutting: A Political Biography" (Master's thesis, New Mexico, 1940); Patricia Cadigan Armstrong, *A Portrait of Bronson Cutting through His Papers, 1910–1927* (Albuquerque: University of New Mexico Department of Government, 1959); Arthur M. Schlesinger, Jr., *The Politics of Upheaval* (London: Heinemann, 1961), 139–41; Jack E. Holmes, *Politics in New Mexico* (Albuquerque: University of New Mexico Press, 1967); Iris Origo, *Images and Shadows: Part of a Life* (New York: Harcourt Brace Jovanovich, 1970); Robert W. Larson, "The Profile of a New Mexico Progressive," *New Mexico Historical Review* 45, 3 (July 1970), 233–44; William H. Pickens, "Bronson Cutting vs. Dennis Chavez: Battle of the Patrones in New Mexico, 1934," *New Mexico Historical Review* 46, 1 (January 1971), 5–36; Richard Fox, "Cutting and His Coalitions," *Century: A Southwest Journal of Observation and Opinion*, 16 February 1983, pp. 18–23; and Corinne Sze, "The Bronson M. Cutting House," *Bulletin of the Historic Santa Fe Foundation* 16, 1 (September 1988), 2–11.

25. See Lowitt, *Bronson M. Cutting*, 4–5; Origo, *Images and Shadows*, 21–22, 26; and George Lockhart Reeves, "William Bayard Cutting," *Columbia University Quarterly* 14, 3 (June 1912), 286–91, in Cutting Papers, Box 92.

26. Colonel Charles A. Reynolds, "Bronson Cutting," *The Cavalier: A Magazine for New Mexico War Veterans* 2, 2 (Memorial Day, 1940) 8, in Cutting Papers, Box 92.

27. Justine Cutting Ward, typescript entitled "1910–1911–1913," in Cutting Papers, Box 92. See also Origo, *Images and Shadows*, 33.

28. Richard Lowitt, "Bronson Cutting and the Early Years of the American Legion in New Mexico," *New Mexico Historical Review* 64, 2 (April 1989), 143–58; and Lowitt, *Bronson M. Cutting*, 103–9, 114–19, 128–30. Lowitt rightly says that "the melioration of the lot of Spanish-speaking citizens of New Mexico through the expansion of their educational opportunities and through their participation in the political process" was a "major concern" of BC's career, ibid., 88.

29. Lowitt, *Bronson M. Cutting*, xi; see also 189–91.

30. "Inventory of Contents in Los Siete Burros in Santa Fe, New Mexico," in Cutting Papers, Box 22.

31. On BC's role in the fight against customs censorship, see James C. N. Paul and Murray L. Schwartz, *Federal Censorship: Obscenity in the Mail* (New York: The Free Press of Glencoe, 1961) 55–62; Paul S. Boyer, *Purity in Print: The Vice-Society Movement and Book Censorship in America* (New York: Charles Scribner's Sons, 1968), 207–48; Hugh Witemeyer, "Senator Bronson Cutting versus Customs Censorship," *New Mexico Humanities Review* 6, 3 (Fall 1983), 75–82; and Lowitt, *Bronson M. Cutting*, 160–61, 169–70. See also the following issues of the *New York Times:* 29 July 1929, p. 23; 11 October 1929, p. 1; 12 October 1929, pp. 1, 8; 7 March 1930, p. 18; 18 March 1930, p. 5; and 19 March 1930, pp. 1, 5. On the history of the customs censorship law and the role of Morris Ernst, see Michael Moscato and Leslie LeBlanc, eds., *The United States of America* v. *One Book Entitled* Ulysses *by James Joyce: Documents and Commentary—a 50-Year Retrospective* (Frederick, Maryland: University Publications of America, 1984).

32. The debate is recorded in the *Congressional Record,* vol. 71, part 4 (10–11 October 1929), 4445–72; and vol. 72, part 5 (7 and 17–18 March 1930), 4893, 5414–33, 5487–5520. Quotations from the debate are identified in the text of this chapter by page numbers only.

33. See Milton R. Merrill, "Reed Smoot, Apostle in Politics," *Western Humanities Review* 9 (1955), 1–12.

34. For EP's view of Senator Blease, see "Congratulates South Carolina," *New York Herald* (Paris), 15 September 1930, p. 6, and "Pound on Blease," *Chicago Tribune* (Paris), 16 September 1930, p. 4; rpt., *Ezra Pound's Poetry and Prose*, 5: 234.

35. Woolsey's opinion is reprinted as a preface to James Joyce, *Ulysses* (New York: Random House, 1961), vii–xii.

36. "Honor and the United States Senate," *Poetry* 36 (June 1930), 152; rpt., *Ezra Pound's Poetry and Prose*, 5: 225–26.

37. See "Republican Forces Win Tariff Victory on Appraisal Item," *New York Times*, 11 October 1929, p. 1.

Chapter Two

1. Ezra Pound, "Pound for President," *The Nation* (New York) 125 (14 December 1927), 462; rpt., *Ezra Pound's Poetry and Prose*, 4: 393. Early statements of the program may also be found in EP's letters of 1925–26 to John Price. See Barry Alpert, "Ezra Pound, John Price, and *The Exile*," *Paideuma* 2, 3 (Winter 1973), 428–430–31; rpt., *Ezra Pound's Poetry and Prose*, 10: 96, 98–99.

2. See Duff Gilfond, "Arbiters of Obscenity," *The New Republic*, (19 June 1929), pp. 119–20.

3. *35 Statutes at Large* (Washington, D.C.: Government Printing Office, 1909), Chapter 321, Section 211, p. 1129. In the *Postal Laws and Regulations of the United States of America* (Washington, D.C.: Government Printing Office, 1913), the provision is given in Section 480. On the history of postal censorship in the United States, see Lindsay Rogers, *The Postal Power of Congress: A Study in Constitutional Expansion* (Baltimore: The Johns Hopkins Press, 1916), 48–49, and Paul and Schwartz, *Federal Censorship: Obscenity in the Mail*, 17–30, 251–62.

4. See *Pound/The Little Review: The Letters of Ezra Pound to Margaret Anderson*, ed. Thomas L. Scott, Melvin J. Friedman, and Jackson R. Bryer (New York: New Directions, 1988), 173–76, and Boyer, *Purity in Print*, 59.

5. See Moscato and LeBlanc, *The United States of America v. One Book Entitled* Ulysses *by James Joyce*, xvii–xix.

6. "Paris Letter," *The Dial*, 72 (February 1922), 189–90. EP also reprints the law in "The Classics 'Escape,'" *Little Review* 4, 2 (March 1918), 32–34; in "American Book Pirates," *The New Statesman*, 16 April 1927, pp. 10–11; in "Ezra Pound Denounces Idiocy of U. S. Mail Act," *Chicago Tribune* (Paris), 1 November 1927, p. 7; in "Article 211," *Exile* 4 (Autumn 1928), 20–22; and in "Strange Bedfellows," *Chicago Tribune* (Paris), 7 December 1930, p. 4. See *Ezra Pound's Poetry and Prose*, 3: 63–64; 4: 217, 383, 388; and 5: 56, 260.

7. See the *Congressional Record*, vol. 75, part 2 (3 March 1932), 5153. See also Boyer, *Purity in Print*, 242–43, and *The Post Office Censor* (New York: National Council on Freedom from Censorship [1932]).

8. See Margaret Sanger, *My Fight for Birth Control* (London: Faber and Faber, 1932), 323–33, and *Margaret Sanger: An Autobiography* (London: Victor Gollancz, 1939), 408–20; David M. Kennedy, *Birth Control in America: The Career of Margaret Sanger* (New Haven: Yale University Press, 1970), 228–50; and Ellen Chesler, *Woman of Valor: Margaret Sanger and the Birth Control Movement in America* (New York: Simon and Schuster, 1992), 66–68, 99, 329–30.

9. See Abe A. Goldman, "The History of U.S.A. Copyright Law Revision from 1901 to 1954" (1955), in *Copyright Revision Studies* (Washington, D.C.: United States Government Printing Office, 1960), 1: 4–14. These studies were issued by the Subcommittee on Patents, Trademarks, and Copyrights of the U.S. Senate Committee on the Judiciary. Our account of efforts to amend the copyright law is greatly indebted to the work of Goldman.

10. Ezra Pound, "Anent a Senator," *Saturday Review of Literature* 7, 42 (2 May 1931), 805; rpt., *Ezra Pound's Poetry and Prose*, 5: 292. On EP's earlier support of the Vestal Bill, see his letter of 27 April 1927 to H. L. Mencken, whose *American Mercury* had run afoul of Article 211 (*The Selected Letters of Ezra Pound 1907–1941*, ed. D. D. Paige [New York: New Directions, 1971], 223); see also Alpert, "Ezra Pound, John Price, and *The Exile*," 444. EP declared his opposition to "the present American copyright law" and offered his own "sketch of what the copyright law ought to be" in two 1918 articles entitled "Tariff and Copyright" and "Copyright and Tariff." See the *New Age* 23, 22 (26 September 1918), 348–49, and 23 (30 October 1918), 363–64; and the *Little Review* 5, 7 (November 1918), 21–25. These articles are reproduced in *Ezra Pound's Poetry and Prose*, 3: 190–91, 208–9, 226–34.

11. *Congressional Record*, vol. 77, part 6 (10 and 12 June 1933), 5622, 5716. See also Richard Lowitt, *Bronson M. Cutting*, 198.

12. Freeman W. Sharp, *Passports and the Right to Travel: A Story of Administrative Control of the Citizen* (Washington, D.C.: United States Government Printing Office, July 10, 1958), 12. Our account of passport regulations is greatly indebted to Sharp's study, which was

prepared by the Library of Congress Legislative Reference Service for the Committee on Foreign Affairs during the second session of the Eighty-fifth Congress. See also Egidio Reale, "Passport," *Encyclopedia of the Social Sciences*, ed. Edwin R. A. Seligman (New York: Macmillan, 1934), 12: 14–16.

13. See Sharp, *Passports and the Right to Travel*, 5, and *40 Statutes at Large* (1918), 559, 1829–32. An amended version of the 1918 law is still in effect today as *22 U.S. Code*, 223–26.

14. See James Longenbach, *Stone Cottage: Pound, Yeats, and Modernism* (New York: Oxford University Press, 1988), 261; letter of 9 September 1916 from EP to John Quinn, in the John Quinn Memorial Collection, Manuscripts and Archives Division, New York Public Library; and Ezra Pound, "The Passport Nuisance," *The Nation* (New York) 125 (30 November 1927), 600–602, and "Four Steps," *Southern Review* 13, 4 (Autumn 1977), 862–71. The last two are reprinted in *Ezra Pound's Poetry and Prose*, 4: 389–90; 10: 192–93. See also *The Selected Letters of Ezra Pound to John Quinn 1915–1924*, 180–81.

15. "Ezra Speaks Sooth," *Chicago Tribune* (Paris), 2 September 1930, p. 4; rpt., *Ezra Pound's Poetry and Prose*, 5: 234. For other attacks upon passport regulations by EP, see *ibid.*, 4: 77, 140, 264, 348, 352, 355, 370, 393; 5: 17, 50, 62, 189, 200; and 10: 138.

16. Cutting's report on his London service, dated 13 February 1919, is in Box 14 of the Cutting Papers. See also Lowitt, *Bronson M. Cutting*, 83.

17. Oliver La Farge, *Santa Fe: The Autobiography of a Southwestern Town* (Norman: University of Oklahoma Press, 1959), 230.

18. See volume two, page 149, of Dunne's unpublished memoir of Cutting, dated 17 June 1937. The bound typescript, entitled "Personal Recollections of a Friend," is in Box 92 of the Cutting Papers.

19. See La Farge, *Santa Fe*, 230, 244; and James A. Burran, "Prohibition in New Mexico, 1917," *New Mexico Historical Review* 48, 2 (April 1973), 133–49.

20. Cutting Papers, Box 39.

21. See La Farge, *Santa Fe*, 344–45.

22. See "Senators Visit Moscow," *New York Times*, 12 August 1930, p. 11, and Albert Rhys Williams, "The Senators Visit the Soviet Villages," typescript in Box 39 of the Cutting Papers.

23. "Recognition of Russia—Address by Senator Cutting," *Congressional Record*, vol. 74, part 4 (5 February 1931), 4006–7. See also "Soviet Recognition Urged by Cutting," *New York Times*, 1 February 1941, p. 24; and Lowitt, *Bronson M. Cutting*, 198, 375.

24. For a detailed account of Pound's contributions to *Morada* and *Front*, see Walkiewicz and Witemeyer, "Ezra Pound's Contributions."

Chapter Three

1. See John L. Finlay, *Social Credit: The English Origins* (Montreal: McGill-Queen's University Press, 1972), 26–28, 42, 75–83, 120–22, 174; Davis, *Vision Fugitive*, 49–51; Leon Surette, "Ezra Pound and British Radicalism," *English Studies in Canada* 9 (1983), 435–51; and Hugh Witemeyer, "'Of Kings' Treasuries': Pound's Allusion to Ruskin in *Hugh Selwyn Mauberley*," *Paideuma* 15 (Spring 1986), 23–31.

2. The closing lines of Canto 14 condemn "monopolists, obstructors of knowledge,/ obstructors of distribution"; see *The Cantos of Ezra Pound* (New York: New Directions, 1986), 63.

3. See Burns, "'Dear Uncle George': The Pound–Tinkham Letters," 37. EP came nearest to playing such a role in 1944, when his advice to officials in the Ministry of Popular Culture in the short-lived government of the Republic of Salò was heeded and often enacted; see Redman, *Ezra Pound and Italian Fascism*, Chapter 8. Earlier, EP had offered to come to Washington to serve Representative George H. Tinkham as private sec-

retary; see Redman, *ibid.*, 195, and Burns, "'Dear Uncle George': Ezra Pound's Letters," 249–51. In his letters to Senator Borah as well, EP had cast himself as "the unofficial Brains Trust of the next president of the United States"; see Pearlman, "Fighting the World," 421.

4. For a more extended account of EP's changing view of Roosevelt, see Burns, "'Dear Uncle George': The Pound–Tinkham Letters," 44–50. For a general analysis of Populist-Progressive objections to the New Deal, see Hofstadter, *Age of Reform*, 303–9.

5. Roosevelt made this remark when BC appeared with him during a campaign stop in Lamy, New Mexico, on 27 September 1932; see "New Mexico Welcomes Roosevelt," Santa Fe *New Mexican*, 27 September 1932, pp. 1–2. Roosevelt described BC on this occasion as "a very dear friend of the family."

6. See Chapter One, p. 13.

7. For BC's speech of 2 June 1933, see the *Congressional Record*, vol. 77, part 5 (2 June 1933), 4832. See also Lowitt, *Bronson M. Cutting*, 235–42, 260–61, 385, 390. For a report on BC's speech of 28 March 1934, see the *Chicago Tribune* (Paris), 29 March 1934, pp. 1, 3.

8. Cutting Papers, Box 83.

9. Cutting Papers, Box 11. See also Lowitt, *Bronson M. Cutting*, 262.

10. From EP's point of view, as Davis says in *Vision Fugitive*, "what Roosevelt had done to relieve depression was not enough" (134).

11. See the following articles in the Santa Fe *New Mexican:* "State Turns Thumbs Down on Amendment to End Child Labor," 5 February 1935, p. 1; "Child Labor Measure Dead," 7 February 1935, p. 1; "Child Labor Measure Ordered to Graveyard," 8 February 1935, pp. 1, 5; "No Hope for Child Work Act," 26 February 1935, p. 1.

12. See "Ezra Pound Prescribes 5-Hour Work Day," *Chicago Tribune* (Paris), 15 October 1931, p. 2. See also Ezra Pound, "The Depression Has Just Begun," *Contempo* 1, 16 (15 January 1932), 1, 4; rpt., *Ezra Pound's Poetry and Prose*, 5: 336.

13. Ezra Pound, *ABC of Economics* (London: Faber and Faber, 1933), 20–21; see also 42–45, 54–56, and 74.

14. See Hugo Black, "The Shorter Work Week and Work Day," *Annals of the American Academy of Political Science*, 184 (March 1936), 62–67.

15. Ezra Pound, "American Notes," *New English Weekly* 7, 4 (9 May 1935), 65; rpt., *Ezra Pound's Poetry and Prose*, 6: 282. See also "More on Economics," *Chicago Tribune* (Paris), 12 April 1933, p. 5; rpt., *Ezra Pound's Poetry and Prose*, 6: 34–35. For BC's support of S. 5267, see the *Congressional Record*, vol. 77, part 2 (6 April 1933), 1349–50.

16. Ezra Pound, *What Is Money For?* (1939; rpt., *Selected Prose*, p. 264. See also Pound, "Depression Has Just Begun."

17. H. J. Hagerman, "Ducking and Cutting—An Uncensored Review," *New Mexico Tax Bulletin* 11, 9 (November 1932), 212; quoted in Pickens, "Bronson Cutting vs. Dennis Chavez," 20.

18. "Roosevelt Wants Wage Boost," *Chicago Tribune* (Paris), 6 March 1934, pp. 1, 3. For more on this speech and EP's reaction to it, see Letter 19.

19. Ezra Pound, "American Notes," *New English Weekly* 8, 12 (2 January 1936), 225; rpt., *Ezra Pound's Poetry and Prose*, 7: 16. See also "American Notes," *New English Weekly* 6, 14 (17 January 1935), 290, and "American Notes," *New English Weekly* 6, 17 (14 February 1935), 349; rpt., *Ezra Pound's Poetry and Prose*, 6: 246. EP wrote at least one letter to Townsend, dated 10 January [1936?] (Pound Archive).

20. Cutting Papers, Box 34.

21. Robinson (1881–1961) represented Indiana in the Senate from 1925 to 1935. EP corresponded with him from 25 March to 26 August 1934 (Pound Archive). For EP's earlier advocacy of bonus payments, see his "Supports Bonus," *Chicago Tribune* (Paris), 9 March

1922, p. 4; rpt., *Ezra Pound's Poetry and Prose*, 4: 222.

22. Pound Archive.

23. See Ezra Pound, "Senator Long and Father Coughlin: Mr. Ezra Pound's Estimate," *Morning Post* (London), 17 April 1935, p. 14, and "American Notes," *New English Weekly* 6, 24 (28 March 1935), 490: "The NEWS is that Huey Long has a 'magnificent education'; i.e., knowing the popular hatred of highbrows he is clever enough to conceal (etc.)." These items are reproduced in *Ezra Pound's Poetry and Prose*, 6: 277, 259.

24. Pound Archive. In the letter of 13 April, EP asks Long to transmit his "regards to Ole Bronson Cutting"; the passage is reproduced in Redman's *Ezra Pound and Italian Fascism*, 161. See also the unpublished manuscript entitled "HUEY, God bless him," which EP sent to *New Democracy* on "13 or 14 Aug." 1935 (Harry Ransom Research Center, University of Texas at Austin). One of the unpublished "Ez Sez" editorials (Pound Archive), undated but written after Long's death, likewise emphasizes the affinities between Long and Cutting.

25. Ezra Pound, "American Notes," *New English Weekly* 7, 20 (26 September 1935), 385. See also "American Notes," *New English Weekly* 7, 18 (12 September 1935), 345. These items are reproduced in *Ezra Pound's Poetry and Prose*, 6: 315, 312.

26. See, for example, an editorial ironically entitled "The Huey Long Menace," *Santa Fe New Mexican*, 8 March 1935, p. 4: "The only answer to Huey Long is not to denounce him as a nut and a demagogue, but to begin to do something about the condition which gives him his dynamite." EP liked this piece so well that he reprinted it in the *New English Weekly* 7, 4 (9 May 1935), 65; rpt., *Ezra Pound's Poetry and Prose*, 6: 282. In "Ez Sez" for 1 June 1935, EP mocks those who fear Long; see Chapter Four, pp. 200–01. On Long's relations with other Progressive senators, see Alan Brinkley, *Voices of Protest: Huey Long, Father Coughlin, and the Great Depression* (New York: Alfred A. Knopf, 1982), 77–78.

27. Hugh Russell Fraser, "Bronson Cutting: Aristocrat in Politics," typescript, Cutting Papers, Box 92.

28. In *Ezra Pound and Italian Fascism*, Tim Redman describes the gold purchase as "the only action taken by Roosevelt that could be considered in accord with Social Credit principles" (201). The purchase, Redman notes, resulted in a new supply of debt-free dollars. See also Davis, *Vision Fugitive*, 191. For useful discussions of EP's "quantity theory of money," see Leon Surette, *A Light from Eleusis: A Study of Ezra Pound's* Cantos (Oxford: Clarendon Press, 1979), 86–90, and Flory, *American Ezra Pound*, 55–58.

29. See Ezra Pound, "American Notes," *New English Weekly* 6, 20 (28 February 1935), 409; rpt., *Ezra Pound's Poetry and Prose*, 6: 250.

30. For expositions of Gesell's theories, see Davis, *Vision Fugitive*, 108–9; Surette, *Light from Eleusis*, 86–87; and Flory, *American Ezra Pound*, 70–73. As for stamp scrip in Monte Carlo, in Letter 23, EP calls BC's attention to a story which appeared on 10 May 1934 in *Lavoro*, a non-fascist newspaper published in Genoa, under the title "Singolare progetto per favorire la rinascita economica del Principato di Monaco" ["Unusual plan to promote the economic recovery of the Principality of Monaco"]. According to this story, "*L'Unione dei Commercianti ed Industriali* di Monaco ha adottato un progetto per favorire il risorgimento economico del Principato, mediante la creazione di una moneta ausiliara monegasca. Il progetto, che è stato patrocinato presso le Autorità locali, prevede l'emissione di 'buoni del tesoro' del valore di 5, 10, 50 e 100 franchi, che tutti dovrebbero accettare in pagamento e che dovrebbo essere convertibili in moneta francese previo un prelevamento del 2% nel ammontare del buono. Inoltre questi titoli ogni mese verrebbero deprezzati dell' uno per cento, quindi del 12% all' anno, e ciò per sovvenzionare anche l'ufficio di propaganda turisticà." [*The League of Merchants and Industrialists* of Monaco

has adopted a plan to promote the economic recovery of the Principality through the creation of an auxiliary Monegasque currency. The plan, which has been approved by the local government, envisions the issuance of 'treasury notes' in denominations of 5, 10, 50 and 100 francs, which everybody should accept in payment and which can be converted into French money upon prepayment of 2% of the amount of the note. Furthermore these bills will be depreciated each month by one per cent, or 12% a year, in order to subsidize the office of tourist information.] EP also mentions this article in "From Italy," *New English Weekly* 5, 6 (24 May 1934), 143–44; rpt., *Ezra Pound's Poetry and Prose*, 6: 178; and in "Cheers for Monte Carlo or the Stamp Cat Is Out of the Bag," unpublished manuscript in the Harry Ransom Humanities Research Center, University of Texas at Austin.

31. Democrat John Hollis Bankhead II (1872–1946) represented Alabama in the Senate from 1931 until his death. He became a close adviser to President Roosevelt on agricultural matters and was cosponsor of the Bankhead Cotton Control Act of 1934. He was a member of the most prominent political family in Alabama and an uncle of actress Tallulah Bankhead. Another niece, Tallulah's sister Jean Bankhead, was a prominent member of the foreign community in Rapallo. EP corresponded with Bankhead from 1934 to 1940 (Pound Archive), met him in Washington in 1939, and quoted him in Canto 84 on the subject of President Roosevelt.

32. *Congressional Record*, vol. 76, part 4 (17 and 20 February 1933), 4327–34, 4460. Bankhead had introduced and then withdrawn the measure on 17 February.

33. Ezra Pound, "A Visiting Card" (1942); rpt., *Impact*, 52.

34. For one of them, see the *Congressional Record*, vol. 77, part 1 (30 March 1933), 1027–35.

35. See Ezra Pound, "Stamp Script," *New English Weekly* 2, 2 (26 October 1933), 31–32; "Woergl Stamp Scrip," *Chicago Tribune* (Paris), 8 November 1933, p. 4; "Letters to Woodward," *Paideuma* 15 (Spring 1986), 113; "Demurrage Money," *Morning Post* (London), 21 September 1934, p. 9; "Inexcusable Darkness," *Delphian Quarterly* 21, 3 (July 1938), 14–17; and "Pound risponde," *Il Popolo di Alessandria*, 2 July 1944, p. 2. See *Ezra Pound's Poetry and Prose*, 6: 86–87, 99, 197; 7: 356–59; 8: 237.

36. Ezra Pound, "The Individual in His Milieu: A Study of Relations and Gesell," *Criterion* 15, 58 (October 1935); rpt., *Selected Prose*, 250, and *Ezra Pound's Poetry and Prose*, 6: 324. See also EP's *What Is Money For?* in *Selected Prose*, 300–301, in which he describes Bankhead's bill as "possibly the only 100 per cent honest monetary proposal made in U.S. legislature" since the Civil War. In a letter of 5 May 1937 to Representative George Tinkham, EP described Bankhead's bill as "the high water mark of his career . . . the one spout that is likely to putt [*sic*] him [on] historical map as a forerunner." See Burns, "'Dear Uncle George': Ezra Pound's Letters," 175; Bankhead is also mentioned on 85 and 188. See also Ezra Pound, "A Matter of Modesty," *Esquire* 3, 5 (May 1935), 31; rpt., *Ezra Pound's Poetry and Prose*, 6: 279. An unpublished, thirteen-page typescript by EP in the Pound Archive is entitled "Honour to John H. Bankhead."

37. Ezra Pound, "Mug's Game?" *Esquire* 3, 2 (February 1935), 148; rpt., *Ezra Pound's Poetry and Prose*, 6: 244.

38. *New English Weekly* 4, 23 (22 March 1934), 535–38. EP responded to the bill in two letters to the editor, published in the issues of 5 April and 1 June 1934; see *Ezra Pound's Poetry and Prose*, 6: 167, 179.

39. See Munson, *Aladdin's Lamp*, 362–63, and Flory, *American Ezra Pound*, 78–79. See also Ezra Pound, "Sense v. Sadism—Or Vice Versa," *Action* 117 (14 May 1938), 13; "Inexcusable Darkness," and "Suggesting a Kindergarten for British M.P.s," *Action* 131 (20 August 1938), 13. EP's articles are reproduced in *Ezra Pound's Poetry and Prose*, 7: 322, 356–59, 366–67.

40. C. H. Douglas, "The Mechanism of Consumer Control," *New Age*, 28 (23 December 1920), 88; quoted by Surette, *Light from Eleusis*, 85. Other useful expositions of Douglas's thought are Davis, *Vision Fugitive*, Chapters 4 and 5, and Flory, *American Ezra Pound*, Chapter 2. According to Flory's succinct summary, "the Social Credit system had three main requirements: that the government assume the issuing of all kinds of money, that the just price be established, and that provision be made for issuing a national dividend" (68). EP believed in all three of these requirements; BC, in the first only.

41. These quotations come from a speech that BC delivered to the People's Lobby in Washington on 19 May 1934; see "Government Bank Urged by Cutting," *New York Times*, 20 May 1934, p. 32.

42. Letter from BC to Herbert Bruce Brougham dated 23 July 1934, in Cutting Papers, Box 20. In *Vision Fugitive*, Davis observes that "Social Credit became mixed in the public mind with extreme and rabid panaceas: religious revivalism, professional rabble-rousing, populist revolution against the established community…; the share-the-wealth slogans of Huey Long; Townsendism; even the diatribes of Father Coughlin…" (108).

43. Letter from BC to Mrs. H. E. Luderer dated 1 March 1934, in Cutting Papers, Box 19.

44. Letter from BC to David Warren Ryder dated 24 April 1934, in Cutting Papers, Box 19.

45. See three-page letter from A. R. Orage to BC dated 8 January 1934, Cutting Papers, Box 11. For Orage's lecture-visit to Santa Fe, see "Orage, Former Visitor Here, Dies in London," Santa Fe *New Mexican*, 7 November 1934, p. 1, and Dunne's memoir of BC, "Personal Recollections of a Friend," Cutting Papers, Box 92, 29–30. For a fund-raising visit by Orage's disciple, Mrs. Meredith Hare, see the letter from BC to Clifford McCarthy dated 21 December 1933, Cutting Papers, Box 32.

46. For BC's contributions to these magazines, see the anonymous article entitled "A Tribute to Senator Cutting," *New Democracy* 4, 6 (15 May 1935); Letters 20 and 21; and letters from the editors of *New Democracy* to BC dated 21 May 1934, 28 May 1934, and 17 January 1935, in Cutting Papers, Box 20. By 11 September 1934 BC was a lifetime subscriber to *New Democracy*, and on 11 January 1935 he pledged additional support of ten dollars a month for six months.

47. For BC's correspondence with the New Economics Group of Pasadena, see the letter from Mrs. H. E. Luderer to BC dated 23 February 1934 and BC's reply of 1 March 1934, in Cutting Papers, Box 19. For his correspondence with the equivalent group in San Francisco, see the letters from the New Economics Group to BC dated 22 January 1934, from David Warren Ryder to BC dated 26 March 1934, from BC to Ryder dated 24 April 1934, and from Harold L. Mack of the California State Social Credit Association to BC dated 21 December 1934 and 12 February 1935, in Boxes 19 and 20. BC was quoted and mentioned frequently in the pages of Mack's Social Credit journal, *Controversy*; see Chapter Four, pp. 179–80. In *Bronson M. Cutting*, 261, 263–64, Richard Lowitt describes some of BC's contacts with "proponents of social-credit legislation."

48. See the *Congressional Record*, vol. 78, part 2 (27 January 1934), 1476–77. BC enclosed a copy of this speech in a letter to EP of 8 March 1934. In a letter of 24 March 1934 to Senator William Borah (Pound Archive), EP writes: "I have at last got hold of the Congressional Record for Jan. 27 with Senator Cutting's speech. That was spoken like a man and an honest one." He also praised the speech in "A Retrospect," *Chicago Tribune* (Paris), 14 March 1934, p. 5; in "Trusting the President," *Chicago Tribune* (Paris), 22 March 1934, p. 5; and in "Light," *New Democracy* 3, 2 (15 September 1934), 30. See *Ezra Pound's Poetry and Prose*, 6: 141, 143, 197.

49. Bronson Cutting (as told to Frederick C. Painton), "Is Private Banking Doomed?" *Liberty* (31 March 1934); rpt., *New English Weekly* 5, 1 (19 April 1934), 6–9, and *Congressional Record*, vol. 78, part 8 (1 May 1934), 8051–53.

50. *Congressional Record*, vol. 78, part 9 (22 May 1934), 9225–27, and *New Democracy* 3, 6 (1 June 1934), 1–3.

51. *Congressional Record*, vol. 78, part 10 (6 June 1934), 10557.

52. On the projected effects of S. 3744 (later renumbered S. 2204), see "Merger of Reserve Banks into a Centralized System under Federal Rule Urged," *New York World-Telegram*, 3 February 1934, clipping in Cutting Papers, Box 19; and "Sweeping Change in Money System Plan of Senator Cutting," Santa Fe *New Mexican*, 26 March 1935, p. 1. See also Lowitt, *Bronson M. Cutting*, 256–60, 301. A copy of BC's letter to G. L. Moody, dated 25 January 1934, is in the Cutting Papers, Box 19.

53. Letter from BC to David Warren Ryder dated 24 April 1934, in Cutting Papers, Box 19. EP's cavils are registered in Letter 27.

54. Ezra Pound, "Letters to John Buchan, 1934–1935," ed. S. Namjoshi, *Paideuma* 8 (Winter 1979), 467, and "Ez Sez," Santa Fe *New Mexican*, 3 August 1935, p. 4; rpt., *Ezra Pound's Poetry and Prose*, 6: 308, and Chapter Four, p. 206.

55. Ezra Pound, "American Notes," *New English Weekly* 7, 13 (11 July 1935), 245; rpt., *Ezra Pound's Poetry and Prose*, 6: 302. In his obituary on BC (see Chapter Four, p. 225), EP asked: "who will take over the leadership, meaning the intellectual economic leadership of the senate...?"

Chapter Four

1. For the flavor of the *New Mexican* at the time, see Walkiewicz and Witemeyer, "Ezra Pound's Contributions," 453–54; and William Bedford Clark, " 'Ez Sez': Pound's Pithy Promulgations," 420.

2. See Ezra Pound, letter of 5 October 1934, to Betty Hare; and Gorham Munson, letter of 11 September 1934, to Ezra Pound (Pound Archive). For Elizabeth Sage (Mrs. Meredith) Hare, see the note on "Mrs. H," letter 30, p. 147.

3. Clark, " 'Ez Sez,' " 426.

4. The complete list of EP's contributions to *Esquire* includes: "Gaudier: A Postscript," 2, 3 (August 1934), 72–75; "Riposte from Rapallo," 2, 5 (October 1934), 12; "Reflexshuns on Iggurunce: Being a Seminar with Ole Ez to which Only the Very Brightest Readers are Invited," 3, 1 (January 1935), 55, 133; "Mug's Game?" 3, 2 (February 1935), 35, 148; "A Matter of Modesty," 3, 5 (May 1935), 31; "Hickory—Old and New," 3, 6 (June 1935), 40, 156; "A Thing of Beauty," 4, 5 (November 1935), 49, 195–97; "How to Save Business," 5, 1 (January 1936), 35, 195–96. These items are reproduced in *Ezra Pound's Poetry and Prose*, 6: 190–93, 202, 232–33, 243–44, 279, 292–93, 336–38; 7: 14–16. Subsequent to our drafting of this chapter, Donald Gallup published a short article on this series. See "Ezra Pound's Experiment for *Esquire*," *Yale University Library Gazette* 67, 1–2 (October 1992), 37–45.

5. "A Matter of Modesty"; EP later lambasted Sinclair again in "A Thing of Beauty."

6. In "Hickory—Old and New," EP "confesses": "I'm no angel. So I wrote sister Perkins a valentine. No sonnet, but a nice little poEM. Cause I just CAN'T EAT work. And I don't believe Sis Perkins can either" (40).

7. See, for example, E. P. Walkiewicz and Hugh Witemeyer, "A Public Bank in Canto 40," *Paideuma* 19, 3 (Winter 1990), 91–98.

8. Our edition of "Ez Sez" was originally based on a transcription of microfilm copies of the *New Mexican* housed in the New Mexico State Library. Subsequently, facsimiles of the column were published in Garland's multivolume collection of EP's periodical poetry and prose. See *Ezra Pound's Poetry and Prose*, 6: 258–59, 261, 286, 288–89, 294, 308–10, 328. The carbon copies of the two letters to Johnson reproduced in this chapter are contained in the Pound Archive. The page that seems out of place among the unpub-

lished "Ez Sez" typescripts begins as follows: "Dynamo, as I see it, is the most active poetry magazine in America." This page seems to be addressed to the audience of a literary magazine rather than the general readership of the *New Mexican*.

9. "A Matter of Modesty," p. 31.

10. "American Notes," *New English Weekly* 6, 13 (10 January 1935), 270; 6, 14 (17 Jan. 1935), 290. Rpt. in *Ezra Pound's Poetry and Prose*, 6: 236, 239. In an April column EP referred to Perkins as a "half-wit" ("American Notes," *New English Weekly* 7, 2 [25 April 1935], 25; rpt. in *Ezra Pound's Poetry and Prose*, 6: 278). Later in the year EP again ridiculed Perkins before his English readers: "Anyone (let us say our admired colleague McNair Wilson) who has fallen or is still falling for the Roosevelt entourage, might have been cured by the sight of Sister Perkins (Madame Secretary of Labour) on the newsreel, the solemn settlement—house visage enunciating: 'What we need to do is CONCENTRATE on preparing for the next depression'" ("American Notes," *New English Weekly* 7, 6 [23 May 1935], 105; rpt. in *Ezra Pound's Poetry and Prose*, 6: 287).

11. See also Clark, "'Ez Sez,'" 423; Walkiewicz and Witemeyer, "Ezra Pound's Contributions," 454–55, and Introduction to Chapter Three, pp. 90–91 above.

12. Frances Perkins, *People at Work* (New York: John Day, 1934), 283–84. Emphasis added.

13. Davis, *Vision Fugitive*, 190.

14. Tugwell, *The Industrial Discipline*; qtd. in Davis, *Vision Fugitive*, 193.

15. "The Hullabaloo Over the Brain Trust," *Literary Digest* 96 (1933), 8–9; rpt. in *The New Deal: A Documentary History*, ed. William E. Leuchtenburg (Columbia: University of South Carolina Press, 1968), 50.

16. "American Notes," *New English Weekly* 7, 4 (9 May 1935), 65; rpt. *Ezra Pound's Poetry and Prose*, 6: 282. EP follows this up with a reiteration of his "Ez Sez" comment: "His ideal was the 'Saturday Evening Post.'" EP once referred to the *Saturday Evening Post* as "one of the few American publications bloated enough to be on sale on almost every European bookstall" ("American Notes," *New English Weekly* 6, 13 [10 Jan. 1935], 270; rpt. in *Ezra Pound's Poetry and Prose*, 6: 236).

17. "American Notes," *New English Weekly* 6, 26 (11 April 1935), 529–30; rpt. in *Ezra Pound's Poetry and Prose*, 6: 275. The Johnson EP refers to here is General Hugh Johnson, head of the NRA, not Hiram Johnson.

18. "Farley: Cheap Imperforates Puncture Philatelists' Marts," *News Week*, 16 February 1935, p. 9.

19. "Farley: Twenty-Three Occupants of Room 1701 Worry Kingfish," *News Week*, 23 February 1935, p. 9.

20. "Farley: Postmaster General to Resign for the Sake of 1936," *News Week*, 13 April 1935, p. 10; "'Big Jim,' Head-Liner," *Literary Digest*, 20 April 1935, p. 15.

21. "Long Excoriates President's Aides; Talks Secession," *New York Times*, 23 April 1935, p. 11.

22. "American Notes," *New English Weekly* 7, 11 (27 June 1935), 205; rpt. in *Ezra Pound's Poetry and Prose*, 6: 299.

23. "Birth Control Curb Hits Congress Snag," *New York Times*, 27 June 1935, p. 23.

24. "American Notes," *New English Weekly* 7, 6 (23 May 1935), 105; rpt. in *Ezra Pound's Poetry and Prose*, 6: 287.

25. "Long Excoriates President's Aides," p. 11.

26. See Munson, *Aladdin's Lamp*, p. 232.

27. See Tytell, *Ezra Pound*, p. 257.

28. "American Notes," *New English Weekly* 7, 6 (23 May 1935), 105; rpt., *Ezra Pound's Poetry and Prose*, 6: 287.

29. Ezra Pound, *Guide to Kulchur* (New York: New Directions: 1938), 250.

30. "Long and Coughlin Classed by Ickes as 'Contemptible,'" *New York Times*, 23 April 1935, p. 1.

31. "American Notes," *New English Weekly* 7, 3 (2 May 1935), 45.

32. Davis, *Vision Fugitive*, pp. 186–87.

33. See "American Notes," *New English Weekly* 6, 25 (4 April 1935), 509–10; rpt., *Ezra Pound's Poetry and Prose*, 6: 274.

34. "American Notes," *New English Weekly* 7, 6 (23 May 1935), 105; rpt., *Ezra Pound's Poetry and Prose*, 6: 287. See Davis, *Vision Fugitive*, 186.

35. "Bulletin," *New English Weekly* 9, 26 (8 Oct. 1936), 425–26; rpt., *Ezra Pound's Poetry and Prose*, 6: 100.

36. Arthur Krock, "Compromise Is Possible in Banking Bill Conflict," *New York Times*, 21 May 1935, p. 18.

37. "Bankers Terrorized, Vanderlip Charges," *New York Times*, 3 May 1935, p. 35.

38. "Social Credit Prophet Will Rule a Province," *New York Times*, 1 Sept. 1935, sec. 4, p. 12. For more on Aberhart, see Lewis H. Thomas, ed., *William Aberhart and Social Credit in Alberta* (Toronto: Copp Clark Pub., 1977), and David R. Elliott and Iris Miller, *Bible Bill: A Biography of William Aberhart* (Edmonton: Reidmore Books, 1987).

39. Munson, *Aladdin's Lamp*, 206–7.

40. "Alberta and the British Press," *Kingwood Review* 2, 21 (15 Nov. 1935), 10; rpt., *Ezra Pound's Poetry and Prose*, 6:, 342.

41. "Hands Off Alberta," *New Democracy* 5, 6 (15 Nov. 1935), 99–100; rpt., *Ezra Pound's Poetry and Prose*, 6: 342.

42. Upton Sinclair, *I, Governor of California and How I Ended Poverty: A True Story of the Future* (Los Angeles: Upton Sinclair, 1934).

43. John Caughey, *California* (New York: Prentice-Hall, 1940), 586.

44. Royce D. Delmatier, Clarence F. McIntosh, and Earl G. Waters, *The Rumble of California Politics, 1848–1970* (New York: Wiley, 1970), 273.

45. Newton Gilmore, ed., *Readings in California History* (New York: Crowell, 1966), 293.

46. "American Notes," *New English Weekly* 6, 12 (3 Jan. 1935), 251; rpt., *Ezra Pound's Poetry and Prose*, 6: 235.

47. Carey Williams, "Upton Sinclair and His E.P.I.C." *The New Republic*, 22 August 1934, pp. 39–41.

48. "Sinclair, La Follette, and Cutting," *The Nation*, 7 Nov. 1934, p. 522.

49. Upton Sinclair, *I, Candidate for Governor: And How I Got Licked* (Pasadena, Calif.: Upton Sinclair, 1935).

50. Robert Cleland, *California in Our Time, 1900–1940* (New York: Knopf, 1947), 226.

51. Caughey, *California*, 587.

52. Cleland, *California in Our Time*, 226.

53. Upton Sinclair, "We Choose Our Future," *Esquire* 4, 2 (Aug. 1935), 49, 167–68.

54. George E. Sokolsky, "We Solve Our Present," *Esquire* 4, 2 (Aug. 1935), 21, 170–72.

55. "A Thing of Beauty," 49, 195–97.

56. See, for example, Ian F. A. Bell, *Critic as Scientist: The Modernist Poetics of Ezra Pound* (London: Methuen, 1981); E. P. Walkiewicz, "'and Agassiz for Gestalt Seed': Pound's American Taxonomy," *Kenyon Review* 11, 4 (1989), 116–22.

57. Louis Herbert Bannister, *When We Become Scientific: This book gives the cause of financial panics, and offers a Scientific Remedy* (Pasadena, Calif.: L. H. Bannister, 1933).

58. "American Notes," *New English Weekly* 7, 16 (1 August 1935), 305; rpt., *Ezra Pound's Poetry and Prose*, 6: 307.

59. "American Notes," *New English Weekly* 7, 17 (5 September 1935), 325; rpt. in *Ezra Pound's Poetry and Prose*, 6: 311.

60. "A Thing of Beauty," 195.

61. "The Credit Forum," *New English Weekly* 6, 17 (7 Feb. 1935), 348.

62. Luther Whiteman, "A Social Credit Synopsis," *Controversy* 3, 5 (1 June 1935), 4, and "Correspondence," *Controversy* 3, 6 (15 June 1935), 15. The second of these items does not appear in Gallup's *Ezra Pound: A Bibliography*.

63. See the letters of 21 December 1934 and 12 February 1935 in Box 20 of the Cutting Papers.

64. "A New Thrust," *Controversy* 1, 6 (30 November 1934), 79; "Cutting to Serve," *Controversy* 2, 3 (1 February 1935), 6; "As Others Say It," *Controversy* 3, 2 (15 April 1935), 13.

65. "Postscript," *Controversy* 3, 4 (15 May 1935), 17.

66. See Walkiewicz and Witemeyer, "Ezra Pound's Contributions," 456–57.

67. Malcolm Cowley, *Exile's Return: A Literary Odyssey of the 1920s* (New York: Viking, 1956), p. 119.

68. There are hints that EP himself considered his relationship with his Santa Fe audience problematic from the start. Before he officially began contributing to the *New Mexican*, for instance, he confided to Elizabeth Sage Hare that he had no "indication whether it is worth while trying to edderkate Santa Fe" (letter of 1 January 1935 to Betty Hare, Pound Archive).

69. "Child's Guide to Economics 1934," *G. K.'s Weekly* 20, 505 (15 Nov. 1934), 177–78; rpt., *Ezra Pound's Poetry and Prose*, 6: 212.

Chapter Five

1. See Pearlman, "Fighting the World," 419: "Borah, though replying but little, never once threw a letter from Pound into his 'crank' file. . . . their goals were too similar for Borah simply to be able to write him off as a nuisance."

2. See Burns, "'Dear Uncle George': Ezra Pound's Letters," 57. In a letter to Tinkham of 2 September 1935, EP writes: "If the following summary of Financial News, Morn. Post, different French papers, Temps, Matin, etc. and the Italian Press is any use to you, go on and wade thru it."

3. Starting in May of 1934, EP also urged Senator Borah to enter the lists against Roosevelt in 1936, with BC as his vice presidential running-mate; see Pearlman, "Fighting the World," 420–21.

4. See Chapter Four, p. 225 above.

5. Ezra Pound, "American Notes," *New English Weekly* 7, 13 (11 July 1935), 245; rpt., *Ezra Pound's Poetry and Prose*, 6: 302.

6. Ezra Pound, "American Notes," *New English Weekly* 7, 20 (26 September 1935), 385; rpt., *Ezra Pound's Poetry and Prose*, 6: 315. To Dorothy Pound EP wrote on 12 September 1935: "As near as I can make out, Long's shooting was local. whether anyone can carry on, I dunno" (Lilly Library, Indiana University).

7. Carpenter, *Serious Character*, 534–35; Tytell, *Ezra Pound*, 241; Pearlman, "Fighting the World," 426. In *American Ezra Pound*, 82–87, 92, 103, 105–6, Flory argues that, after the invasion of Abyssinia, EP's perception of public events was systematically colored by self-deception, as he began to rationalize or deny truths which were incompatible with his continuing faith in Mussolini.

8. Carpenter, *Serious Character*, 540–41.

9. See Charles Norman, *Ezra Pound* (New York: Macmillan, 1960) 326, and Carpenter, *Serious Character*, 545.

10. Burns, "'Dear Uncle George': The Pound-Tinkham Letters," 48. See also Leon Surette, "Ezra Pound's Fascism: Aberration or Essence? The Correspondence with William Bird," *Queen's Quarterly* 96, 3 (Autumn 1989), 619–20.

11. Norman, *Ezra Pound*, 359–61; Carpenter, *Serious Character*, 560–61; Tytell, *Ezra Pound*, 251–52. All three quote the passage from Canto 84.

12. *"Ezra Pound Speaking,"* 97.

13. Ibid., 60, 223. These passages and others in the same vein are quoted by Robert Casillo, *The Genealogy of Demons: Anti- Semitism, Fascism, and the Myths of Ezra Pound* (Evanston, Ill.: Northwestern University Press, 1988), 350–51.

14. Ezra Pound, "I Gather the Limbs of Osiris [II]," *New Age* 10, 16 (7 December 1911), 130–31; rpt., *Selected Prose*, 21–23.

15. Ezra Pound, *The Cantos*, 568.

16. Ibid., 685–86.

17. Ibid., 728.

18. Chapter Four, p. 225; quoted by Pearlman, "Fighting the World," 422.

INDEX